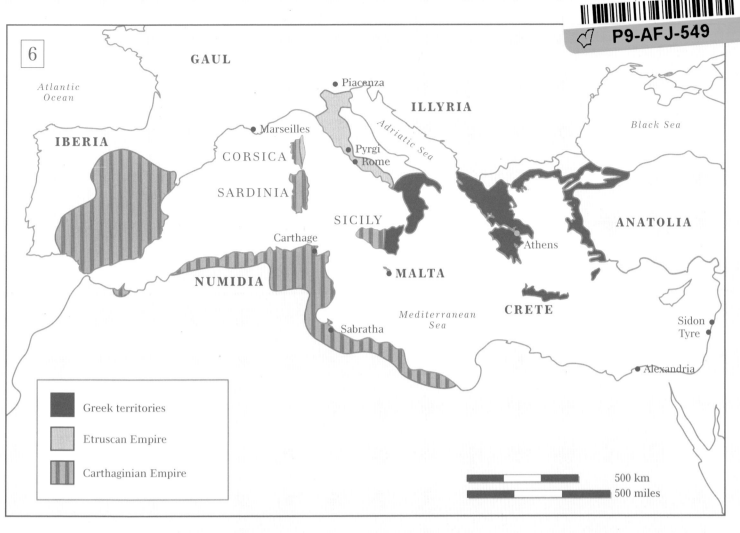

6

GAUL

Atlantic Ocean

IBERIA

Marseilles

CORSICA

SARDINIA

Piacenza

ILLYRIA

Adriatic Sea

Pyrgi
Rome

SICILY

Carthage

NUMIDIA

MALTA

Sabratha

Mediterranean Sea

CRETE

Athens

ANATOLIA

Black Sea

Sidon
Tyre

Alexandria

	Greek territories
	Etruscan Empire
	Carthaginian Empire

500 km
500 miles

7

SCANDINAVIA

BRITANNIA

GERMANIA

SARMATIA

Atlantic Ocean

GAUL

ROMAN EMPIRE

ILLYRICUM

DACIA

Sarmizegetusa

Black Sea

Caspian Sea

Spoleto
Rome
Pompeii

HISPANIA

SARDINIA

Cannae

ARMENIA

SICILY

Corinth

Athens

Thyatira

GALATIA

ASSYRIA

Cadiz
Gibraltar

Carthage

Palmyra

MAURITANIA

Mediterranean Sea

Sidon
Tyre

CYRENAICA

MESOPOTAMIA

Red Sea

500 km
500 miles

THE ANCIENTS
IN THEIR
OWN WORDS

Michael Kerrigan

© 2009 Amber Books Ltd

This 2009 edition published by 3C Publishing Ltd
by arrangement with Amber Books Ltd.

3C Publishing Ltd
Sky House
Raans Road
Amersham
Bucks, HP6 6JQ

Editorial and design by:
Amber Books Ltd
Bradley's Close
74–77 White Lion St
London N1 9PF
United Kingdom
www.amberbooks.co.uk

Project Editor: Michael Spilling
Designer: Joe Conneally
Picture Research: Natascha Spargo

ISBN: 978-1-906842-00-0

Printed and bound in Thailand

1 3 5 7 9 10 8 6 4 2

CONTENTS

Mesopotamia

What we call 'civilization' started, archeologists agree, approximately 11,000 years ago in the Middle East. Here, a Fertile Crescent sweeps from Lebanon through Syria into what is now Iraq along the course of the Euphrates and Tigris Rivers. It was here that the Neolithic Revolution took place, the hunter-gatherer lifestyle of the Paleolithic (Old Stone Age) giving way to the agricultural economy of the Neolithic (New Stone Age).

Although it seems to have been in the uplands that foragers first became farmers, agriculture really took a hold in the open flats of 'Mesopotamia' – from the Greek *meso*, 'in the middle', and *potamia*, 'rivers'. Doused with floodwater after the springtime thaw in the Anatolian mountains, the plains between the rivers were enriched with fresh alluvial deposits every year. A more rewarding agricultural environment could hardly be imagined. Forms of wheat, barley, flax, chickpeas and lentils were gradually domesticated, along with livestock such as cattle, sheep, goats and pigs.

The implications of the Neolithic Revolution extended far beyond the area of diet: nomadism was abandoned for a settled lifestyle. Agricultural production allowed the accumulation of surpluses, the generation of wealth and the emergence of social hierarchies, with elites and subjects: societies became more complex, early states emerged. The first cities are believed to have arisen around Uruk in the Sumer region of Lower Mesopotamia in 3000 BC – give or take a few centuries.

Left: Mesopotamia means literally the country 'between the rivers': land and history alike have been formed by the ageless flow of the Tigris and (shown here) the Euphrates. This photograph was taken near the Seleucid ruins of Dura Europos on the upper Euphrates in Syria.

BY THAT TIME, writing of a sort was already extremely well established. Archeologists in Mesopotamia have discovered what are assumed to be 'tokens', of moulded clay, scored over with tally marks. Perhaps recording head of livestock or measurements of grain, they date back as far as 8000 BC. Examples of 'proto-writing' from the millennia that followed take the form of pictograms – literally, stylized pictorial representations of what they were supposed to depict.

'One cow'; 'five bushels of grain' – we are clearly quite some way still from the sort of literacy that produces a Thucydides, a Sophocles, a Seneca. But writing was clearly on the march; Mesopotamia was already at work constructing that culture which, within the space of a few thousand years, would yield the rich poetry of the *Epic of Gilgamesh* (*see pp. 32–33*).

It seems safe to assume, however, that if works of the imagination alone had been at stake, the Mesopotamian peoples would have continued to be cheerfully illiterate. Not so much because literature would have been regarded as a luxury – then as now – but because poetic culture did not then depend on being written down for its survival. As modern research among preliterate tribes has shown, such cultures have an extraordinary facility for committing to memory enormous screeds of narrative and verse. It is only in those lettered societies with written texts that the memorizing 'muscle' in the mind has atrophied.

THE COMING OF CUNEIFORM

First and foremost, writing was needed for accounting and inventorying property and for keeping track of trading deals and tax contributions. Scribes, in these early states, were not littérateurs or scholars but civil servants responsible for overseeing the collection, storage and distribution of produce on the king's behalf. Tablets found in Uruk in 3000 BC show that an early written script had been developed but that its use was restricted to record-keeping.

Known as 'cuneiform' – from the Latin *cuneus*, 'wedge', in reference to its characteristic wedge-shaped characters – this script was inscribed in moist clay using a sharpened stick or stylus. The pictographic impulse was still strong: though these early tablets have resisted deciphering, their subject matter can easily be seen from the use of symbols that unmistakably represent, for example, ears of barley.

FROM CITIES TO EMPIRES

Other cities rose in the wake of Uruk: first Ur, then Kish, and then Umma. By the middle of the third millennium BC, Umma's neighbour Lagash was in the ascendant. By 2350 BC, Umma had reasserted its supremacy in Sumer – but the region as a whole was facing a new threat. For centuries now, Semitic herders had been drifting into Mesopotamia from the north, settling down as farmers in the region around Baghdad. Akkad, as this kingdom was called, grew steadily in power and influence until the accession of King Sargon I some time in the twenty-fourth century. Sargon the Great made Akkad an imperial power – and, incidentally, made himself a model for a new breed of ruthlessly expansionist Mesopotamian rulers.

The centuries that followed saw empires rising and falling in continuous succession. Akkad itself lasted till the late twenty-first century, when it was supplanted by a briefly resurgent Lagash. A league of Sumerian cities under the

Above: Beautifully picked out in glazed terracotta brick, a lion stalks across a wall of the grand processional way which ran through the ceremonial centre of Babylon.

leadership of the Dynasty of Ur came to power in 2111 and stayed in place until 2003 BC. By 1800, a new power had emerged, centred on the city of Assur, on the west bank of the Tigris to the north of the great Sumerian cities. Under Shamshi-Adad an empire was built, though this was quickly overthrown by the all-conquering forces of Babylon's King Hammurabi.

Hammurabi's reign marked something of a golden age, not just for Babylon but for Mesopotamia as a whole: it was a time of cultural creativity, economic development and social progress. Hammurabi's successors were not made of the same stuff, however, and their kingdom was quickly conquered in the sixteenth century BC by the Hittites, whose empire centred on Anatolia and northern Syria. In turn, they were displaced by the Kassites, Indo-European invaders originating in a region of what is now Iran. The Kassites were toppled themselves, in about 1165 BC, when King Shutruk-Nahhunte of the Elamites placed most of Mesopotamia under his rule.

SECOND TIME AROUND
In the thirteenth century BC, the Assyrian state was rebuilt by Adad-nirari I and his son Shalmaneser I; their successors carried on strengthening Assur's influence in the north. By the time Tukulti-Ninurta I came to the throne in 1243, Assyria was a mighty power: Tukulti-Ninurta began his reign by going to war with what had till then been an also-resurgent Babylon. This was no contest: Babylon's military strength was smashed and Assyria was established as the dominant power across the entire region. It was to maintain that authority with cruel effectiveness in the centuries that followed.

By 1000 BC, the Assyrians were faltering, but in the ninth century their power took on a new lease of life. Reviving under Adad-nirari II, Assyria was led to victory again and again by its warlike rulers, including Ashurnasirpal II, Shalmaneser III, Sargon II and Sennacherib. This Neo-Assyrian Empire reached its

height in the reign of Tiglathpileser III, which lasted from 745 to 727 BC. Not until 612 BC was this period of Assyrian overlordship brought to an end when Assyria's forces were decisively defeated by the army of King Nabopolassar I (625–05 BC).

Under him, the Neo-Assyrian Empire was forced to make way for a Neo-Babylonian one. Restored to glory by Nabopolassar I, this new Babylon was steered to unprecedented triumphs under the leadership of his son Nebuchadnezzar II (605–562 BC).

ANNALS OF WAR
Farming is supposed to be a peaceful business, but that agricultural idyll was never quite to come about in the Middle East. Sedentary populations could accumulate wealth in a way their nomadic forebears could never have imagined – which meant that they could covet one another's wealth and territory, mindful of the status and power they brought. War became routine; indeed, there was a season for fighting, just as there was for ploughing, sowing and the harvest. Tucked in to the summer schedule – when the ground was dry

Above: War was as much a way of life as agriculture in ancient Mesopotamia. Cities needed strong defences, as seen here at the old Assyrian site of Nineveh.

and passable but before the grain had to be gathered – the military campaign season became a fixture in the calendar.

But then, like it or not, this was the 'civilized' way: where old-style 'savages' had been content to survive, the new elites wanted wealth and rank. Hand in hand with this development, the function of writing was gradually changing, its uses diversifying. Though records of production, payments and debts remained important, there were now new matters – often less tangible – to describe: the nobility of kings, their building projects and their military victories. New dictions and tones were found, far removed from the matter-of-fact 'one-cow, two-cow' style. Sublimely portentous, extravagantly high-flown, this was a style of language that we have learned in modern times to suspect and deprecate as 'propaganda', but in which the poetic impulse found its expression – was even, perhaps, born.

Born to Rule: Sargon of Akkad

A legend in his own lifetime, still more so in his posterity, Sargon the Great did all he could to help his own cult along. But this should not blind us to the genuine achievements of the founder of Mesopotamia's first great empire.

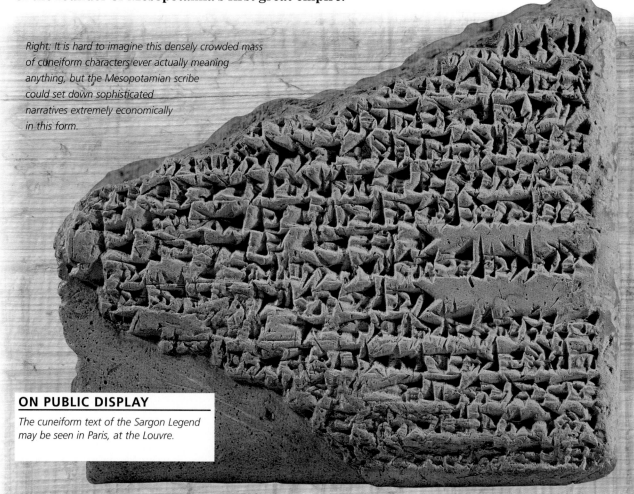

Right: It is hard to imagine this densely crowded mass of cuneiform characters ever actually meaning anything, but the Mesopotamian scribe could set down sophisticated narratives extremely economically in this form.

ON PUBLIC DISPLAY

The cuneiform text of the Sargon Legend may be seen in Paris, at the Louvre.

Sargon's obscure origins became an important part of his mystique. By the first millennium BC, Neo-Assyrian rulers were finding inspiration in his conquests – and, at least in the case of Sargon II (*see pp. 28–29*), his antecedents. An inscription of the time describes the circumstances of his birth in strikingly similar terms to those of Moses in the Jewish Bible, though he is protected not by Jehovah but by the goddess Ishtar:

> **66** *I am Sargon, the great ruler, the mighty King of Akkad. My mother was low-born; I never knew my father...After I was conceived, my mother had to keep my existence hidden: she gave birth to me in secret. She placed me in a basket of reeds, the gaps caulked up with tar. So, when she consigned me to the waters of the river, I was not overwhelmed but floated. The current carried me along to where Akki, the water-carrier, found me. He reared me as his own son and subsequently made me his gardener. The goddess Ishtar loved me...* **99**

The first and original Sargon the Great emerged from nowhere in the twenty-fourth century BC, seizing power in the city-state of Kish. His antecedents are uncertain to say the least: he appears to have been serving as an official before his coup. His real name too remains a mystery. He took the title Sharru-kin, or Sargon, by adoption: it means 'The King is Legitimate' – though, of course, he was anything but.

BELOVED OF INANA

The story known as the Legend of Sargon makes no secret of his humble origins, no attempt to deny his usurpation. It does, however, insist that he was backed and assisted at every turn by Inana, the Sumerian goddess of love and war. The equivalent to the later Ishtar and Astarte, Inana advances his career. She also protects him when Ur-Zababa, who has become aware of the upstart's ambition, sends him off with a message containing secret instructions to have him killed.

THE EMPIRE OF AKKAD

Sargon's achievements as king were real enough: having made himself the king of Kish, around 2334 BC, he set about building an empire in the northern part of Mesopotamia. This region was united culturally to some extent since all its peoples spoke languages belonging to the Semitic language-family, unlike the Sumerian region to the south. Overthrowing Uruk, Sargon quickly conquered the cities of Sumer before going on to take territories beyond the Tigris and Euphrates, in Elam to the east and into Syria and other territories to the west. He made his capital at Agade, after which the name of his empire – Akkad – was to be named. Though his empire did not long outlive him, his reputation remained a powerful force in Mesopotamian culture, as did the Akkadian language, the region's lingua franca for the next 2000 years.

Above: Inana-Ishtar was the Mesopotamian goddess of love and war. Always shown with wings – and with her pubic area bare – she was identified with the waxing and waning of the moon, then as now associated with fertility.

" *As evening fell one day, Sargon came to the royal palace with his regular deliveries. Ur-Zababa was sleeping in his sacred chamber. He had a dream, whose meaning he understood, but did not choose to relate to anyone…He made Sargon his cupbearer, giving him charge of drinks. Inana still stood by him.*

Between five and ten days later, King Ur-Zababa…was gripped by fear in his palace. He urinated like a lion, all down his own legs, and there was blood and pus mixed in. In his fear and distress, he was like a fish thrashing about in stagnant water.

Then the cupbearer Sargon had his own dream: he saw the goddess Inana drowning Ur-Zababa in a torrent of blood. As he slept, he moaned and chewed the earth. Hearing of his moaning, King Ur-Zababa had him summoned to his sacred presence and said: 'Cupbearer, did you have a vision in the night?' Sargon replied: 'My lord: here is the dream I had. I saw a young woman, standing to the heavens, her body as vast as the earth, as firm in her stance as the bottom of a wall. She drowned you in a terrible torrent, a river of blood – and for my sake.' "

In the Name of Ningursu

From the city of Lagash comes an extraordinary inscription, as important from a literary perspective as from a historical one. It describes how King Gudea came to build and dedicate a shrine to Ningursu at the command of the god himself.

> *On a day when the destinies of heaven and earth were being laid down, Lagash lifted its head, towering towards heaven in its immense stature…Certainly the heart overbrimmed its banks; certainly the heart of Enlil overbrimmed its banks; for certain, the heart overbrimmed its banks; for certain, the floodwater sparkled as it rose in splendour; certainly, the heart of Enlil, the Tigris, poured sweet water…*
>
> *In my dream, a solitary man appeared, huge as the heavens, vast as earth; his head seemed that of a god; his arms were the wings of the Anzu bird, but his lower parts were the storming floodwaters. To his right and left, lions lay down. He gave me his command to build his temple, but I could not fully comprehend his plans.*

Right: Carved into a ceramic cylinder when wet and then fired to provide a lasting record, Ningursu's inscription has kept his name alive through more than forty centuries.

ON PUBLIC DISPLAY

Both the Cylinders of Gudea are among the exhibits in the Louvre, in Paris.

From Ngirsu to Nippur

The patron deity of Lagash, Ngirsu was adopted as the divine protector of the entire Akkadian realm after the kingdom's conquest by Sargon the Great. He became known as Ninurta, in which new guise his head shrine moved some way to the north to the city of Nippur, at that time on the banks of the Euphrates. This city was already ancient and already a sacred centre, site of the great shrine to Enlil, Sumerian god of life and space and air. Here Ninurta was worshipped as one of a sort of trinity with his father Enlil and his mother Ninlil, goddess of the wind.

Below: Gudea himself is shown seated in prayer – apparently to Ningishzida, god of the underworld and of medicine – in this diorite statue of the twenty-second century.

It has been suggested that, at the time when the so-called Gudea Cylinders were fashioned, Lagash was the greatest city in the world. That was a long time ago, of course: this southern Sumerian city-state, not far from the mouth of the Tigris, had its heyday towards the end of the third millennium BC. Its ruins were initially thought to have been discovered in 1877, when excavations at Telloh by the French archeologist-diplomat Ernest de Sazec – then his country's vice-consul in nearby Basra – turned up traces of what had clearly been a major city.

Experts now believe that de Sazec had found not Lagash itself but another city, Ngirsu. However, by the time of Gudea's reign, around the twenty-second century BC, Ngirsu was the capital of the kingdom of Lagash, so the distinction may seem academic. Certainly, this was a site of treasures. The most significant were two ceramic cylinders, inscribed with a lengthy text. This sang the praises of Ningursu, god of thunder and protector of the state, and described how King Gudea came to build him the great temple that came to be known as Eninnu.

He did so, the text relates, on the express instructions of the god himself, though Ningursu was apparently not as explicit as he might have been.

The Wings of Anzu

It is interesting to find the divine figure of Ningursu incorporating features of the ferocious Anzu bird – a demonic and destructive monster in Sumerian tradition. In one story, this fearsome fire-breathing bird steals the tablets of destiny from Enlil, compromising the orderly conduct of the cosmos. Fortunately, he is conquered and killed – by the courageous action of Ningursu, who has apparently taken on some of the monster's powers, but for the benefit of creation.

The World's First Medical Text?

Fashioned 4000 years ago in Sumer, a clay tablet covered with cuneiform inscriptions constitutes the first known manual for medical practitioners. This extraordinary document gives us a fascinating insight into the knowledge ancient doctors had at their command.

Grind pear-tree bark and moonplant-flower into a powder together before pouring on Kushumma wine; then mix in plain oil and heated oil of cedar.

Grind up the seeds of the carpenter plant with Markazi resin and thyme. Dissolve the resulting mess in beer and give it to a man to drink.

Add hot water to powdered dried water snake mixed with Amama-Shumkaspal plant, thorn roots, powdered Naga-plant and powdered turpentine…Rub it into the affected area after it has been bathed.

ON PUBLIC DISPLAY

This remarkable document may be viewed at the University of Pennsylvania Museum, Philadelphia.

Right: Beautifully set out, as though for clarity and for ease of practical reference, this ancient tablet might easily have been held in the hand of a doctor as he worked.

Nippur was one of the oldest cities in Babylonia, dating back to 5000 BC or even further. It was already very old, then, when some ancient scribe sat down here to make a tablet recording some of the pharmacological wisdom of his time. In a careful cuneiform script believed to date from around 2100 BC, he set down no fewer than 15 different prescriptions in some detail. Among the ingredients in the Sumerian medical cabinet were 'moonplant-flower' and turtleshell, along with more familiar items like thyme and turpentine.

A RELIGIOUS DIMENSION?
It may or may not be significant that Nippur was the sacred city of Enlil, the lord of the cosmos: the city and the god were both represented by the same cuneiform sign. Was there a religious dimension to Sumerian medicine? Could that be why the pharmacopeia was found here?

Tempting as it may be to jump to such conclusions, there is evidence that points the other way. Conspicuous by their absence on this tablet are the sort of incantations we are accustomed to seeing in comparable sources from elsewhere in the ancient world (the Metternich Stela, for example). These treatments were expected to work on their own merits, not as ritual accompaniments to healing spells. Were these remedies the start of scientific medicine?

MAGIC AND MEDICINE
The truth appears to have been less clear-cut. The Sumerians had two kinds of healer: the first, the ashipu, was what we might today call a 'witch-doctor'. He examined the patient and, according to which area of the body had been affected and which particular symptoms were exhibited, made a judgment on which demon was responsible or which deity the sufferer had offended. His prescriptions belonged firmly in the realm of ritual: sacrifices of propitiation to the gods, and spells and chants designed to draw out the malignant spirit.

In certain cases, though, the ashipu seems to have referred his patients to a practitioner of another sort, the asu. His work was practical, his treatments, as far as we can tell, empirically based. The evidence we have from other sources suggests that he prepared drugs to tried-and-tested recipes – rather like those recorded here.

AN EFFECTIVE COMBINATION
In hindsight, then, we can see something of a 'twin-track' system at work in Sumer. First, a loosely scientific approach, offering genuine relief against a range of maladies. Then, for those ills that could not be cured, there was a second tier of magical treatments.

To the mind of the modern medic, these may have been

Ancient Aspirin

The use of powdered willow bark by the Sumerian pharmacists would not have surprised healers from other ancient cultures: it contains salicylic acid, the active ingredient of aspirin. This mainstay of modern medicine was actually among the earliest drugs to be discovered – not just in the Old World but in the Americas. The Sumerians, living in damp alluvial plains, were particularly plagued by rheumatism, and appreciated the anti-inflammatory properties of this drug.

'mumbo-jumbo', but they may well have had some efficaciousness, thanks to the 'placebo effect'.

Right: Over 40,000 inscribed tablets have been uncovered in the course of excavations at Nippur, including everything from temple records to mathematical tables – even school texts and exercise 'books'.

The Kings of Sumer

A mix of outright myth and hazy history, the document known as the Sumerian King List records the reigns of Sumer's earliest rulers.

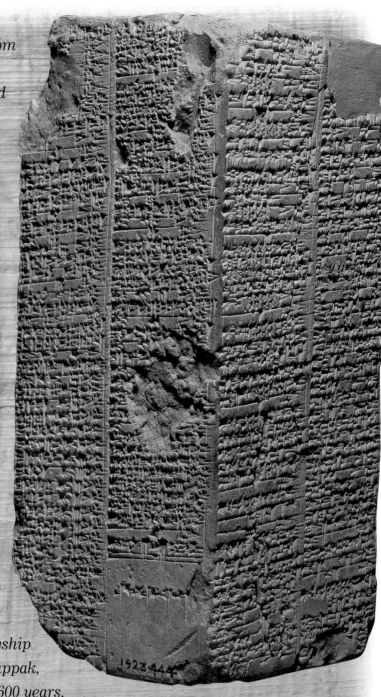

" The office of King came down from heaven, alighting at Eridu. At Eridu, Alulim was King. His reign lasted 28,800 years. Alagar reigned for 36,000 years. Two kings. They reigned for 64,800 years.

Eridu was conquered. Power passed to Badtibira. At Badtibira, Enmenluanna reigned for 43,200 years. Enmengalanna ruled for 28,800 years. Dumuzisib ruled for 36,000 years. Three kings. They reigned for 108,000 years.

Badtibira was conquered. The place of kingship was established at Larak. At Larak, Ensibzianna ruled for 28,800 years. One king. He reigned for 28,800 years.

Larak was conquered. Power passed to Sippar. At Sippar, Enmenduranna was King, reigning for 21,000 years. One king. He reigned for 21,000 years.

Sippar was conquered. The place of kingship was established at Shuruppak. At Shuruppak, Ubardudu was King and reigned for 18,600 years. One king. He ruled for 18,600 years.

Five cities. Eight kings. They ruled for 241,200 years.

The Flood came up over the earth. After the flood, the office of King, which had come down from heaven, established itself at Kish... "

ON PUBLIC DISPLAY

The Weld-Blundell Prism can be found in the Ashmolean Museum in Oxford, England. It stands just 20cm (8in) tall and is 9cm (3.5in) wide.

Above: The Weld-Blundell Prism lay hidden in the rubble of Babylon for almost 4000 years.

Discovered in Babylon in 1922, what is known as the Weld-Blundell Prism is a four-sided ceramic prism, inscribed with two tightly written columns on every face. Its text, in cuneiform, is that of what is known as the Sumerian King List, a record of the Sumerian rulers of the earliest age.

AN UNSTABLE SUMER
It is believed to have been composed around 1800 BC in the city of Larsa. This was a time of increasing instability in Sumer. The region had enjoyed a resurgence. Towards the end of the third millennium, the Empire of Akkad had collapsed in chaos and the southern city of Ur had risen once again. Ur-Nammu, enthroned in 2112 BC, founded the Third Dynasty. He and his son Shulgi emulated the achievements of Sargon the Great, patiently piecing together a major empire through a combination of conquest and diplomacy. This one, though, was centred on the south in Sumer. Now it, too, passed, and Isin and Larsa struggled for supremacy in the south before being eclipsed in their turn by Manana, Kazullu and finally by Babylon. Hammurabi, who came to the throne of Babylon around 1792 BC, was to make the city-state the centre of an economic and political superstate.

ACCOUNTING FOR THE PAST
Exciting but difficult times for Sumer, then – perhaps difficult enough to foster a nostalgia for the certainties of a mythic age gone by? We can only speculate, but this would help account for the odd (to the modern reader, at least) combination of bureaucratic pedantry and extravagant myth in this list of kings. It is not so much a history as a chronological accounting, each king's reign recorded with pernickety exactitude. Yet this precision contrasts with the wildly fantastical duration of the rulers' lives – not to mention the matter-of-fact inclusion of the flood.

Scanty Evidence

In some cases, the archeological record seems hazily to confirm the contents of the Sumerian King List; in others, it does not exist at all. Eridu does appear to have been Sumer's earliest city: archeological remains at Tell Abu Shahrain, near modern Basra, date back to about 5570 BC. Its temples were clearly important, lending credence to the idea that it was a major ceremonial centre.

Badtibira is harder to place, though it is believed to have lain further to the north, near Umma. Larak was another name for Larsa – it is no surprise that a clerk from this city would have wished to transcribe a king list that gave his home-state such a special place in history. It had waned in influence since then, to re-emerge with the start of the second century BC – though it was finding its status difficult to maintain.

Sippar was some way to the north, on the Euphrates: the temple of Shamash here is believed to have functioned as the world's first bank, though it dates back only as far as about 1800 BC. Shuruppak, now Tell Fara, is in the south-central region of Iraq: it was sacred to Ninlil, the goddess of grain and air. Excavations here have revealed remains from around 3000 BC – certainly long enough ago to tie in with the King List's chronology.

The Code of Hammurabi

Standing 2.25m (7ft) tall, a magnificent basalt pillar proclaims the law of Babylon in all its majesty. King Hammurabi had it created during the eighteenth century BC: it offers all sorts of insights into the life and society of his age.

> *Anyone who accuses someone of a crime in the presence of the elders but fails to prove his claim is – if the charge is a capital one – to be put to death.*
>
> *If he manages to prove his claim to the extent of getting the elders to levy a fine of grain or money, that fine will go to him…*
>
> *Anyone who steals property belonging either to a shrine or the royal court is to pay with his life; whoever receives that item shall also be executed.*
>
> *Anyone who makes a deal with someone's son or slave, without either witnesses or a written contract, to buy silver or gold, a male or female slave, an ox, sheep, ass or anything else, shall be regarded as a thief and therefore be executed.*
>
> *Anyone who breaks into a house is to be executed at the spot where he effected his entry and buried there.*
>
> *Anyone who commits a robbery is to be executed.*
>
> *If he is not caught, then his victim will report the extent of his loss under oath; the community shall then pay him compensation for what was taken.*
>
> *If, when a house is on fire, one of those who has come to help put it out notices valuables among the property of the house and takes them, he is to be thrown into that very fire…*
>
> *If conspirators meet in a tavern to plot a crime, and the tavern-keeper does not give them up, then she is guilty of their crime and shall be put to death…*

ON PUBLIC DISPLAY

Visitors to the Louvre, in Paris, may see the Code of Hammurabi amongst other ancient treasures.

Left: One of the earliest known codes of law, the Code of Hammurabi was created over 3750 years ago. It contains almost 300 separate provisions over a range of legal areas.

The medium is the message, wrote the modern commentator Marshall McLuhan, and that is certainly the case with the Code of Hammurabi. A work both of beauty and magnificence, the tapered black basalt stela with its carved reliefs and cuneiform text announces not just the actual provisions but the awesome splendour of the law. At the top, we see the king, his right arm raised in respect as he stands before the sun god Shamash to receive his laws. Below, in Akkadian (Old Babylonian) cuneiform, comes the code itself – 282 laws in all, dealing with everything from land and property to marriage and family relations.

Whilst the punishments stipulated are frequently draconian, one striking aspect of the code is the way in which it places the onus of proving guilt upon the accuser; mischievous allegations suffer severe penalties, even death. The code also places considerable faith on the sworn testimony of the accused – though whether this is a faith based on the decency of human nature or fear of the gods is hard to know.

THE EMPIRE BUILDER
The sixth king of Babylon, Hammurabi became the first ruler of the Babylonian Empire: his reign lasted from about 1792 BC to about 1750 BC. During that time, he pursued a policy of expansionism by both military and diplomatic means, extending his rule through the realms of Isin, Larsa, Eshnunna and Mari until he controlled the whole of greater Babylonia. His empire was not long to survive him, however. When the Hammurabi Law Code was discovered, it was not in Babylon but in Susa, where the Elamites had taken it as a trophy.

Not the First

The Code of Hammurabi may be the fullest and most magnificently presented, but it is by no means the first of the Mesopotamian law codes to be written down. King Ur-Nammu of Ur recorded his as early as 2050 BC, whilst Lipit-Ishtar of Isin set one down around 1930 BC.

Above: Hammurabi, some cynical scholars have said, was more concerned with justifying his own depredations in his law code, legitimizing his confiscations of property and land. Be that as it may, it strikes us as in many ways surprisingly enlightened in its understanding of justice and how it should be done.

Ugarit: A Blind Alphabetical Alley?

A busy seaport, Ugarit traded with both east and west – with Mesopotamia, the Mediterranean and Egypt. Its cosmopolitan culture accordingly looked both ways. This is clearly apparent in the unique script developed in the city: cuneiform symbols marshalled into a Phoenician-style alphabet.

One day in 1928, a peasant was ploughing his land outside Ras Shamra, a place in present-day Syria, on the Mediterranean coast. A vault opened up beneath him where the blade sank in: it turned out that he had discovered an ancient necropolis. Soon archeologists had found the city to which it belonged, a site of almost unbelievable antiquity: there was an urban settlement here 8000 years ago.

COSMOPOLIS

It was a bustling port: rich finds of pottery and other craft-items tell the story of Ugarit's trading links across the ancient world. From here, vessels plied back and forth to Cyprus and the Greek islands, which were by the late second millennium BC under the cultural and economic influence of the Mycenaean civilization. There is evidence of trade with Egypt too, albeit at a time of crisis when the Nile Delta region had fallen under the control of the Hyksos. These invaders, who occupied Lower Egypt for several generations, from around

1650 to 1540 BC, are believed to have been of Semitic origin themselves. (If, as many scholars believe, they hailed from the city of Byblos, just down the coast from Ugarit in modern Lebanon, the two peoples were once practically next-door neighbours.) But Ugarit's network of trading links also extended eastward and inland, along the Fertile Crescent to the Tigris and Euphrates Rivers and so into Mesopotamia, from where derived its first cuneiform script.

LIMITED BY LITERACY

Literacy is liberating, but over time the people of Ugarit appear to have found their writing a mixed blessing. With hindsight, it is easy enough to work out why. Cuneiform, with all its virtues, was quite the wrong sort of script for a busy seaport. Pictographic writing forms may be admirably clear once mastered, but that process can take a considerable amount of time. Sumerian cuneiform script comprised well over 500 different characters: a great deal of schooling

Above: Found at the site of Ugarit, Syria, this cast records some of the earliest alphabetical figures ever known, inscribed some time towards 1400 BC. By that time, cuneiform was commonplace through much of the Middle East, but the alphabet offered a whole new flexibility.

was required before an individual could learn to write.

In well-established, stable centres of culture, such practicalities mattered much less than might be imagined: a steady supply of scribes was constantly being trained. Their function was largely predictable, moreover: keeping track of tribute and taxes and recording the events of the court and the wider society. The rhythms of life moved slowly and predictably, in time with the rhythms of the growing season: there was no particular need for adaptability or haste.

A SOUND SCHEME

Ugarit could hardly have been more different. Like any port, it was full of foreigners: merchants, seafarers,

adventurers, many just passing through. Ships came and went on a daily basis; merchants made deals, payments were made and consignments dispatched. Those recording them were often not working in their first language. Hence, it seems, the adoption, in around 1400 BC, of an alphabet with letters corresponding to the most frequently used sounds. This system enabled words to be written out quickly and easily, so that even the comparatively uneducated could use it: if you knew how it sounded, you knew how it was written. One version, employed in commercial accounts and tax records, has 30 different letters; another, used for religious and literary texts, just 27. The latter was used, among other things, to record stories that were written down, centuries later, in the Bible. Ugarit's alphabet was an extraordinary breakthrough – and an inestimable boon for the seaport's clerks and captains.

Historically, though, it was destined for oblivion. It is not known for certain which came first, but another trading people, the Phoenicians, were developing their own alphabet at around the same time (*see pp. 152–153*): they used their own symbols, rather than adapting cuneiform. These were the letters which, later adopted by the Greeks, became the basis for the written scripts of the modern West.

ON PUBLIC DISPLAY

Entire rooms are dedicated to the treasures of Ugarit at Damascus' National Museum, including not just written tablets but sacred statues and imported luxuries.

A Missing Link?

More than a thousand examples of Ugarit script have been found: these have included several 'abecedaries', in which the alphabet-sequence is set out in order for the benefit of young learners. From this we learn, intriguingly, that Ugarit followed the same basic 'Alpha, Beta, Gamma…' order as the Greeks were to use, following on from their Phoenician model. This suggests the existence of a pre-existing alphabet, now lost – perhaps a proto-Canaanite one – on which both the Phoenician and Ugarit alphabets were ultimately based.

Right: That the scribes of Ugarit could cope with cuneiform is clear from finds like this clay tablet: here the Mesopotamian script is overlaid with the impression of the seal of King Mursil II (1345–20 BC).

The World's First Peace Treaty

In 1274 BC, the Egyptian and Hittite armies clashed at Kadesh: both sides emerged from the fighting badly bruised. Fifteen years later, they negotiated the terms of an agreement which would prevent any further wars between them, a paradigm for peace treaties ever since.

The Battle of Kadesh was fought not far from the city of that name on the banks of Syria's Orontes River, in 1274 BC or thereabouts. The army of Egypt and its allies was led by Rameses II, on an exploratory foray into the region. Egypt had only re-engaged with the wider Middle East relatively recently in the aftermath of the expulsion of the Hyksos (*see pp. 52–53*). The Amarna Letters (*see pp. 56–57*) reveal the reluctance of Egypt's Pharaohs to involve themselves in the region as recently as the mid-fourteenth century. But from about 1290, Rameses' father Seti I had consciously set about rebuilding Egyptian imperial power and had taken extensive territories – including Kadesh. The city had since been lost, but Rameses was determined to retake it and to continue pursuing Seti's expansionist strategy.

AMBUSH!

Two captives taken near Kadesh told him the Hittites' main force was far away, near Aleppo.

Emboldened, Rameses pushed on towards the city at breakneck speed. The Pharaoh's advance guard began to pull away from the main body of his force, so the Egyptian army was now stretched out over some distance, and – crucially – divided by the river. Even so, with 20,000 infantry and well over 2000 chariots at his disposal, Rameses would have been ready for most eventualities. Not, however, for the fact that – despite the assurances of his prisoners, clearly enemy agents – the Hittites were in reality close at hand, with almost 40,000 foot soldiers and 3000 chariots.

His heavy three-horse chariots leading the attack, Muwatallis, the Hittite king, sent his force smashing into the Egyptian army, which broke in the shock and confusion of the assault. An easy victory appeared to have been won, but as the Hittite forces paused to plunder, Rameses kept his nerve and managed to marshal his troops to mount a courageous counterattack in which his light and manoeuvrable chariots proved decisive.

TRUTH THE FIRST CASUALTY

The outcome appears to have been an honourable draw, though you would never have guessed this from the reactions of the propaganda machines of the respective sides. The first casualty of war, they always say, is truth. The Hittites claimed the victory, and with some justice: they did hold on to Kadesh, while those conquests the Egyptians did succeed in making were quickly to be recovered. Even so, they must have been disgusted to have had the power of Egypt's Pharaoh in their grasp and then somehow have contrived to let him go.

Rameses, meanwhile, bedecked the temple complexes at Thebes and Abu Simbel with celebratory inscriptions and reliefs of the battle. The Pharaoh had, it was true, shown heroism in extricating his army

ON PUBLIC DISPLAY

The Hittite Treaty of Kadesh is on display in the Archeological Museum, Istanbul.

Right: The treaty we have today, inscribed in clay, is believed to be a contemporary copy of an original which was made in solid silver. Its rhetoric may have a hollow ring, its eloquence may sound impossibly insincere, but the Treaty of Kadesh was still an inspiring first. Not only is it the earliest-known peace treaty; never before, it is believed, had the representatives of two states sat down to make a binding, written agreement of any kind.

from a desperate spot, and in the years that followed he managed to consolidate his position in the Middle East.

FROM ENMITY TO ALLIANCE
The real significance of the battle may have been that it showed the two sides that they could not defeat one another, except at enormous – and prohibitive – cost. The result was a 'balance of power' in the region; the establishment of mutual respect, if not affection. That respect was (literally) set in stone 15 years later at Kadesh itself when the 'Eternal Treaty' of the two states was formally agreed. It committed them not just to non-aggression but to an alliance in which each would come to the assistance of the other in the event of an attack by a third party. The Akkadian version (the only one still extant) is shown above the entrance to the chamber of the Security Council at the United Nations in New York.

Who Were the Hittites?

The Hittites appear to have originated somewhere in the region to the east of the Black Sea, and to have wandered into Anatolia between 5000 and 3000 BC. They made their home in the land called Hatti, from which they took their name. They make an elusive subject for study since they cheerfully adopted many of the customs and deities of the areas they settled and conquered. By the middle of the second millennium BC, they had built an empire extending into Syria, Lebanon, Palestine and Mesopotamia and made themselves credible rivals to the might of neighbouring Egypt.

Left: Rameses II rides into battle in his chariot, a stirring sight, as depicted in his own propagandist art: the Egyptians saw Kadesh as a great victory. The reality was less cut-and-dried, though there is no doubt that Rameses and his army conducted themselves with courage and decision.

“ *Previously, from the beginnings of time, the gods did not let enmity arise between Egypt's mighty ruler and the High Prince of Hatti. During the reign of my brother Muwatallis, High Prince of Hatti, though, there was war with Rameses Meri-Amon, great Pharaoh. But from this day on, Hattusilis, Great Prince of Hatti, is committed to making a lasting contract of the deal which Re and Seth made on Egypt's behalf with the realm of Hatti, so that further fighting should forever be prevented.*

Peace and fraternity shall forever prevail between us…
The children of the children of the Great Prince of Hatti will be at peace with the children of the children of Rameses Meri-Amon, great Pharaoh, for they too will live in fraternity and peace. ”

The Black Obelisk of Shalmaneser III

The exploits of Shalmaneser go on and on; high rhetoric becomes routine: victory after victory, triumph after triumph. Yet this is no boast but an end-of-reign report, a reckoning for an Assyria that saw waging war as the business of the state.

It was towards the end of the 1840s that the French-born British diplomat and archeologist Austen Henry Layard began his excavations at Nimrud – the ancient Assyrian capital of Kalhu, beside the Tigris in what is now Iraq. Among the extraordinary finds he made was a black marble obelisk 1.5m (5ft) tall, with pictorial designs and inscribed text on every face. Translated in the years that followed, this proved to be a sustained and detailed account of the military campaigns conducted by the Assyrian king Shalmaneser III in a reign that lasted from 859 to 842 BC. The son and successor to Ashurnasirpal II, Shalmaneser made the conquests that made Assyria the pre-eminent power in Mesopotamia and the Middle East.

A CATALOGUE OF CONQUESTS
'I am Shalmaneser, King of multitudes of men, prince and hero of Assur,' the inscription starts,

ON PUBLIC DISPLAY

The Black Obelisk of Shalmaneser III is currently displayed at the British Museum in London.

> **❝** *...the strong King, King of all the four zones of the Sun and of multitudes of men, the marcher over the whole world; son of Ashurnasirpal, the supreme hero, who...has caused all the world to kiss his feet...who has laid his yoke on all lands hostile to him and has swept them like a whirlwind.* **❞**

Right: Kings queue up to abase themselves before Shalmaneser in the figurative panels which continue round all four faces of the obelisk.

An impressive opening, but the modern reader soon tires of the relentlessly heroic rhetoric in the apparently unending catalogue of victories which follows:

> *In my eleventh year for the ninth time the Euphrates I crossed. Cities to a countless number I captured. To the cities of the Hittites of the land of the Hamathites I went down. Eighty-nine cities I took. Rimmon-idri of Damascus and twelve of the Kings of the Hittites with one another's forces strengthened themselves. A destruction of them I made.*

Below: The detail is stunning: five different kings have been identified from the carved reliefs, from Anatolia, Syria, Iran, Israel and Egypt.

The ritual or symbolic importance of all these crossings of the Euphrates remains unclear. What is apparent, though, is that Shalmaneser was practically commuting back and forth across the river with his armies:

> *In my nineteenth campaign for the eighteenth time the Euphrates I crossed. To the land of Amanus I ascended. Logs of cedar I cut. In my twentieth year for the twentieth time the Euphrates I crossed. To the land of Kahue I went down. Their cities I captured. Their spoil I carried off. In my twenty-first campaign, for the twenty-first time the Euphrates I crossed. To the cities of Hazael of Damascus I went. Four of his fortresses I took. The tribute of the Tyrians, the Sidonians and the Gebalites I received.*

Five friezes around the obelisk show subject rulers bringing tribute to the Assyrian king, among them Jehu, the king of Israel, subjugated in 841 BC.

WAR AS A WAY OF LIFE

Today what strikes us about the inscription is the way it makes the heroic first monotonous and then finally mundane, banal even, but then war had become the business of the Assyrian state. As important as agriculture, campaigning had its own place in the seasonal cycle, between the spring planting and the autumn harvest. The Assyrians were ruthlessly matter-of-fact in their prosecution of war: civilians were slaughtered, captives killed and prisoners sometimes suspended in cages from the walls of the cities they had bravely defended. Such outrages seem to have been inspired less by sheer sadism or bloodlust than by a practical sense that they would encourage cooperation from other peoples. Whether this makes their atrocities more justified is highly questionable, of course. Almost 3000 years before Hannah Arendt saw it at work in the Nazi Holocaust, the 'banality of evil' was in evidence in the Middle East.

Protesting Too Much?
A CV for Sargon

Sargon II was to be remembered as one of Assyria's greatest kings, but his accession was wrapped in controversy and doubt. Ancient rulers were never shy of discussing their achievements, but there is perhaps an anxious air about Sargon's insistent self-advertisement.

ON PUBLIC DISPLAY

Sargon's inscription is among the exhibits at the Louvre Museum in Paris.

Who was Sargon II? Suddenly, in 722 BC, he turned up as co-ruler to Assyria's Shalmaneser V. Was he the younger brother? No one knew. The Assyrian court was remote and, as the people now realized, its political ins and outs were far from clear. Shalmaneser's background was not in doubt; he was unquestionably the son of the great Tiglathpileser III.

Sargon, however, seemed to have emerged out of nowhere. Not that Assyrians were to have the luxury of puzzling over his pedigree for long. Shalmaneser died that same year while campaigning in Samaria: the breath had barely left his body before Sargon had himself crowned.

THE 'TRUE KING'

Sargon did not dwell much on his antecedents: the inscriptions with which he festooned his palaces suggest egocentric rather than dynastic pride; that of the 'self-made man' perhaps. He preferred to look to the future rather than to the past, except in one crucial matter – that of his choice of regnal name.

'Sargon', as the whole of Mesopotamia knew, was a title which until then had been hallowed to Sargon the Great, still revered for his rule of Akkad almost a thousand years before.

He was famed for having built what amounted to the region's first great empire, conquering all the cities of Sumer. But his name had another important resonance: literally, Sargon meant 'The King is Legitimate' or 'The True King'. So was the new Assyrian ruler protesting too much?

Left: All the doings of a ruler's reign could be recorded around a barrel cylinder like this, which, when buried in the foundations of a new building, became a sort of 'time capsule'.

Right: For the man who had so coolly helped himself to Shalmaneser's kingdom, the appropriation of a dead man's name would hardly have signified, but all Mesopotamia understood the connotations of the title 'Sargon'.

"These are my actions from the commencement of my reign to its fifteenth year: I crushed Khumbanigas, the King of Elam, on Kalu's plains.

I besieged the city of Samaria, took it and captured 27,280 of its people. I took 50 chariots but left them the rest of their possessions. I placed my officials in charge; I restored the tributary arrangement imposed by one of my predecessors…

I took tribute from the Pharaoh of Egypt and from Samsie, Arabian Queen; It-amar of Sabea gave me gold, fragrant herbs, horses and camels.

When Kiakku of Sinukhta blasphemed against the god Assur and refused to do him homage, I took him captive, along with 30 chariots and 7350 soldiers. I gave his city, Sinukhta, to the governorship of Matti of Tuna and increased the tribute, including some horses and asses.

I mounted a punitive expedition against the unholy and insubordinate Chaldeans. Merodach-Baladan heard that my force was approaching and, fearing that his own army would crumble in its cowardice, fell back, flying like an owl in the night, and took refuge in Ikbibel, Babylonia. He brought together the gods and oracles from all the cities around and placed them in the citadel of Dur-Iakin, whose walls he reinforced. Calling on assistance from the tribes of Gambul, Pukud, Tamun, Ruhua and Khindar, he dug in with them, preparing for a fight. He created a great ditch 2000 spans in width and a fathom and a half deep before his wall and, by digging canals, filled it with water diverted from the Euphrates so that his city was an island. …I deployed my warriors in small groups all around the edge of the water along the canals and they conquered their enemies. The waters were coloured red, like dyed wool, by the rebels' blood."

The 'City of Sargon'

Sargon II's claims to be a 'true' Assyrian king could not have been maintained without the construction of a new capital like Ashurnasirpal's Nimrud. Dur-Sarrukin (the 'City of Sargon') was a fittingly grandiose construction, conceived as a memorial to his reign.

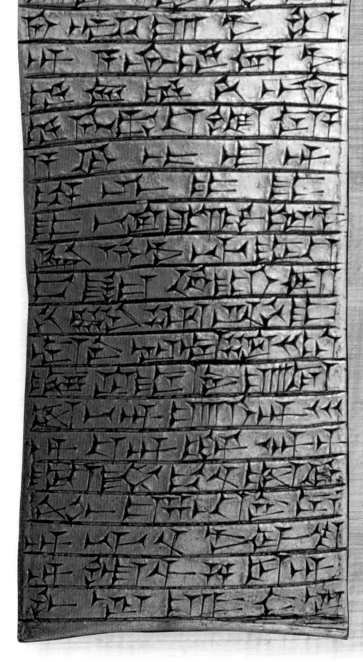

ON PUBLIC DISPLAY

This inscription is one of the treasures of the Vatican Museum in Rome.

> *At that time, these peoples and these states whose submission I had compelled with the help of the gods Assur, Nebo and Merodach, had been set upon the path of piety. With the assistance of the gods, following both their will and the wishes of my own heart, I built…a city that I called Dur-Sarrukin as a replacement for Nineveh. Nisroch, Sin, Samas, Nebo, Bin, Ninip and their divine spouses who live and reproduce eternally in the heights of heaven and the depths of the underworld all gave its stupendous buildings and glittering streets their blessing. I reformed all those rites and ceremonies which were not to the gods' liking: after much learned debate about the different divinities and the sacrifices due to them, my priests devised new rituals.*
>
> *I built in Dur-Sarrukin palaces roofed with the hide of the sea-calf and from the timbers of sandalwood, ebony, mastic cedar, cypress, pistachio I created a palace of unequalled magnificence. This was to be my royal seat. I inscribed as foundation-documents tablets of gold, silver, alabaster…copper, lead, iron, tin and clay. I recorded on these the glory of the gods.*

Left: Discovered in the ruins of Dur-Sarrukin, at Khorsabad, this tablet was found carefully concealed within a wall: it records Sargon's self-justifying account of his life and reign.

Sargon II's right to play the part of Assyrian king may have been distinctly dubious, but there is no doubt that he was convincing in the role. Continuing the conquests of Tiglathpileser III, he pushed eastward against the power of Elam, and northwest up the Euphrates Valley. Following the curve of the ancient Fertile Crescent, he extended his country's territory through western Syria and then onward down the Mediterranean seaboard. He scored important victories over the Medes and the Egyptians.

MEGALOMANIAC MONUMENT
It is no surprise that a ruler simultaneously so strong and so insecure should have wanted to create a lasting memorial to his reign. He did so by building himself a new capital, Dur-Sarrukin, or 'City of Sargon', northeast of Nineveh – in today's terms, 15km (9 miles) north of Mosul, at Khorsabad. Though there was a precedent for this in Ashurnasirpal's Nimrud, built a century or so before, the need for Sargon was the more pressing as he sought to stake his own individual

claim to imperial glory. The new city was to give architectural form to all its builder's pretensions as monarch: at its heart was a palace-complex, with more than 200 rooms and 30 courtyards and with temples for all the great Assyrian gods. Its construction reflected the scale of Sargon's conquests – not just in its magnificence but in the range of materials used. Gold, silver, copper, cedar wood, and other more exotic materials were brought from every corner of the empire. The city, rectangular in plan, occupied an area of 280 hectares (700 acres). There were seven great gateways in the massive wall that surrounded it; this was further fortified by over 150 towers. The royal palace and its shrines had their own wall, along with a ziggurat – a spiral tower. There were stupendous statues and sculpted wall-reliefs throughout.

Everything was built on a colossal scale, but even so there is one wall so gigantic as to be almost absurd. Found by the French archeologist who began excavating the complex in the mid-nineteenth century, it was built to a thickness of 8m (26ft). It was the hiding place for a stone box

Above: Sargon's palace-complex at Khorsabad was conceived on a colossal scale, as befitted the greatest (and most self-advertising) ruler of his age.

holding inscribed tablets of gold, silver, copper, and other materials. These, the foundation tablets, describe, in Sargon's own words, the course of this extravagant project from start to finish.

Sadly, the city remained uncompleted at his death, and his son Sennacherib preferred to create his own capital, a rebuilt Nineveh. In the end, then, Sargon's boasts have a hollow ring – as, for that matter, do the halls and passages of his palace, which appear to have been something of an empty shell. The architecture, integral inscriptions and heavy sculptures apart, archeologists found surprisingly few artefacts here. Certainly, very little in the way of moveable items: the strong impression left is that the city may never even have been occupied. As impressive as it is, there is a faintly ludicrous melancholy about the complex. Had the 'City of Sargon' really just been Sargon's Folly?

Sennacherib's Prism

The son of Sargon II, Sennacherib was in his way to prove as controversial a ruler as his father. Uncertainty surrounds several aspects of his reign. The so-called Taylor Prism gives the official line on his campaigns, including his war against Judah in 701 BC.

The Assyrian who came down on Jerusalem 'like a wolf on the fold' (to use the poet Byron's words) is now regarded very much as a soldier-king. As, indeed, was every Assyrian ruler, and Sennacharib's career – round after round of wars, apparently without end – is documented by the Taylor Prism (so-called after the British Consul General in Baghdad who came by it in 1830).

A LEGACY OF DOUBT
But questions surround many of his conquests – even his most famous one, the Sack of Jerusalem

Left: Sennacherib's Prism, also known as the Taylor Prism, was found in 1830, amidst the ruins of Nineveh – now Nebi Yunus, near Mosul, in Iraq. Sennacherib built this city partly as a way of inscribing himself a fresh identity as something other than Sargon II's son.

ON PUBLIC DISPLAY

The Taylor Prism may today be seen at London's British Museum.

❝ *Sennacherib the great, the magnificent world-ruler, King of Assyria and of the four quarters of the world. Wise shepherd to his people; beloved of the gods; protector of right, overseer of justice; friend of the poor; pious in his offices; great hero, strong warrior, foremost among princes. He it is whose rage destroys the rebellious, whose thunderbolt fells the wicked. The god of Assur, the mighty mountain, has a special kinship with me and my court; he has ensured that my weapons have prevailed everywhere, from the upper sea of the sunset to the lower sea of the rising sun...*

in 701 BC. The cliché would have it that history is 'written by the victors', but it is hard to know who was victorious in this case. Whilst Sennacherib's version leaves no room for ambiguity, neither do those of the Jewish scribes. The Second Book of Kings (Chapters 18–19) accepts that Sennacherib's forces did to begin with gain a stranglehold on Hezekiah's Judah, but insists that the Jewish capital was then saved. The Angel of the Lord came down in the night and cut down the Assyrians' leading warriors, it says. Sennacherib was forced to withdraw, returning home, where he was promptly assassinated by two of his own sons. This account is repeated in the Second Book of Chronicles (Chapter 32).

Sennacherib's campaign in Egypt was also controversial: again a successful venture is said to have been cut short by an unforeseen disaster. According to the Greek historian Herodotus (albeit writing almost three centuries later), the Pharaoh's kingdom was defenceless, its army in mutiny. Before Sennacherib's coup de grâce could be delivered, though, an army of field-mice stole into the Assyrian tents in the dead of night and chewed up their bowstrings and the thongs of their shields, leaving them effectively unarmed.

THE BUILDER
A controversial career in the field of battle, then, but in truth it seems that Sennacherib wanted to be remembered not just as a sacker of cities but as a builder too.

The great project of his life was the rebuilding of Assyria's old capital at Nineveh. Whilst this was clearly a bid to distance himself from the memory of his father Sargon II (who is seldom mentioned in his

Above: Sennacherib's reign was plagued by persistent unrest in the Assyrian Empire. He was forced to intervene in Babylon and Egypt – and, notoriously, in Judah.

inscriptions), he plainly wanted to leave himself a more constructive monument.

> " *Hezekiah of Judah would not bow down to me. Forty-six of his strongholds – all walled cities – as well as innumerable smaller towns in his territory were taken. My men brought up siege-engines, razed them to the ground with battering-rams, attacked and took them by storm, stole in through breaches made in the surrounding walls or undermined their fortifications with mines and tunnels. One way or another, I laid siege to them and took them. 200,150 people of high and low estate, both men and women were taken captive. I carried off as booty countless horses, mules, asses, camels, cattle and sheep. The King himself was holed up in his royal city, caught like a bird in a cage. I built ramps and fortifications to prevent people from leaving the city, imprisoning them in their wretchedness. Having sacked his [other] cities, I cut them off from their hinterlands…The glory of my greatness overwhelmed Hezekiah in his terror: the Arabs and other mercenaries who had come to serve him deserted him. In the end he had to submit to my yoke and to pay me tribute: 30 talents of gold; 800 talents of silver; gems; antimony; jewels; carnelian; couches and chairs inlaid with ivory; elephant hides and tusks; ebony, boxwood and other rich treasures, along with his daughters, his wives, his musicians – men and women…All these things I had brought to me in Nineveh.* "

The First Flood

From the *Epic of Gilgamesh* comes the terrifying story of the flood that overwhelmed the world, washing away a humanity steeped in sin. This is real literature – dramatically constructed, poetically expressed and morally challenging in the most fascinating way.

The world's first work of literature, the *Epic of Gilgamesh* is thought to have been first written down in Sumer in the second half of the third millennium BC. The poem itself may be much older: many of the great mythological epics of the ancient past circulated in the oral tradition for many centuries before anyone actually got round to writing them down. The version we are most familiar with today is a comparatively 'late' one, recorded over a thousand years later in the Neo-Assyrian Era. Written on a series of clay tablets, this text was one of the great glories of the seventh-century Royal Library of Ashurbanipal at Nineveh.

A FLAWED HERO
The poem's protagonist, Gilgamesh, is supposed to have been a king of the ancient city of Uruk, who reigned some time around 2600 BC. He was the son of the goddess Ninsun, the poem tells us, and thus semi-divine. The epic describes his adventures and misadventures. Gilgamesh is a morally complex figure – certainly when seen from a modern perspective.

As the story begins, his own people have asked for the gods' protection from Gilgamesh, a lord who bullies the men and violently seduces their young brides. Hearing their prayers, the earth-goddess Shamhat sends a wild man, Enkidu, to try to control him. Through their various struggles, the two grow from being enemies and opponents to fast friends – and, finally, brothers, when Gilgamesh's mother adopts Enkidu as her own son.

The wild man's death leaves the hero devastated, both by bereavement and by fear for himself, and he sets out on a quest to find the secret of immortality. It is in the course of this that he meets Utnapishtim and his wife, the only human survivors of the great flood sent by the angry gods to drown the earth.

A Deluge of Floods

The parallels between Utnapishtim and the biblical Noah are very obvious: the more so when we read the details of how he constructs his 'ark', to strict specifications ordained by Shamash, the sun-god. There is little doubt that the writers of the Jewish scripture, if not actually influenced by the *Gilgamesh* account, were at least drawing upon a common stock of inherited stories. Deluge legends exist in other ancient cultures too, from the Greek myth of Deucalion to that of Matya in Hindu tradition. But in Mesopotamia the idea of a primal, purging inundation appears to have loomed particularly large – perhaps because, in these alluvial plains, the risk of catastrophic flooding was never far away. Suffice it to say that the old Sumerian King List (*see pp. 16–17*) features the flood as part of its historical chronology.

Left: Flanked by two impressive demigods who hold a winged sun in triumph above his head, the hero Gilgamesh has an oddly stunted look. But he towered in his achievements – that this Syrio-Hittite stela should have been created 1500 years or more after his exploits were first written down is testimony to the hold his story had.

Right: The Gilgamesh deluge story as it appears in a tablet of the first millennium BC. The fullest text we have was found in the Royal Library of Ashurbanipal at Nineveh.

> *The angry gods felt in their hearts the urge to send a mighty flood…All day the wind blew from the south; fast and strong it came, plunging the mountain deep in water; the torrent rushed over the people like an advancing army. They could not see each other or distinguish one another for the flood. The gods themselves were struck with terror: they withdrew to Anu's heaven, where they crouched, cowering like frightened dogs. Ishtar screamed like a woman giving birth: her voice, usually so soft and gentle, screeched…'How could I have called for a catastrophe to destroy my people? Hardly have I given birth to my people than the world becomes an ocean, and they like fish!'…For six days and seven nights, the storm continued to rage without abating, the wind and rain assaulting the earth. By the seventh day, the deluge was more like a war, striving against itself, like a woman racked by the agonies of labour.*

Rebuilding Babylon

In 689 BC, Sennacherib's army sacked Babylon so thoroughly that little more than a smoking ruin was left. That did not stop his son, Esarhaddon, claiming the plaudits when he rebuilt the city – and the shrine of Esagila – in the 670s.

" Great king, mighty monarch, lord of all, king of the land of Assur, ruler of Babylon, faithful shepherd, beloved of Marduk, lord of lords…dutiful leader, loved by Zurpanitum [Marduk's consort]…humble, obedient, full of praise for their strength and awestruck from his earliest days in the presence of their divine greatness…When in the reign of an earlier king there were ill omens, the city offended its gods and was destroyed at their command, it was me, Esarhaddon, whom they chose to restore everything to its rightful place, to calm their anger, to assuage their wrath. You, Marduk, entrusted the protection of the land of Assur to me. The Gods of Babylon meanwhile told me to rebuild their shrines and renew the proper religious observances of their palace, Esagila…I called up all my workmen and conscripted all the people of Babylonia. I set them to work, digging up the ground and carrying the earth away in baskets. "

Left: Esarhaddon, Assyrian king (680–669 BC). A dominant Esarhaddon dwarfs the kneeling figure of the Pharaoh Taharqa's son Ushanakhuru and (standing behind him) the king of Tyre.

Esarhaddon believed in leading from the front, taking a central role in what we would nowadays call the 'groundbreaking ceremony' for the new Esagila. Once the damaged temple had been demolished and its site fully cleared, he says:

> *I poured libations of the finest oil, honey, ghee, red wine, white wine…To instil respect and fear for the power of Marduk in the people, I myself picked up the first basket of earth, raised it on to my head and carried it…*

Sennacherib's sacking of Babylon may have been a major military triumph, but it had badly dented the image of Assyria in the region. The destruction of the city – and, especially, of Esagila – had widely been seen as an act of sacrilege. Rebuilding was the very least his son could do, if he was to reconstruct the reputation of his kingdom: Esarhaddon had a great deal of making-up to do. You would never guess that, though, from the tone and terminology of his dedicatory account.

PUTTING THE WORLD TO RIGHTS
His father's actions are passed over just about completely, apart from a coy reference to 'the reign of an earlier king'. No mention is made of Assyria's part in the destruction. On the contrary, the blame for the disaster is placed on the presiding deities of the metropolis – and ultimately, given the provocation these gods are said to have received, on the city's people. Esarhaddon's own role, he would have us believe, is that of conciliator, salving the wounds made by mortal transgression and divine wrath. Determined to renew the covenant between Babylon and its gods, he has mobilized the people into rebuilding their shrine so that this relationship might be cemented.

ON PUBLIC DISPLAY

Esarhaddon's account of Babylon's rebuilding may be seen at the British Museum in London.

Sacred Precincts

The home shrine to the great god Marduk, the Esagila temple complex had been the religious centre of Babylon since the eighteenth century BC. At that time, Babylon was emerging as the main power in Mesopotamia, so Marduk – the supreme deity of the Babylonian pantheon – was more widely adopted by the region's different cultures. Successive Assyrian kings were to affirm their loyalty to Marduk, so Esarhaddon's praises need not be dismissed as cynical. At the same time, though, to identify himself so closely with Marduk's cult was politically shrewd.

   The temple at Babylon was square in plan, with an outer and an inner court, inside which was the actual shrine, where the statues of Marduk and Zurpanitum were housed in a 'holy of holies'. To the north of the temple was a great ziggurat (sacred spiral tower), reported to have been up to 92m (300ft) high – the original, perhaps, for the fabled Tower of Babel.

Babylonian Map of the World

One of Mesopotamia's most intriguing legacies dates from around 600 BC: a map of the world with Babylon at its centre. It represents the world not as it measurably was but as it was mythologically conceived, its starlike form opening a window on the ancient imagination.

World Centre

In presenting a view of the world, any map at the same time presents a 'worldview' – an ordered set of assumptions and attitudes. This one, with its breezy metro-centrism, its apparently unquestioning assumption that Babylon was the hub at the heart of things, speaks volumes for the self-confidence of the city. (A modern equivalent might be the satirical map of 'America from Manhattan', which, while reluctantly acknowledging the existence of Los Angeles and San Francisco, excludes the Midwest in its entirety.) Of course, the Babylon rebuilt by Nabopolassar and Nebuchadnezzar had a great deal to be self-confident about: it was no great exaggeration to see it as the centre of the world.

ON PUBLIC DISPLAY

This marvellous map is one of the highlights of the British Museum's incomparable collection.

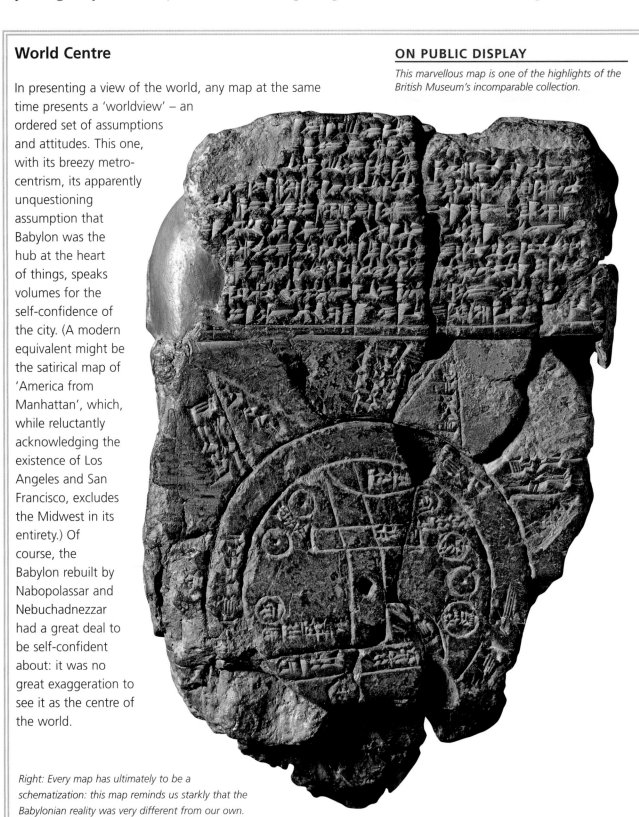

Right: Every map has ultimately to be a schematization: this map reminds us starkly that the Babylonian reality was very different from our own.

This inscribed clay tablet was discovered at Sippar, in southern Iraq. At first glance, it hardly seems a map at all. On closer examination, things become clearer, though the contents are set out in a highly stylized, schematic form. The world (or, at least, its land area, the earth as trodden by humanity) is circular in shape and surrounded by a 'river' of 'bitter' water – in other words, the salt sea. Just above its centre, a rectangular Babylon spans the straight lines presumably intended to represent the Euphrates River; around the edge of the landmass are seven small circles – presumably cities. Assyria, Armenia and Elam are all named in the cuneiform inscription, along with several cities, but none of these can clearly be identified on the map. A curve cutting in from the top of the map appears to show the rising eminence of the Zagros Mountains, while parallel lines near the bottom seem to represent the southern marshes.

To modern eyes, the map is tantalizing: there are clear cartographical correspondences to be traced, yet the overall effect still seems fantastical. Tempting as it is to see the points of the compass in the starlike shape of the map, the reality is that its guiding principles are more mythological than geographical in the modern sense.

AMBIGUOUS ISLANDS

That being the case, it is hard to know whether the seven islands or regions (the triangular points) are supposed to be literal geographical entities, lying beyond the sea, or more spiritual realms, removed in some more transcendent way. The inscription seems to support both interpretations: one island is identified as the 'place of the rising sun' – because, prosaically enough, it lies in the east; on another island, a monstrous bull stomps and snorts, attacking and goring the unwary

Above: An atmospheric view across the ruined walls of Ur underlines the remoteness of the civilization they represent. The world has been transformed – and transformed again, many times over – in the millennia since Mesopotamia was at its height.

trespasser. The other descriptions can be read either way, too: in one, for instance, 'the sun is hidden and nothing can be seen'... Is this some pit of existential despair or moral banishment, or simply a place far to the north?

Is the island that is said to be 'beyond the flight of birds' just a long way off or remote in some more fundamental sense? And what of the island whose light, we are told, is 'brighter than the stars'?

Setting the World to Rights

Many in Mesopotamia must have felt alienated by the arrogance of the Babylonian worldview; today we are more likely to be touched by its naivety. In truth, though, the Neo-Babylonian state could be forgiven a bit of chauvinism – especially because its glory had been so recently and so hard won. A thousand years had passed since 'Old Babylon' had flourished; for much of the interim, Babylon had been a subject state, most often to the mighty Assyrian Empire. It must have been especially satisfying for the map's creator to relegate Assyria to the margins.

The Boaster of Babylon

Under the guise of a dedication to the god Marduk, Nebuchadnezzar II launched an extraordinary paean of praise to himself. The ancient conqueror's boasts appealed to modern empire builders: the British took the inscribed column back for exhibition in London's East India House.

 Nebuchadnezzar, King of Babylon, renowned ruler, worshipper of Marduk, honourer of the great one, glorifier of Nebu, the wise…I am the heroic son of Nabopolassar, King of Babylon…

ON PUBLIC DISPLAY

The East India House Inscription can be viewed in Room 55: 'Mesopotamia' at East India House, London.

Above: This stone block with finely carved cuneiform was found in the ruins of Babylon and was presented to the representative of the East India Company in Baghdad, hence its modern name – the East India House Inscription.

Towards the end of the eighteenth century, a black basalt column was discovered during the excavation of Babylon. It came into the hands of Sir Harford Jones Bridges, the local representative of the East India Company. He sent it back to London in 1801, whereafter it was exhibited in the company's City headquarters, East India House. The scholars who first unpicked its cuneiform inscription were fascinated by what it revealed of a king who while not quite the unmitigated tyrant described in the Bible still has much in common with the man the Jews loved to hate.

> *The walls of Babylon...I extended all the way round the city. I dug out a deep defensive ditch and threw up massive ramparts of brick and cement. To one side stood a lofty tower like a mountain. Great gates of pine wood covered with copper kept the enemy out of unvanquished Babylon. I brought deep waters before the city, as vast as the sea: there was no way through. I carefully fortified these defences and fitted Babylon out to be a city of treasures.*

PRIDE AND PREJUDICE

'Is not this great Babylon, which I have built for the royal dwelling-place, by the might of my power and for the glory of my majesty?' The Nebuchadnezzar of the Book of Daniel is punished for his pride by being driven out into the fields 'to eat grass like oxen...until his hair was grown like eagles' feathers and his nails like birds' claws'. His historical model seems to have suffered no worse humiliation than a military defeat or two. An attempt to invade Egypt in 601 BC was beaten back and several subject nations – including the Jews – took the opportunity of rebelling. All were severely put down.

When the Jews rose in revolt just a few years later, the Babylonian ruler reacted by destroying their Temple and abducting their political and intellectual elite, in what became known as the Babylonian Captivity. Hence, of course, the portrayal this extraordinary monarch receives in scripture.

The real Nebuchadnezzar was named for Nebu, the Mesopotamian god of wisdom and son of the great deity Marduk. However toxic his relations with Judah, he restored his own state to regional dominance after centuries of Assyrian hegemony in Mesopotamia and the Middle East. Though Babylon had held sway about a millennium before, it had soon been eclipsed by the rise of Assyria. In 626, however, Nabopolassar had successfully risen against Assyrian rule and in 612 he had even sacked the Assyrian capital, Nineveh. Assyria itself, along with its possessions, passed under the control of what was now a powerful Neo-Babylonian Empire.

REBUILDING BABYLON

Fact and symbolism seem to flow together in the life and personality of his son, Nebuchadnezzar. Having succeeded his father at some time around 605 BC, he became, both literally and figuratively, the rebuilder of Babylon. The East India House Inscription describes in detail how he repaired the flood damage to a temple his father had built. It relates too how he mobilized the people in an unprecedented programme of public works: soon, it says, enormous new buildings were rising up 'like mountains'.

This, the chroniclers agree, was no empty boast: as reconstructed by Nebuchadnezzar, Babylon was among the most spectacular cities of ancient times. That it has come down to us as the ultimate in big, bad, decadent cities, corrupt and cynical, is once again due to the – understandable, yet unfortunate – prejudice of the Jewish scribes. Less hostile observers describe a city of immense wealth and great magnificence, whose celebrated 'hanging gardens' (supposedly built by the king for his wife, Amytis of

Above: A reconstruction of the outer entrance of the Ishtar Gate, Pergamon Museum, Berlin. The original was built in the reign of Nebuchadnezzar II and was first excavated in 1902 by German archeologists.

Media, who missed her mountain homeland) were later ranked among the Seven Wonders of the World.

A MIRACULOUS CONCEPTION

To modern eyes, Nebuchadnezzar's pronouncement reveals an extraordinary blend of self-advertisement and self-effacement as the king boasts his own achievements under the guise of fulsomely thanking the gods who helped him. In the end, the piety he is at such pains to stress and the vainglory he actually ends up showing can scarcely be separated.

There is no doubting his conviction that he was divinely chosen. Having documented his efforts to foster the worship of the gods among his people, his rich refurbishments of the major temples Esagila and Ezida, and his assiduousness in constructing new shrines, Nebuchadnezzar recalls the moment of his own conception. No ordinary child, he says, he was the conscious creation of the greatest of the gods:

> *When Marduk, my divine creator, made me, he planted my seed inside my mother: then was I conceived.*

Egypt

The Pyramids and the Great Sphinx at Giza; the treasure-crammed tombs of the Valley of the Kings; the temples and palaces of Luxor; the massive royal statues at Abu Simbel – the majesty of Egyptian civilization is most obviously announced in incomparable monuments such as these, still awe-inspiring so many centuries after they were built.

Yet the greatest achievement of the Egyptians, arguably, was the sheer longevity of their culture, the striking continuity it showed over almost 3000 years. The Pyramids were well over a thousand years old when Tutankhamun ascended the Pharaonic throne; a further thousand years would elapse before the invasion of Alexander the Great. Even then, the Egyptian spirit endured: the heirs of Alexander's general Ptolemy showed great sensitivity towards the country's native culture. Only in 30 BC, when Octavian (later Augustus) brought the territory into the Roman Empire, could the history of Pharaonic Egypt really be said to be at an end.

That history had to a considerable extent already been written. As in Mesopotamia, a bureaucratic culture excelled in record-keeping. The result is that we can date dynasties, reigns and even individual events far more accurately than might be imagined. Even so, the Egyptian record – as preserved in the Palermo Stone, inscribed in the second half of the third millennium BC (*see pp. 46–47*) – becomes less reliable the further back it goes. 'Predynastic' times are certainly represented – in voluminous and extravagant detail – but the god-kings listed are clearly mythical.

Left: Backed by the bulk of the Great Pyramid, the Sphinx gazes inscrutably out across the desert. But, unmistakably familiar though the images are, much in Egyptian civilization remains mysterious. Fortunately, inscriptions can shed some light.

THE ARCHEOLOGICAL evidence suggests that by about 4000 BC an identifiable 'Egyptian' culture was taking shape along the Nile. Excavations at Nagada, north of Luxor, have found what appear to be traces of an early urban centre. Around it were the fields that were refreshed with water and replenished with fertile silt each year when the river flooded, thereby enabling abundant harvests. Such settlements set the pattern for a way of life that continued across the following millennia, conforming with the rhythms of the Nile, its rising and retreating waters.

It did not, however, make much sense at this point to talk of 'Egypt' – chiefly, because there were two Egypts, an Upper and a Lower. The former was based upriver in the main valley of the Nile itself; the latter along the muddy channels of the Delta. The first had its capital at Nekhen or Hierakonpolis, where remains of a fourth-millennium temple of Horus, the falcon-god, have been found; the second was ruled from Buto, modern Tell el-Fara'in, now some way inland but at that time a coastal city. Each of these two states developed its own distinct identity and culture through what we now call the 'Predynastic' period.

The two states were brought together, supposedly, by King Narmer, a hazy figure who straddles the worlds of history and myth. Whether he actually existed, or whether the chroniclers felt compelled to come up with a fittingly heroic story to account for a union that happened for more complex economic and political reasons, we have no way of being sure (*see pp. 44–45*). Suffice it to say that from this time on, Egypt was for the most part ruled as a single realm, though the Upper and Lower states did to some extent retain their separate character.

BUILT ON LITERACY

Tantalizing evidence has appeared recently to support the view that there was indeed a 'Dynasty Zero' – perhaps of Narmer's successors – before Egyptian history began with what is still called the First Dynasty. Even the First and Second Dynasties are shrouded in mystery, however: the official chronicles of the 'Old Kingdom' are not generally considered to begin until the reign of Nebka (2686–2613 BC), which ushered in the time of the Third Dynasty. The Old Kingdom was the age of the pyramids: the earliest, Djoser's so-called 'Step Pyramid',

was built at Saqqara around 2610 BC. Sneferu's 'Bent Pyramid' at Dahshur followed in about 2575 BC, whilst Khufu's 'Great Pyramid' at Giza was built around 2550 BC.

By this time, however, the history of writing in Egypt was well advanced. Early hieroglyphics are a feature of the Narmer Palette. A label above his head identifies the ruler, punning visually upon his name, the sign of the catfish, *n'r*, followed by that of the chisel, *mr*, to give 'Narmer'. Contrary to what scholars long assumed, the hieroglyphics employed were indeed mostly pictograms (literally, stylized depictions of what they represented) but certain phonetic (sound-based) symbols were also used.

Writing had an important ceremonial function in Egyptian culture, but its practical applications were far-reaching. The Pharaohs are now famous for ambitious construction projects – not just pyramids but also palaces and temples, built on an extensive scale – and none of these could have been accomplished without an efficient army of clerks or scribes. They kept meticulous records to keep track of the collection of grain given as tax and tribute, its storage and distribution. They organized the call-up for the corvée – the conscription of labour. And, for a society now built on the use of writing, they also kept careful chronicles, some of which have survived.

Hieroglyphic script, in its solemn stateliness, is awesome to behold. But, by its very nature, it is elaborate and formal. For jotting down quick notes, functional records, personal messages and even religious texts, the scribes began to use a streamlined version called 'hieratic'. This looks much more like what we might call 'writing', although the 'alphabetical' element is extremely limited for this is still a simplified form of hieroglyphic script.

TROUBLED TIMES

By the twenty-second century BC, there had already been six successive ruling dynasties. The Seventh and Eighth, however, found themselves

Above: Written around 1600 BC in an elegant hieratic script, the Edwin Smith Papyrus is the world's earliest surviving surgical text, with anatomical information and guidance on procedures.

presiding over mounting chaos. The year 2160 BC is generally seen as marking the collapse of the Old Kingdom and the start of the 'First Intermediate Period'. The Egyptian union broke up, and rival royal houses set up in Upper and Lower Egypt. Inscriptions testify to failures of the Nile flood and resultant famine, but whether this caused the crisis – or merely exacerbated it – is unclear. In the north, in Lower Egypt, the rulers of the Ninth and Tenth Dynasties came to power. They are known as the Herakleopolitan Pharaohs, since they reigned from Herakleopolis Magna, just above the Delta. Upriver, in the south, the Theban Pharaohs of the Eleventh Dynasty held sway till their ruler Mentuhotep II imposed his authority over the whole of Egypt.

The 'Middle Kingdom' brought 400 years of stability and strength, from 2055 to 1650 BC. The regular rhythms of the year – the Nile floods; the growing season – gave an extraordinary continuity to Egyptian life. In the final reigns of the Thirteenth Dynasty, however, the centre was clearly weakening; the Fourteenth Dynasty was a time of disintegration. The 'Second Intermediate Period' saw Egypt once more divided – and, more shocking still, an alien people in control in the north. The so-called Hyksos, of Levantine origin, reigned as Pharaohs in Lower Egypt: not until the sixteenth century BC did Kamose and his successors start to push them back. It was Kamose's brother Ahmose who established the 'New Kingdom' in the 1540s. The Egyptian achievement was set to reach its height.

ZENITH…AND DECLINE

This period saw the construction of some of Egypt's most famous monuments – the great tombs; the temple complexes at Karnak and Luxor. The renown of the Pharaohs was now, if anything, more glorious than it had ever been. The so-called Amarna Letters (*see pp. 56–57*) show just how far Egypt's diplomatic reach in the region extended at this time, while the reigns of Seti I, Rameses II and Merneptah saw military expeditions deep into Syria (*see pp. 22–23 and pp. 58–59*).

Rameses III, however, faced a more difficult struggle, against foreign and domestic adversaries; he was ultimately toppled in a palace coup. More Pharaohs were to follow in the Ramesid line and in dynasties thereafter, but a sense of inertia characterizes these years, marked only by gradual decline. Yet Egypt was still by any normal standards a powerful state with a magnificent culture, its prosperity underwritten by the yearly inundations of the Nile.

PTOLEMAIC TIMES

It seems to have been in the seventh century BC that 'demotic' script first came to be written by scribes looking for greater fluency than even hieratic writing could afford. It was the visiting historian Herodotus who gave this script its Greek name (*demos* means 'people') in the fifth century BC, but, though

Above: Egyptian art is notorious for its 'flat' figures. But, as here at the Dendera Temple, they were intended to accompany inscriptions, together comprising a three-dimensional whole.

undoubtedly less formal, this was hardly the 'people's script'.

Herodotus came as a tourist, but in 332 BC Alexander the Great led his forces into Egypt; this time, the Greeks were here to stay. Years of fighting followed the conqueror's death, but finally his general Ptolemy came to power: he reigned as Ptolemy I, and his descendants followed him onto the throne. In Ptolemaic times, Greek and Egyptian cultural traditions were fused to some extent; though demotic became prevalent in the legal and administrative documents of this time, Greek appears also to have been used. Hence the inscription, in 196 BC, of a trilingual text of a royal decree on what was to become known as the Rosetta Stone. Intrinsically, it could hardly have been less important – an announcement on tax-cuts and instructions for statues of gods to be set up in certain temples. But given that a Greek translation was offered for versions in both demotic and formal hieroglyphics, it provided a crucial key for the unlocking of Egyptian script. As it turned out (*see pp. 68–69*), it was to take some of Europe's most brilliant scholars several decades to discover just how to turn the key. When they finally succeeded, though, they opened up a treasure-house of history.

Egypt's Violent Birth: The Narmer Palette

A conquering king holds up a club to smite a kneeling captive; beheaded bodies are lined up in their rows. This scene, appalling as it is, may well represent the moment 5000 years ago when the state of Egypt first came into being.

Hierakonpolis was already believed to be one of the earliest centres of Egyptian civilization when British archeologists James E. Quibell and Frederick W. Green were excavating in the 1890s. The evidence was mounting up that this had been an important ceremonial centre in the days of the Second Dynasty, early in the third millennium BC. In 1897, however, they started unearthing objects that appeared to point to an origin even earlier in Egypt's history, in what are now called 'Predynastic' times.

A Historic Drama

On what is now regarded as the reverse of the palette, a standing figure prepares to strike the prisoner kneeling before him; slaughtered prisoners or battle-casualties sprawl beneath his feet. The falcon-god Horus stands atop a clump of papyrus, looking on; in one claw he holds a rope, betokening bondage. The whole scene is surmounted by what appears to be the king's *serekh* (a sort of punning pictorial representation of his name): a catfish (*n'r*), above a chisel (*mr*). Hence the name, 'Narmer', given to the ruler shown.

His *serekh* appears at the top of the obverse too. Below are the anthropomorphized cows' heads of the goddess Bat. Narmer appears again, in a triumphal procession. This time, however, he is wearing a different crown: lower, sloping back, and with a serpentlike projection from the rear. To one side are a row of bound and decapitated figures – apparently, executed prisoners of war.

Above: Narmer raises his hand to smite a kneeling captive, symbolically enforcing the unification of Upper and Lower Egypt.

The so-called Narmer Palette, a shaped green siltstone of the kind used for grinding up powders for cosmetics or religious offerings, was the most striking of these finds: its sheer beauty and perfect preservation are still perhaps its most extraordinary features. Once we have marvelled at the skill with which it was fashioned, however, we can hardly help recoiling at the bloodthirsty subject matter. As researchers were to find, though, neither of these reactions is really adequate: the palette repays much more careful examination. For depicted here, it seems, is the drama acted out more than 5000 years ago when Egypt was united under its first Pharaoh.

A TALE OF TWO EGYPTS
Hierakonpolis, at that time, was the capital of 'Upper Egypt'. This kingdom occupied the main valley of the Nile, as opposed to 'Lower Egypt', the Delta, whose capital was

at Buto. The former's conquest of the latter under Narmer is the explicit subject of the palette. On the reverse, Narmer wears the tall and bulbous crown of Upper Egypt; on the obverse, the 'red crown' of Lower Egypt. Backward-sloping, this sits lower on the head, apart from a projection from the rear, the symbolic representation of a serpent. The two crowns were later combined to form the Pharaonic 'double crown'.

Although from this time onwards Egypt was to be governed as a unified state, a sense of duality persisted. The ideas of Upper and Lower Egypt remained important for centuries after they had ceased

to exist as separate states, emblematic of the triumph of order over chaos.

Scholars disagree as to where literal representation leaves off and symbolism starts in the Narmer Palette. Upper Egypt was wealthier and more technologically advanced than the Delta region. Was this story of conquest just a triumphant way of dramatizing a takeover that happened more peacefully over a period of time?

ON PUBLIC DISPLAY

The Narmer Palette is just one of the many hundreds of astonishing artefacts to be seen at the Egyptian Museum in Cairo.

Strange Creatures

Necks entwined, and held back by tethers, a pair of 'serpopards' face one another at the centre of the obverse of the palette. Their winding necks provide a raised border for what might well have been the grinding area if the palette was indeed used for this purpose in Predynastic times. Half-leopard (or perhaps lioness; there is no sign of any spots) and half-serpent, the serpopard is another example of that Egyptian obsession with duality, which emerges in everything from the imagery of Upper and Lower Egypt to the statues of the Sphinx. Interestingly enough, it is found in Mesopotamian art as well, suggesting possible trade or diplomatic contacts between the two cultures.

Right: The design of the Narmer Palette seems deeply strange to us, and, whilst it was plainly full of significances for its creators, they are meanings at which we can for the most part only guess.

Where History Meets Myth: The Palermo Stone

The Egyptian chroniclers kept meticulous accounts – in many cases, the modern scholarship differs only in details – but beyond a certain point the picture blurs. The Palermo Stone purports to list the country's very first Pharaohs – many of them mythical, it is now thought.

ON PUBLIC DISPLAY

In addition to the section on display at Palermo's Archeological Museum, further fragments may be seen at Cairo's Egyptian Museum and the Petrie Museum in London.

The Palermo Stone gives a wonderfully serendipitous variety of information about Egyptian history, including:

• **A maritime venture** in the reign of Sneferu (2613–2589 BC): forty ships set out to an unreported destination and returned fully laden with timber.

• **Also in Sneferu's reign, a large-scale raid** deep into Nubia, in the hills to the north of Egypt. The army returned with 7000 slaves and 200,000 cattle.

• **The start of copper-smelting** in Egypt as early as the Second Dynasty – by about 2700 BC, in other words.

• **Expeditions to mine turquoise** in the Sinai Peninsula.

Right: The Palermo Stone is not of course Sicilian. It may well have originated in Memphis where what appears to be another fragment has been found. Though part of the Palermo collection since 1866, its importance was only appreciated in the 1890s.

Above: The regular rises and falls in the level of the Nile have been like a life-giving pulse for Egypt. The dry desert begins just a stone's throw back from the river's banks.

Though named for the Sicilian city in which its largest extant fragment is to be found, the Palermo Stone is one of the most fascinating relics of Egyptian archeology. A sizeable chunk of basalt, it remains the largest surviving fragment of a stela that is believed to have originally stood over 2m (6ft 6in) tall and to have been about 60cm (2ft) across. (Other fragments are to be found in London and in Cairo.) Essentially a history in hieroglyphics, it gives details about the succession of Pharaohs and about Nile flood-levels – the two great variables of Egyptian history. There are data too on such subjects as taxation, cattle numbers and military campaigns, as well as important ceremonies and construction projects.

BEGINNINGS AND ENDINGS

Incomplete as it is, we cannot be sure exactly where the king list originally ended. The last ruler included in the Palermo fragment is Neferirkare Kakar, third Pharaoh of the Fifth Dynasty, who reigned from 2474 to 2464 BC – within a few generations, it is believed, of when the stela was actually made. More surprisingly, perhaps, the chronicle provided by the stone pushes the historical start point far beyond its conventional beginning. Its king list accounts for thousands of years of 'god-pharaohs' and other legendary rulers before we get to the merely semi-mythical figure of Menes. The traditional inaugurator of Pharaonic rule, he is identified with the first of the 'Predynastic' Pharaohs to have been more or less securely identified by modern archeological scholarship: Narmer (*see pp. 44–45*).

A HISTORICAL HABIT

This bold schematization of an impossibly blurry past should not perhaps surprise us. The Egyptians expected to be able to account for their origins. They had started keeping records early and had kept them well. When, in the third century BC, King Ptolemy II commissioned his priest Manetho to compile a history of Egypt, he was able to call on temple records that have since been lost. His *Aegyptiaca* went back almost 3000 years: the listing of the different Pharaohs and dynasties he identified is substantially the same as the one we use today.

We speak glibly of 'Ancient Egypt' without recalling that this single civilization endured for more than three millennia. An identifiable 'Egyptian' culture was emerging by about 4000 BC. And when the country was conquered by Alexander the Great in 332 BC, the Greek-descended Ptolemaic Dynasty maintained many of the old Pharaonic ways until the invasion of the Romans in 30 BC. In other words, Ancient Egypt was a culture that lasted for more time than has even now elapsed since Homer wrote his *Iliad* or since the Latin tribes thought about establishing a city of their own.

This astonishing longevity is so easily forgotten because, for all its ups and downs, Egyptian culture showed such remarkable continuity. The essentials of economic life changed comparatively little as dynasties came and went. With a few cataclysmic interruptions (owing, it is now suggested, to El Niño events), the Nile kept up the never-ending cycle of inundation and retreat on which the economy was based; cultural and ceremonial life evolved only slowly. The conditions were thus ideal for the emergence of the sort of palace-based bureaucracy that we see so triumphantly achieved in the Egypt of the Pharaohs.

Tjetji the Treasurer

A functionary fulfilled, Tjetji went to his rest a happy man, if the inscription on his funerary stela is to be believed. The right-hand man to Intef II and then to Intef III, he held a position of the utmost power and trust.

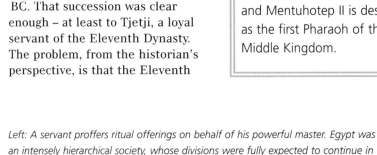

Standing 1.5m (5ft) tall, the Stela of Tjetji the Treasurer is an impressive memorial to a man who spent his whole life in the service of the state. His own authority underlined by the two servant-figures standing in attendance behind him, the official himself is shown facing to the right, where a vertical inscription records offerings and a prayer. Dominating the stela, however, and occupying its upper half is the personal testament of Tjetji. Set out horizontally, this is the proud proclamation of the Pharaoh's humble servant.

A POSITIVE SPIN

There is clearly an element of idealization here: how far the text exaggerates Ttetji's own importance we can hardly know, but its account of his masters' reigns certainly accentuate the positive. No one would ever guess, reading this inscription, that Tjetji was describing a time of division and relative anarchy in Egypt, known to historians as the First Intermediate Period. The Old Kingdom had fallen into economic and political decline soon after the start of the twenty-second century BC, leaving two separate states jostling for supremacy in Egypt.

Egypt's Eleventh Dynasty was established by Mentuhotep I, who reigned from 2134 BC; his grandson, Intef II, ascended the throne just fourteen years later. On his death in 2069 BC, after an eight-year reign, Intef was succeeded by his son, Intef III, who remained as Pharaoh until 2061 BC. That succession was clear enough – at least to Tjetji, a loyal servant of the Eleventh Dynasty. The problem, from the historian's perspective, is that the Eleventh Dynasty came to power before the Tenth Dynasty had reached its end. While Tjetji's masters held sway in Thebes, the Pharaohs of the Tenth Dynasty continued to rule Lower Egypt from their capital at Herakleopolis Magna.

On the Up

If Tjetji's confidence was premature, his optimism was justified: he had enlisted in the service of what was to be the winning side. For decades, the advantage see-sawed between the two Egypts, but eventually Intef II prevailed, taking possession of the Nile Valley, from the First Cataract, on the borders of Nubia, all the way down to Abydos in the north. Considerable progress – even if it hardly amounts to the hold over Lower Egypt implied by Tjetji's inscription. Time would bring the victory: the reign of Intef III seems to have constituted a pause for breath, but the struggle was resumed by his son and successor Mentuhotep II. At some point, he managed to reunite the whole of Egypt. Thus his reign is regarded as bringing the First Intermediate Period to an end, and Mentuhotep II is described as the first Pharaoh of the Middle Kingdom.

Left: A servant proffers ritual offerings on behalf of his powerful master. Egypt was an intensely hierarchical society, whose divisions were fully expected to continue in the underworld after death.

Right: The text at the top, reading horizontally, represents the testament of Tjetji. The vertical lines below and to the right, are spells or prayers.

" *I was a man beloved of his lord and master, given daily praises. For many years I served his majesty Horus Wahankh, King of Upper and Lower Egypts, son of Re, Intef, while this country was under his authority…I was his personal attendant, his chamberlain. He raised me up; he exalted me in rank; he made me his right-hand-man, admitting me to his constant company in the privacy of his palace. He entrusted his wealth and treasures to me, investing my seal with his authority, giving me power over all the tribute brought in from Upper and Lower Egypt alike – all the good things brought to him for fear of his wrath from throughout this country and all those things brought to his majesty by the chiefs of the Red Land for fear of his wrath through the kingdoms of the hill country. I kept track of everything and accounted for it fully, without ever making a significant slip, such were my skill and reliability.*

This made me the Pharaoh's faithful confidant…I am a man who loves good and hates evil, a person beloved by all in his master's house, who did everything he did in accordance with his master's will. I did everything aright…I never overstepped my authority…Never once did I act in arrogance; nor did I ever take personal advantage of my trusted position. I improved the functioning of every department I was given charge of…When his son succeeded him…he gave me all the offices I had held under his father, asking me to continue with my work in them under his rule… "

ON PUBLIC DISPLAY

The Stela of Tjetji is one of the largest (and finest) stelae in the British Museum's collection.

An Egyptian Artist

The Stela of Irtysen at Abydos is an Egyptian artist's advertisement for himself, listing his various accomplishments, setting out his stall. Yet it was directed not towards living employers but towards Osiris, god of death, in hope of preferential treatment in the underworld.

Abydos was one of the great cities of early Egypt. From the end of the Old Kingdom, it was starting to take on a new role as a religious centre. It was sacred to Osiris, the god of death and rebirth, who was believed to have

ON PUBLIC DISPLAY

Irtysen's Stela may be seen today in Paris, at the Louvre.

I know the secrets of the hieroglyphs, the workings of sacred rituals; I know all the magic spells and how they work. I am supremely skilled in my art, and knowledgeable in all its mysteries: I can estimate measurements, cut things and fit them into place. I know the right posture for a male statue and how the female should look as well...the squirmings of the terrified captive; a squint; a frightened enemy; the way a hippo hunter holds his arm and how man moves his legs when he is running...I know the formulae for the different pigments.... Only I know these things – I and my eldest son, whom the god has ordered me to initiate into my arts. I have seen how skilful he is in all the most precious materials – everything from silver and gold to ivory and ebony.

Above: A work of art in itself, the Stela of Irtysen offers an exciting and intriguing insight into how an Egyptian artist viewed his vocation.

Above: This relief from the tomb of the vizier Nespeqashuty from the 26th Dynasty depicts the dead vizier and his wife KetjKetj making the journey to the holy city Abydos.

been buried here himself. By the time of the Middle Kingdom (2040–1803 BC), its primary importance was as a place of pilgrimage: people flocked from up and down the realm to worship at the Great Temple of Osiris. Pilgrims erected stelae around the temple to list their own virtues for the benefit of the god, preparing him in advance for their eventual arrival in his realm.

'I AM SUPREMELY SKILLED…'
Irtysen's recitation of his skills gives his stela something of the flavour of a job application: was he putting in his bid for a privileged position in the afterlife?

All except the royal dead were expected to work for Osiris, just as they had been expected to work for the Pharaoh in this life. For most, of course, that meant hard labour in the fields or on construction projects. It is clear that artists and skilled artisans were highly valued in Egyptian society, and Irtysen would have been eager to ensure that he suffered no loss of status in the hereafter.

The pictures below the text appear to show Irtysen, with his wife Hepu, being given funereal offerings by their sons, behind whom are their daughter and their grandson.

The rod and sceptre held by the artist are the symbols of his paternal authority within the family. Below this, we see the couple again, framed as though by a window: Irtysen is sniffing at some sort of perfume. Offerings of food and drink have been set before them on a table.

Concrete Evidence?

Irtysen's claim, 'to know how to make mixtures which melt without the need for fire and which will not dissolve in water' is taken by some modern experts to be evidence of the early use of a form of concrete. 'Cast stone' of this sort might easily have been used for making monumental statues: a blend of crushed limestone, gypsum and water would have been poured into pre-prepared moulds and allowed to harden. The suggestion has even been advanced that the blocks used for building the Pyramids were made this way.

Kamose the Conqueror

Two stelae at Karnak bear eloquent testimony to the life of Kamose and his struggles against the Asiatic Hyksos. The story they tell is a stirring one, but should this narrative be read as a historical document or as mere bluster?

Saviour of his country? The chronological divisions conventionally used in Egyptian history are undoubtedly useful, but they are sadly lacking in glamour or romance. To say that Kamose's reign as the final Pharaoh of the Eighteenth Dynasty brought the Second Intermediate Period to an end is to sell short an exciting and important life. Even the assurance that his death was to bring about the start of the New Kingdom hardly hints at the historic significance of the man.

His two stelae at Karnak, outside Thebes, help explain the scholars' caution. Historical sources have seldom seemed less reliable. The accumulated evidence suggests that, thrilling though it is, Kamose's own account of his epic achievements is wildly exaggerated. Kamose's victories over the Hyksos, though real, were far more limited than is acknowledged here; he certainly never got as far as Avaris, the Hyksos' stronghold down in the Delta. Yet his reign still mattered because, even if he never managed to press it to its conclusion, he did seize the initiative in the fight against the Hyksos.

Though he fell on the field of battle in 1549, his mother and his brother Ahmose were able to follow through, fighting on until the Asiatic invaders were finally expelled. Egypt was Egyptian again: Ahmose came to the throne as the Pharaoh Ahmose I, and the way was clear for the achievements of the New Kingdom.

Under Occupation

The Second Intermediate Period was, behind its bland academic title, a time of drama – even if what happened remains obscure. Lower Egypt was under foreign occupation from around 1650 to 1540 BC. The Hyksos, a Semitic people believed to have come from Byblos, on the coast of Lebanon, established their own kingdom in the Delta. Did they invade in overwhelming force? It is certainly possible. There was a significant 'weapons gap' between the Egyptians and the Hyksos, given the latter's chariots and composite bows. But it could be, too, that they moved unopposed into the political vacuum left by the implosion of the Middle Kingdom. Either way, they established themselves as rulers in the north, whilst the Theban kingdom had to pay tribute. Not until the Seventeenth Dynasty did a serious fightback begin, led by Tao II Seqenrere, Kamose's father.

Left: Kamose's stelae were set up in the spectacular temple complex of Karnak, in Thebes, or Luxor, so he could claim his place among the great historic Pharaohs.

ON PUBLIC DISPLAY

Kamose's stelae are still to be seen in the Karnak temple-complex, outside Luxor (ancient Thebes).

> *The great ruler of Thebes, Kamose the Mighty, guardian of Egypt, says: I headed north since I knew I had the strength to tackle the Hyksos. Amun, giver of good advice, gave me my orders. My brave army went before me like a searing flame…The east and west gave up their produce as my army lived off the land…He holed up in Nefrusi with his Hyksos. I stayed in my ship overnight and in the morning I attacked. I reduced his walls to rubble; I slaughtered his people; I made his wife come down to the banks of the river. Like lions with their prey, my men set about their plunder, taking slaves, cattle, produce, sharing out the spoils, happy at heart…I landed at Perdjedken, happy myself at heart, to torment Apophis, that Syrian weakling, hatcher of bold plans that he will never execute. Reaching Yenyet on the way to the south, I crossed to the other shore to meet his forces, my ships in battle-order, my heroes flying like falcons over the waves, my golden flagship leading like a god…*
>
> *See, I come in triumph!…Does your courage fail you, wretched Asian? See how I drink the wine from your vineyards, whose grapes your own Asians I forced to tread for me. I demolished your residence; I cut your timber; I drove your women into my ships; I rounded up your horses; I smashed to smithereens your ships and took all the limitless gold, lapis lazuli, silver, turquoise and bronze axes they had in them…Avaris…I destroyed with all its people, laying waste their towns and reducing their houses to smouldering ashes, since they had given their loyalty to the Asians, abandoning Lady Egypt.*

Tiy's Wedding Scarab

A third-millennium mésalliance ended up in what would appear to have been one of Egypt's more successful Pharaonic marriages. But not only was Tiy destined to serve as her royal husband's constant companion: she became a religious figurehead for his realm.

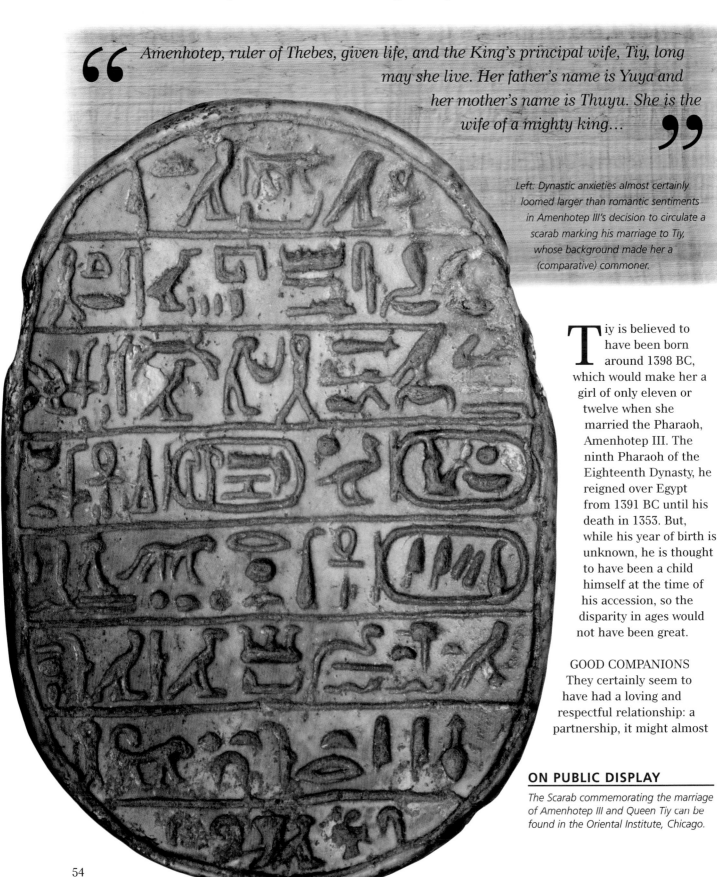

> *Amenhotep, ruler of Thebes, given life, and the King's principal wife, Tiy, long may she live. Her father's name is Yuya and her mother's name is Thuyu. She is the wife of a mighty king…*

Left: Dynastic anxieties almost certainly loomed larger than romantic sentiments in Amenhotep III's decision to circulate a scarab marking his marriage to Tiy, whose background made her a (comparative) commoner.

Tiy is believed to have been born around 1398 BC, which would make her a girl of only eleven or twelve when she married the Pharaoh, Amenhotep III. The ninth Pharaoh of the Eighteenth Dynasty, he reigned over Egypt from 1391 BC until his death in 1353. But, while his year of birth is unknown, he is thought to have been a child himself at the time of his accession, so the disparity in ages would not have been great.

GOOD COMPANIONS
They certainly seem to have had a loving and respectful relationship: a partnership, it might almost

ON PUBLIC DISPLAY

The Scarab commemorating the marriage of Amenhotep III and Queen Tiy can be found in the Oriental Institute, Chicago.

before his father and thus never had the chance to ascend the throne. Their second son did reign, however, succeeding his father in 1351 as Amenhotep IV, or Akhenaten.

A WOMAN OF INFLUENCE

But it is hard to believe that any sons of Tiy could ever really have been overlooked: she was not just an important figurehead but a political player – perhaps even the power behind the throne. The extent to which Amenhotep relied on her is clear from the fact that she became the first Egyptian queen to have her name placed alongside the Pharaoh's on imperial decrees. Her importance seems only to have grown after her husband's death, in the reign of Akhenaten: it is clear from some of the Amarna Letters (*see pp. 56–57*) that she wielded considerable power at court.

Hallowed to Hathor

In his eagerness to boost the profile of his beloved wife, Amenhotep gave her a new ritual role as the earthly embodiment of the cow-goddess, Hathor. This was anything but an insult. One of Egypt's most ancient deities, Hathor was associated not just with the milk of motherhood but with the Milky Way, the great starry 'Nile of the Sky'. Tiy's headdress was decorated with the long, curved horns that symbolized not just the cow-goddess herself but the universe-enveloping sweep of the Milky Way. Amenhotep had several shrines built to Hathor-Tiy, as well as a major temple at Sedeinga, in Nubia, not far away from his own temple at Soleb.

---

be said, of equals. Unusually, Amenhotep had Tiy portrayed along with him in his official statues and pictorial inscriptions. Quite unprecedentedly, moreover, he has her shown at roughly the same size as himself. By normal convention, whatever her actual stature, she would automatically have been shown far smaller than her royal husband, in deference to his gender and his royal rank.

This is the more remarkable given that Amenhotep had been taking a chance by marrying Tiy in the first place: she was considered far too 'common' for a Pharaoh's wife. Though her father Yuya was wealthy in land and cattle, and even held ceremonial office as a priest, he was not a member of the highest aristocracy. Her mother, Thuyu, was a high priestess, and of royal blood, thanks to her descent from Amenhotep I's regent, Ahmose-

Nefertari, but this pedigree was not enough to give Tiy status at the Pharaonic court.

PUBLIC ACKNOWLEDGEMENT

It is thought to have been for this reason that Amenhotep III issued a series of 'wedding scarabs', announcing his marriage, for circulation throughout the empire. This too was an unprecedented move: till now, royal marriages had generally not been announced at all – the Pharaoh's domestic arrangements did not concern the people. Amenhotep's insistence on advertising this union may well have stemmed from a fear that his sons by Tiy might not be accepted as legitimate by Egypt's establishment: so public a declaration could hardly be ignored.

As it turned out, their two sons were generally acknowledged, though the elder, Thutmose, died

The Amarna Letters

Some of the most intriguing inscriptions discovered in Egypt were written not in hieroglyphics but in cuneiform on clay tablets. The Amarna Letters represent what amounts to a diplomatic correspondence, dating from the fourteenth century BC.

Local villagers unearthed the tablets on the site of ancient Amarna in the 1880s. A city in Upper Egypt, Amarna had briefly been the capital under Amenhotep IV, or Akhenaten, who reigned from 1351 to 1334 BC.

Before any serious attempts were made to investigate their origins, the tablets had been sold piecemeal to collectors, and ended up being dispersed around the world. Only from the 1890s were attempts made to excavate more scientifically, first by British archeologist Sir William Flinders Petrie and then by France's Emile Chassinat. Efforts were made to bring the whole collection together, to be subjected to more systematic study.

In all, 382 letters have been discovered: though most were written to Akhenaten, some had been sent to his predecessor, Amenhotep III (*see pp. 54–55*). Sent to Amarna by the Pharaohs' various Middle Eastern vassals, they relate to the history of the Middle East as much as Egypt. They are inscribed in Akkadian, the diplomatic lingua franca of the day.

CRIES FOR HELP

If the letters have a common theme, beyond their authors' competitively extravagant declarations of loyalty and admiration, it is the stridency of their complaints about one another. Hence, King Rib-Hadda writes no fewer than sixty letters, begging Akhenaten to come to his rescue against the expansionism of Amurru. The king of Byblos had a reputation as a mischief-maker, and the growing desperation of his letters suggests that Akhenaten may have taken a grim satisfaction in hanging him out to dry. But the ruler of Amurru also presses his own pleas for support: the general impression in the Amarna Letters is of a region in turmoil.

This was hardly surprising. The sixteenth century BC had seen the rise to regional prominence of Mitanni, a city-state on the plains of northwestern Mesopotamia. From about 1550 BC, it had been expanding its territories towards the Mediterranean. This represented a clear challenge to Egyptian influence in the wider region, and was resented as such. After a century and a half of diplomatic rivalry between the two powers,

Below: Amarna, Akhenaten's capital, was founded in about 1345 BC by the Pharaoh himself, at a time when, after a period of expansionism, Egypt was retrenching.

punctuated by outbreaks of all-out war, Egypt and Mitanni were compelled to come – however uneasily – to terms. The reason was the rise, in the uplands of the north, of a powerful and aggressive Hittite Empire.

NOTES OF DESPERATION
Rather than producing calm, however, the withdrawal of Egypt and Mitanni from Canaan only exacerbated the instability. Hence, perhaps, the grovelling tone adopted by one of Akhenaten's correspondents, Tagu, the ruler of Ginti (or Gath).

ON PUBLIC DISPLAY

Sadly for scholars, the Amarna Letters have been dispersed, with examples at Berlin's Vorderasiatisches Museum, Cairo's Egyptian Museum, the Louvre in Paris and elsewhere.

Above: Inscribed in Akkadian, the Amarna Letters make an unlikely item of Egyptological research, but the light they shed on the Egyptian foreign policy of their time is fascinating.

> *I prostrate myself at your feet, my lord – seven times and then seven times more. As your loyal servant, I arranged to send my brother with a caravan with tribute to you, but it was attacked and he was almost killed…Ask your own official if this is not so. My eyes are always directed towards you. Whether we should soar into the heavens or dive deep into the earth, our fate would be in your hands. With this tablet, therefore, I am trying to send another caravan to my lord and king under the leadership of my friend. Let the King be secure in the knowledge that I serve him and am ever at the ready…*
>
> *Your servant, the dirt beneath your feet, I prostrate myself before you my lord, my god, my sun, seven times and then seven times more. I looked one way; I looked the other: there was no light to be seen. Then I looked at my king, my lord and suddenly there was light. I am resolved to serve my lord and king: the brick may shift beneath its fellow but I shall not shift beneath the feet of my lord, my king.*

The 'Israel Stela'

The Stela of Merneptah, as it is more properly called, is a record of the conquests of an Egyptian Pharaoh of the Nineteenth Dynasty. It takes its popular name from a glancing mention of Israel – the earliest known reference we have.

Merneptah reigned from 1213 to 1203 BC, the fourth Pharaoh of the Nineteenth Dynasty. His name meant 'Beloved of Ptah' (Ptah being the creator-god). His accession could hardly have been described as auspicious: the eleventh or twelfth son of his father Rameses II and the fourth by his mother Istnofret (Rameses' second-principal wife), he ascended the throne only because his elder brothers and half-brothers had died before him. He finally became Pharaoh at the age of around 60 – though it seems possible that he had for some time previously acted as regent for his ageing father.

ON PUBLIC DISPLAY

The 'Israel Stela' is just one of many extraordinary ancient artefacts on display in the Egyptian Museum in Cairo.

❝ *He gave courage to his armies in their hundreds of thousands, restored the breath to those who panted in their fear…he vanquished the Libyans and sent them packing from Egyptian soil: now the fear of Egypt is deep within their hearts. Their vanguard was routed; their legs would serve them only for flight; their*

Left: Merneptah, unsurprisingly, emerges as very much the hero in his own inscription. Despite this, we have no real reason to doubt the importance of the victory he had won.

A HEROIC TRIUMPH

But there is no gainsaying that Merneptah appears to have been an effective military leader, restoring Egyptian ascendancy after a period of weakness. A stone some 3m (10ft) tall, the monument popularly known as the 'Israel Stela' was found at Thebes at the end of the nineteenth century. It is decorated at the top with a representation of Merneptah meeting the god Amun along with the god's wife, Mut, and their son, Khonsu.

The inscription is one of two to commemorate what does appear to have been a significant victory won by Merneptah's forces over the Libyans and their allies, the 'Sea Peoples'. (These mysterious maritime raiders appear to have cast a shadow over the whole eastern Mediterranean towards the end of the second millennium BC, but their origins remain maddeningly obscure.)

This particular inscription downplays their role, however, focusing instead on the fight with the Libyans. Battle was joined outside Perire, in the western Delta, an area which was so literally devastated by the depredations of foreign raiders that it 'had to be abandoned as pasture for cattle', according to the second inscription, carved into a wall at Karnak. In the event, we learn from other sources, almost 10,000 of the enemy were killed.

Right: Merneptah meets falcon-headed Horus, the god of royal rule, in this tomb-painting from the Valley of the Kings. Though he came late to the throne, Merneptah proved a natural ruler, decisive and strong.

The Question of Israel

Little more than an aside in the inscription itself, the reference to Israel has created enormous interest among biblical scholars ever since this stone was found by Flinders Petrie in 1896. Its precise meaning is a matter of controversy; it has even been suggested that the identification of Israel in the inscription is based on a mistranslation. In so far as a consensus exists, however, it is that this reference, not just to Israel but to its 'seed', is the first known source explicitly to name a people of Israel – the Jews.

---

bowmen threw down their weapons in fear; running for their lives, their morale failed them and they discarded their water-skins and kitbags to speed their flight. The Libyan leader, basest of men, ran for his life through the darkness of the night, without his regal headdress – or even the sandals from his feet. Without food or water he fled, fearful of the anger of his own family and of his generals, now turning on one another, their tents reduced to ashes, their supplies seized by our men. No hero's welcome awaited him at home but fear and loathing for a leader marked out as unlucky, damned to defeat by the power of Egypt's Pharaoh…

A prodigious deed has been done for Egypt. Those who attacked her have been made her prisoners, thanks to the judgment and generalship of the divine Pharaoh…He has freed those who were held captive in their cities; he has had sacrifices brought to the shrines and incense burned before the gods; he has given the nobility back their estates and the poor people their homes…There is rejoicing in Egypt. From all her cities come cries of acclamation for Merneptah's triumphs over the Libyans…

Canaan weeps in her captivity; Ashkelon has been taken and Gezer seized. Yanoam no longer endures; Israel lies devastated, bereft of its seed.

Ani in the Underworld

Some time in the Nineteenth Dynasty, a scribe went to his grave, equipped with a guide to entering eternity. Several copies of the Egyptian 'Book of the Dead' have been discovered, but Ani's is among the fullest and the most beautiful.

Above: The Necropolis at Thebes was the obvious place to find a copy of the 'Book of the Dead'. Ani's underlines the profound poetry – and complexity – of the Egyptians' relationship with death.

Every Egyptian of any rank went to his or her grave with a copy of a text known nowadays as the 'Book of the Dead', though its literal translation is more like the 'Book of Going Out by Day'. It set out to coach the departing soul on how the whole process of death and judgment should be dealt with: the journey to the underworld; the weighing of the soul; what to say when meeting Osiris Un-Nefer, Death as Judge. A more or less standard text was used, though there were variations, and the document was personalized to a degree with the individual's name and details. Copies have been found in which the name of the deceased has been added in gaps left in pre-prepared documents.

SCRIPTED FOR A SCRIBE
Found at Thebes in the late nineteenth century, the Papyrus of

Ani was a fine example: fully unrolled, it came to almost 24m (80ft) in length. It is written in a beautiful hand – or, rather, three. The cursive hieroglyphs used are typical of this sort of solemn and portentous religious document, for which fully formed hieroglyphs would have been impracticable but a more cursive hieratic script would have seemed overly informal.

Ani, it tells us, was a 'true royal scribe'; a 'collector and accountant' of the Pharaoh's taxes; 'governor of the granaries of the Lords of Abydos; recorder of the taxes of the lords of Thebes'. His lady Thuthu is said to have been one of the priestesses of Amun-Ra.

Below: The cursive hieroglyphs of Ani's 'Book of the Dead' display to their best advantage the beauties of Egyptian penmanship: stately, poised and yet at the same time elegantly flowing.

" *Horus, son of Isis, says: I have come to you, Un-Nefer, bringing with me the Osiris Ani. His heart is good: it has been weighed in the scale and no sin against god or goddess has been found. Thoth has weighed it as decreed by the gods, and it has been found to be true and just. Allow him to be given food and drink and permit him to make his appearance in the presence of Osiris and let him be as one of the followers of Horus for the rest of eternity.*

Ani's Speech. And the Osiris Ani says. Here I am in your presence, Lord of the Land of the Dead. My body is without sin. I have not uttered any word which I have known to be dishonest, nor committed any deed in a spirit of falsehood. Allow me to be like those lucky ones admitted to your company, so that I may be an Osiris in the presence of the beautiful god, and win the love of the Lord of the Two Lands. I, the Pharaoh's scribe, Ani, who loves you and whose word to the god Osiris will ever be true. "

An Egyptian Investigation

Over 3000 years ago in the reign of Rameses IX, a spate of robberies was reported from the Pharaonic burial grounds outside Thebes. The Vizier's notes offer intriguing glimpses of the investigative procedures, and of how Egyptians regarded what were already ancient monuments.

Named for the English scholar who originally acquired it in Cairo in the mid-nineteenth century, the Abbott Papyrus is an extraordinary document, prepared on behalf of the Vizier of Rameses IX. Egypt had evidently been shaken by a series of robberies to the royal tombs west of Thebes, at that time the capital.

The report describes the thorough and systematic way in which the investigators went through the necropolis, checking tombs – and, ultimately, making arrests.

PHARAONIC THIRD DEGREE
Among those caught was a coppersmith who admitted to having been in the tomb of Isis, the queen of Rameses III, who had died half a century before. 'I took a few things for myself,' he confessed. Subsequently, he was subjected to what the officials describe as a 'severe examination', but was unable to direct them to any other tombs. We are told that he swore on the name of the Pharaoh that he knew of no other opened tombs, asking that he should have his ears and nose cut off and be stretched on the rack should he be lying.

The guidance is vague (and we do not know which Amenhotep was 'Amenhotep-of-the-Court'), but a word to the wise will sometimes be sufficient. In 2000, some 3000 years after these words were written (and 3500 years after Intef's reign), a joint German-Egyptian team was able to follow the directions they offered and successfully locate and excavate Intef's tomb, beneath the rubble of its collapsed pyramid.

If the circumstances of the discovery were intriguing, directed by a tip given so many centuries before, the find was of intrinsic importance too. Prior to then it had been assumed that pyramid-building had been a feature of the Old Kingdom, and had ended with it: Intef's pyramid had been constructed 600 years later on the eve of the New Kingdom.

Digging Directions

One section of the Abbott Papyrus describes how the investigators checked the tomb of Intef, a Pharaoh of the Seventeenth Dynasty. The tomb stands to the north of the House of Amenhotep-of-the-Court. Its pyramid has been destroyed, but the stela is still there, showing the standing figure of the Pharaoh with his dog Behka between his feet. The tomb was examined but found not to have been disturbed.

Above: The Valley of the Kings came into use in the New Kingdom because it was secluded and comparatively easy to guard. Even so, thieves managed to ransack many of its tombs.

> " The officials of the great and sacred necropolis were dispatched along with the scribes of Pharaoh's Palace and his Vizier to check the tombs and burial places of those former Pharaohs interred to the west of the city...The pyramid of King Nubkheperre, Son of Re, was in the middle of being broken into by the robbers, who had so far managed to tunnel two cubits into its fabric...The tomb of King Sekhemre-Shedtowe, Son of Re, was found to have been broken into. The robbers had dug through the base of its pyramid, from the antechamber to the tomb of Nebamon, the overseer of Thutmose III's granary. The Pharaoh's burial place had been emptied of its lord, as had that of his wife, Nubkhas, the robbers having raided these tombs. The Vizier, the nobles and the inspecting officials checked the chamber over and established how the robbery had been effected. The tombs of the women singers from the temple of the Divine Votress of Amun Re, King of the Gods, were also checked. The result: 2 undisturbed; 2 broken into by robbers. Total 4.
> As for the tombs and burial-places in which have been laid to rest the noblemen and noblewomen and the people of Thebes, the robbers were found to have violated all these, dragging the dead from their sarcophagi and coffins and throwing them on to the ground. They had stolen all the furniture that had been left with them as well as any gold, silver or jewels which were in their coverings. "

ON PUBLIC DISPLAY

The Abbott Papyrus is one of the most intriguing items in the British Museum's Egyptian collection.

Above: Rough and ready; a little hurried, even, the report of Rameses' Vizier is clearly written to the moment, in contrast with the monumentalism of more familiar Egyptian inscriptions.

Spells in Stone: The Metternich Stela

Magic meets medicine in the Metternich Stela – a breathtaking work of art. Now in New York's Metropolitan Museum of Art, the sculpture is certainly a feast for the eyes, but its inscribed messages should not be ignored.

The curators call it the 'Magical Stela', arguing that this sumptuously worked stone has its own romance, far more compelling than its connection with an eighteenth-century Austrian prince and diplomat. And they have a point, though tradition has sanctioned the name, the 'Metternich Stela', in honour of the statesman to whom it was presented. It was the gift of Muhammad Ali, the Ottoman Pasha, or governor, of Egypt, who had risen up against the Sultan to set himself up as ruler in his own right. The Austrian dignitary had more respect for the stela's antiquity and importance

A Spell Against Scorpions

Isis offers this spell to protect her worshippers against the stings of the seven scorpions: Tefenet, Befenet, Meset, Mestetef, Petet, Matet and Tetet.

> *Venom of Tefenet, leave the body and return to the earth; penetrate no further. Befenet's poison, hear me, divine Isis, with my magic powers, my words of enchantment. Every poisonous snake obeys me: you must too. Sink into the soil, poison of Meset; rise no more, poison of Mestetef; cease your working, poison of Petet and Tetet. Drop down, biting venomous mouth on the orders of the goddess Isis…poison give way, withdraw, take flight and leave the body.*

Right: Just how alien the Egyptians' culture was from our own is evident in the various prescriptions offered by the Metternich Stela – part medicine, part magic, part mythological extravaganza.

Left: Nekhebet in her vulture headdress – emblematic of Upper Egypt, of which she was the proprietary goddess – faces the Pharaoh in this detail from the Metternich Stele, also known as the Magical Stela.

an extremely dangerous natural predator but the agent of Osiris, in his capacity as god of death: the souls of the unjust were devoured by these monsters.) In either hand, Horus holds up scorpions and snakes, whose menace he has also conquered; he has a lion by the tail and an antelope by its horns. To the right, ibis-headed Thoth looks on; to the left can be seen Isis. Between them, they hold up the walls of what appears to be a simple shrine.

Beneath this central scene are thirteen lines of incantations, offering protection against bites, stings and poisons of every kind. Around and about, strings of hieroglyphs cover every available part of the stela, telling stories of how the gods dealt with a wide variety of dangerous creatures.

MAGIC UNAVAILING

Great as its magical powers may have been, the stela was unable to save Egypt, or Nectanebo II. His kingdom was finally conquered by the Persian emperor Artaxerxes III. Thereafter, indeed, there were to be no more truly Egyptian Pharaohs, as the country passed from Persian into Greek and then finally into Roman hands.

than did the Egyptian renegade, so perhaps it is fitting that it should bear his name.

A priest named Esatum had the stela carved during the reign of Nactanebo II – a Pharoah of the Thirtieth Dynasty who reigned from 364 to 343 BC. It is thought that he placed it in his temple, where individuals afflicted by illness could come to consult it. Reading those spells which were relevant to their particular plight, they may also have drunk water that had been poured over the stela's sacred stone.

A TRIUMPHANT TABLEAU

At the top of the stela may be seen the disc of Ra, the sun: its nightly journey through the underworld is shown, as is its dawn rebirth, hailed here by an adoring Pharaoh Nectanebo II along with the god Thoth and a group of baboons. The centrepiece of the stela, however, has a sculpted figure of the youthful Horus standing in triumph upon two crocodiles. (The crocodiles are a reference to Sobek, the crocodile-god, who was not just

---

Healing Horus

Around the base of the stela is inscribed the story of how Horus was almost killed by the sting of a scorpion as a young child. It happened at the time when he and his mother Isis were hiding out in the marshes. Osiris, her husband and the father of Horus, had been murdered and his power usurped by his brother Seth, who was now anxious to secure his power by killing Horus. He it was, indeed, who had sent the scorpion. Here on the stela, as though in Isis' own words, we read how she called out from her hiding place in desperation. The sun boat stopped short in the sky, and Thoth, god of wisdom, came down to help. He uttered a series of spells over the ailing infant, each one ending with the tag 'and for the earthly suffering', meaning that mortals could benefit from these cures as well.

The Decree of Canopus

Issued in 239 BC by King Ptolemy III, the Decree of Canopus established a new festival in honour of a dead (and deified) princess. But a rambling, wide-ranging inscription offered a variety of insights into life in the Egypt of the Ptolemies.

" *Given that a daughter had been born to the Benevolent Gods King Ptolemaios and Berenike, Queen of both lands, and since this Princess – also named Berenike – returned suddenly and unexpectedly to heaven in her virgin state, the Priests…decreed that she should from that time forward have the glory of a goddess, to be proclaimed in temples the entire length of Egypt…Accordingly, a festival and procession for her have been ordained …There is also to be a statue of the goddess in gold, adorned with all precious stones in the temples of the first rank and sanctuaries of the second rank throughout and…there shall be made to her a burnt offering and all the sacrifices appropriate to the days of this feast.* "

Left: The trilingual text of the Decree of Canopus can easily be made out: first hieroglyphics, then demotic and then, finally, Greek.

ON PUBLIC DISPLAY

The Decree of Canopus is among the most fascinating exhibits in the Louvre, Paris.

The rise of Egyptology in the nineteenth century coincided with the high-point of European colonialism – and the racial theory that went with it. So Ptolemaic Egypt was long neglected by historians: it was a late, debased episode – not quite the real thing, it seemed. The 'Age of the Pharaohs' had ended in 343 BC with the overthrow of Nactanebo II (*see pp. 64–65*) by the Persians.

For historians of the nineteenth century, Alexander's conquest of 332 had at least saved Egypt for civilization. However, he and his successors had to an alarming degree 'gone native' in their new African and Asian realms. Ptolemy, one of Alexander's generals, had won this part of his Hellenic empire in the wars that followed the great conqueror's death. And as the new ruler of a country that already had an extremely strong sense of its own identity and tradition, he had not hesitated to embrace important aspects of Egyptian tradition. Today it is precisely the hybridity of the Ptolemaic culture that makes it seem so fascinating. Today we live in an age of multiculturalism, after all.

Like the Egyptians, then, the Ptolemies came to see themselves as gods; their dead daughter becomes a temple companion to Osiris. Strange to us too is the incestuous tradition of the Ptolemies. The inscription goes on to mention the king's 'sister and wife', a reference to a single person. The king and queen's commitment to their kingdom is clear in the measures they have taken to relieve the famines caused by a failure of the Nile flood.

The so-called Canopus Decree was issued in 239 BC in Canopus, on the coast of Lower Egypt. For a long time, its main point of interest to scholars was the fact that it was written in the three languages: hieroglyphics, 'the writing of books' (that is, demotic, a more informal and easily written Egyptian script) and Greek. Had it not been for the Rosetta Stone (*see pp. 68-69*), this might have been the key that unlocked the mysteries of ancient Egypt. It would be sad, though, if its intrinsic interest were not recognized.

Below: The Ptolemaic kings and queens had twin identities: their coins characteristically represented them in classical European style; but they were also shown in thoroughly Pharaonic guise.

" *When, moreover, there came a year of low water in the Nile during their reign and all the people of Egypt became fearful, thinking of the famines which poor floods had brought in earlier reigns, the King and his sister and wife took compassion, their hearts full of sympathy for the people and temples of Egypt, who were laid low by the disaster. For the sake of saving lives, their majesties were prepared to forgo many of their taxes and they saw to it that grain was imported from Rutennu [Syria], from Kafatha [Phoenicia] and from the island of Nabinaitt [Cyprus] in the middle of the Great Sea.*

This decree, written by the priests in the temple and their principals and scribes, is to be inscribed in a stele of stone or bronze in hieroglyphics, in the writing of books and the writing of the Greeks, and the stele is to be erected in the great hall, open to all men in the temples, first, second, and third rank, so that all men may be made aware of the honour given by the priests of the temples of Egypt to the Benevolent Gods and their children, as has been appointed. "

The Keystone

Intrinsically, it may seem banal, but no inscription was ever more important than this decree of Ptolemy V. Through its trilingual text, the Rosetta Stone eventually allowed the mysteries of hieroglyphics to be unravelled and the whole history of ancient Egypt to be read.

ON PUBLIC DISPLAY

Ownership of the Rosetta Stone has been hotly contested – first by the French and then more recently by Egypt – but it remains on show in the British Museum in London.

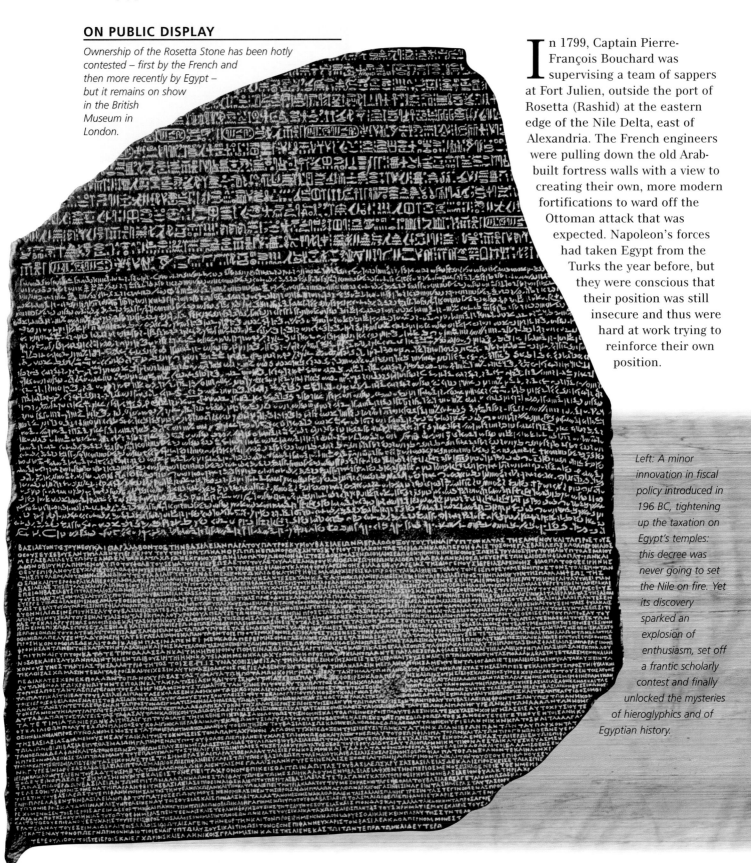

In 1799, Captain Pierre-François Bouchard was supervising a team of sappers at Fort Julien, outside the port of Rosetta (Rashid) at the eastern edge of the Nile Delta, east of Alexandria. The French engineers were pulling down the old Arab-built fortress walls with a view to creating their own, more modern fortifications to ward off the Ottoman attack that was expected. Napoleon's forces had taken Egypt from the Turks the year before, but they were conscious that their position was still insecure and thus were hard at work trying to reinforce their own position.

Left: A minor innovation in fiscal policy introduced in 196 BC, tightening up the taxation on Egypt's temples: this decree was never going to set the Nile on fire. Yet its discovery sparked an explosion of enthusiasm, set off a frantic scholarly contest and finally unlocked the mysteries of hieroglyphics and of Egyptian history.

THE SPOILS OF WAR

Napoleon's Egyptian campaign was a 'military adventure' in the fullest sense of the phrase, conducted in a remarkable spirit of romanticism. Before the Battle of the Pyramids, he reminded his troops, 'From those monuments, forty centuries look down on you', and along with his infantry, cavalry and artillery he brought squadrons of Egyptologists. There was great excitement, then, among Bouchard's men when they unearthed a slab of granite. Its dimensions were 114 x 72 x 28cm (45 x 28 x 11in) and one highly polished side was covered in inscriptions. The Arabs had used it as building-stone, but to the French archeologists it was clearly more than that: they could see it had three closely written texts in three different scripts.

Since one of them was Greek – more or less decipherable to any educated individual of the day – the potential importance of the inscription was immeasurable. Indeed, the stone's significance was sufficiently clear that the French took the trouble to haul it back to Alexandria in March 1801, when they retreated from the British, who had landed on the Egpyptian coast.

By August, however, Egypt's great port city was in British hands and the 'Rosetta Stone' had fallen to them as booty. (It occured to neither French nor English that the rightful home for the Rosetta Stone might be the country where it had actually been created.)

STILL MYSTERIOUS

Given the existence of a Greek translation, the meaning of the Egyptian texts was easily established – but just *how* was that meaning embodied in these two unfathomable scripts? Not until 1823 did the French scholar Jean-François Champollion succeed in showing how the hieroglyphic and demotic scripts should be deciphered. All of a sudden, Egyptian history was an open book.

Sounds vs Symbols

How the inscription was eventually deciphered is a fascinating story in itself – again, a tale of colonial power-conflict. French and British scholars vied with one another for the honour of finding the key to open the door on ancient Egypt. With hindsight we can see that, as Jonathan Downs has pointed out, the real 'obscurity' of these scripts lay in the preconceptions of the nineteenth-century researchers. The magical, mysterious quality of the characters seemed self-evident, so scholars took it as read that they were essentially symbolic rather than phonetic – sound-based – scripts. This thinking held back Britain's Thomas Young, who went halfway to cracking the code but could not find his way past this misapprehension.

" *Decreed during the reign of the young man who has followed his father onto the throne, the most illustrious King of crowns, protector of Egypt, strict in his observances to the gods, victorious over his foes; the ruler who has brought civilization to all his realms…Immortal Ptolemy, beloved of Ptah [Egyptian creator-god], issued this edict in the ninth year of his kingship…in the presence of his chief priests, soothsayers and sacred attendants, royal fan-bearers and religious scribes, and all the other priests from the various shrines across the kingdom, all summoned together at Memphis to mark the accession of the Immortal Ptolemy, beloved of Ptah…A god himself, born of a god and goddess, as King Immortal Ptolemy…has been generous towards the shrines and those who serve them, directing money and grain towards them from his own revenues, so that the temples – and the whole land of Egypt – might rise in prosperity. He has also reduced the tax-burdens so that all might prosper during his reign. He has written off debts owed to the Crown, numerous as they are; he has shown mercy in offering an amnesty for those in prison or those awaiting trial; he has funded the provision of horse and infantry and naval vessels to defend Egypt against those who hoped to invade it, spending vast sums in money and grain to ensure the country's safety…* "

Israel and the Holy Land

The land we know as Israel lies towards the western edge of the Fertile Crescent. As such, it was one of the first parts of the world to see a settled civilization. Jericho, indeed, has a claim to have been the world's first city: a walled centre existed here as early as 7500 BC. The written record begins rather later, not until the end of the third millennium BC, from which time we have finds from Ebla, in modern Syria. The builders of this ancient state adopted a Mesopotamian model of civilization – cuneiform script and all. We know they were a Semitic people, though, from the language that they used.

Other tribes continued to pursue a nomadic pastoralist lifestyle – a rational choice in a semi-arid, sparsely vegetated region. Their wanderings brought them into contact with the empires of Mesopotamia and Egypt along the margins of their territories, but for the most part they were able to carry on unhindered. In periods of tension between the great powers, though, they were liable to find themselves squeezed: at such times, their home-territories became 'no-man's-land'. Indeed, it is a moment of Egyptian expansionism that brings the first explicit reference to Israel: the scribes of the Pharaoh Merneptah crow about the country's conquest in the Israel Stela of around 1210 BC (*see pp. 58–59*).

Left: The sight of the Dome of the Rock – one of Islam's most sacred shrines – atop the Temple Mount is a telling comment on the complex religious history of the 'Holy Land'.

WAR AND CONQUEST were to be the great forces that fashioned the Jews into a people, their various tribes coming together in the course of a series of struggles with their neighbours. By the end of the second millennium, King David had defeated the Philistines and established Jerusalem both as political capital and religious shrine. His successor Solomon built a formidable economic base by fostering trade with Arabia and Egypt. After his death in 926 BC, however, his kingdom split in two: the southern part, Judah, kept Jerusalem as its capital. Established by King Omri, in 885 BC, the northern state of Israel was centred on Samaria.

The two states fought incessantly – and not just with one another but with neighbouring kingdoms like Moab and Edom. The Pharaohs interfered, of course, in what was pretty much Egypt's 'backyard'; in the east, the threat from Assyria was looming. In 853 BC, Ahab of Israel led an alliance of local states, successfully seeing off an Assyrian invasion. But Assyria's kings were not so easily put off, and by 841 BC they had taken Israel in thrall.

Judah, for the moment, appears to have remained unscathed – mainly because it was too small and insignificant to arouse the ancient superpower's interest. In the end, though, the southern kingdom may have paid the price for Israel's stubborn resistance. All the evidence is that the Assyrians were easy-going overlords, content to keep their colonies on a relatively long leash. But a series of revolts in Israel made intervention inevitable. Tiglathpileser III, Shalmaneser V and Sargon II all had to mount punitive expeditions and, in around 730 BC, Judah was brought under Assyrian control. The Jews remained restive, however, even Sennacherib's Sack of Jerusalem in 701 BC failing to tame them.

TWO KINGDOMS, ONE GOD
One reason for the Jews' assertiveness was the fact that – remarkably, for the period – they had embraced a belief in a single universal creating and lawgiving deity, Jehovah. Just when they did this is unclear: tradition has tended to push the start date back into the remotest mists of time, whereas modern scholarship points to clear pagan strains in the early iconography of the Jews. The Menorah – the seven-stemmed candlestick so closely associated with Solomon's Temple, for example – is oddly reminiscent of the trees that served as fertility symbols for earlier Semitic cults.

Certainly, though, by 640 BC, when King Josiah was enthroned in Judah, the Jews were militantly monotheistic. And God, it seemed, was on their side: Assyrian power was on the wane and, in 612 BC, it collapsed completely. But Josiah's successor, Jehoiakim, was dangerously overplaying his hand when he refused to pay tribute to Assyria's conqueror, King Nebuchadnezzar of Babylon. In 597 BC, after a three-month siege, the Babylonians took Jerusalem. Ten years later, after another rebellion, Solomon's Temple was razed to the ground and – to ensure the destruction of the Jewish spirit – leading Jews were carried home by the invader as hostages: the 'Babylonian Captivity' had begun.

SEMITIC SCRIPTS
Sadly, the archeological record suggests that these early centuries of Jewish history went more or less entirely unrecorded by the Jews themselves. Though the Jews flit in and out of the Mesopotamian and Egyptian chronicles of this period, only odds and ends of first-hand Jewish testimony have been found. (The Bible gives a full account, of course, but it was written down in

Above: The walls of Jerusalem, today a holy city for Jews, Christians and Muslims, have been breached many times in 3000 eventful years – though often too they have been held by brave defenders.

retrospect, around the middle of the first millennium BC.)

The first 'Paleo-Hebrew' texts appear to date from around 1000 BC; they include the extraordinary calendar stone found at Gezer. By Middle Eastern standards, this suggests a comparatively late development of literacy. Given that other Semitic peoples – like those of Ebla – had been able to write a thousand years before, it seems on the face of it unlikely that the Jews had not been literate; in the absence of hard evidence, though, we can only speculate. It is striking, all the same, that the earliest Paleo-Hebrew script was relatively advanced, being alphabetical in its organization. Arguably, it was ahead even of its kindred Phoenician script by being less rigid and more flexible about the formation of letters in a way that lent itself to wider, more informal use.

The Jews were not, of course, the only inhabitants of 'Israel'; they were not even the only Semitic inhabitants. The Old Testament tells us how much of their time the people of Abraham and Moses spent defending their territories (and, where possible, extending them). In the eighth-century Tel Dan inscription, we first encounter

Aramaic, as the language of Israel's enemy. The linguistic history of this part of the world is complex: many Jews ended up as Aramaic speakers – including, apparently, Jesus Christ and his Apostles. The Jewish elite picked up Aramaic at the time of the Babylonian Captivity: the Mesopotamians themselves adopted it, appreciating the flexibility its alphabetical script offered in comparison to cuneiform. When Persia's Cyrus the Great brought the Babylonian Captivity to an end on conquering the city in 539 BC, those who returned took Aramaic home with them to Jerusalem.

There, thanks to Cyrus' enlightened generosity, they rebuilt their Temple and also their whole identity. Alexander fought his way through the country in 332–331 BC, but he was so set on reaching Egypt that he seems to have taken little trouble to suppress the Jews or their religion. After his death, his generals warred over his empire: this province fell to Seleucus, and his successors. They ruled unchallenged until 169 BC, when Antiochus outlawed key dietary rules and rituals. In 161 BC, Judas Maccabeus rose up against Seleucid power; ironically, he formed an alliance with the Romans.

Above: The Nimrod Fortress was raised on the Golan Heights by Al-Aziz Uthman in the thirteenth century to keep out the Christian Crusaders. Israel, fought over incessantly by an ever-changing cast of enemies, has yet to succeed in finding a lasting peace.

From 140 BC, Judas' brother Simon Maccabeus was ruler of an independent Jewish state but, as so often before, the Jews were divided amongst themselves. The difficulties continued under Simon's successors of what was known as the Hasmonean Dynasty. In 63 BC, the Romans invaded to restore order. They did so at the cost of at least 12,000 lives, eventually annexing Judaea to the province of Syria. Surprisingly, perhaps, God's Chosen People were given special privileges by Rome: they were granted partial autonomy and, in 49 BC, King Herod was recognized as their ruler.

Unrest continued, however, the resistance fighters known as the Zealots conducting guerrilla operations against the occupiers. A major revolt of AD 66 finally provoked a crushing response: a bloody invasion claimed many thousands of lives. Then, in 70, Jerusalem was sacked and the Temple again destroyed.

The Ebla Enigma: A Royal Archive

Few archeologists get to live the dream of discovering a lost city: Giovanni Pettinato and Paolo Matthiae did that at Tell Mardikh. But this excitement was as nothing to the thrill of unearthing a vast archive there, much of it in a hitherto unknown language.

Southwest of Aleppo in the north of modern Syria, Tell Mardikh had intrigued archeologists for some years. An unpromising rocky mound to the untutored glance, this 'tell' – built up by the accumulated debris of generations of human habitation – announced the presence of an ancient settlement of some size.

In 1963, an Italian team from the University of Rome set to work on the site. They were led by Giovanni Pettinato and Paolo Matthiae. Work was meticulous and progress slow, the days of the treasure-hunting archeologist-adventurers being long gone: this was research in the modern, scientific spirit. Even so, as they toiled doggedly, rewarded by a shaped stone here, a ceramic shard there, they were understandably itching to make some sort of breakthrough.

A LOST CITY FOUND?

After five long years, it came. A basalt statue was unearthed amidst the rubble. This clearly represented Ishtar, Mesopotamian goddess of love and fertility. An Akkadian inscription at its base referred to Ebla – the 'City of White Stones'. This place had been known to scholars from Assyrian inscriptions; it is mentioned too in the chronicles of Thutmose III inscribed on walls at Karnak, Egypt. Had they truly discovered this lost city?

Giovanni Pettinato decided that they had: Tell Mardikh was actually the site of Ebla, he announced. In the circumstances, this was something of a stretch. Had his understandable impatience caused him to jump to conclusions that were not warranted by the actual evidence? Perhaps. In 1975, however, and some seven years later, came a discovery as spectacular as any in the history of archeology – and one that supported Pettinato. Working by now in what was clearly part of an ancient palace, the team found a hoard of almost 17,000 tablets.

A ROYAL ARCHIVE

As in the Assyrian king Ashurbanipal's later library at Nineveh, these records had apparently been carefully stacked up in wooden shelf-units; again, as at Nineveh, this supporting structure had been destroyed in a fire at some ancient date. The entire archive thus ended up in a gigantic heap, any organizing logic lost. As the first inscriptions were deciphered, it became apparent that Pettinato's hunch had been correct: this pile of tablets was, in fact, Ebla's Royal Archive.

THE FIRST BILINGUAL DICTIONARY?

Among the finds in the Ebla archive have been several 'lexicotexts' – lists of Sumerian words, apparently for study. More intriguing still are

Below: At first an apparently unpromising site, Tell Mardikh turned out to be a treasure-house, archeologically speaking at least, the site of what was literally a 'lost civilization' from the third millennium BC.

vocabularies of Eblaite words with their Sumerian equivalents – over a thousand in all and even more a boon to modern scholars than they must have been to ancient students.

A DISTINCT CULTURE
But most of the tablets could not easily be read. Though written in the classical cuneiform script of Mesopotamia, the language they were in was unfamiliar. Scholars slowly unpicked the complexities of 'Eblaite', establishing that it was an early Semitic dialect: it had similarities with Canaanite, Hebrew and Phoenician, but was very much its own tongue.

The bulk of the record related to a period around the middle of the third millennium BC. One letter from an Eblaite king to one of his generals refers to the conquest of neighbouring Mari, known from Assyrian sources to have happened at this time.

Even now, work on the archive is in its

early stages: great excitement was caused among scriptural scholars by the discovery of what may be allusions to Abraham and some of the prophets. There even appear to be references to the so-called Cities of the Plain, destroyed by an angry God in the Book of Genesis. To some extent, the resulting furore has obscured the wider significance of the Ebla findings, which promise in time to yield an enthralling account of the political, economic and social life of a fascinating civilization. Taken alongside other archeological finds on the site – a

splendid palace, temples and burial-chambers – the tablets underscore our sense of a wealthy and prestigious city. The tablets show how this prosperity and power were buoyed up by the city's textile exports, whilst there are records too of victories in battle and of diplomatic treaties with Assyria and other neighbours.

ON PUBLIC DISPLAY

Many of the Ebla Tablets are to be seen at the museum in nearby Idlib.

Right: Some 17,000 inscribed tablets were found in the ruins of Ebla, a royal archive written in cuneiform but in many cases representing an unfamiliar – yet recognizably Semitic – language.

Several versions of this Creation Hymn have been found among the Ebla Tablets:

> *Lord of heaven and earth: The earth did not exist: you brought it into being. The daylight did not exist: you brought that into being. The dawn did not yet exist – you had not made it.*

A Calendar in Stone

'To everything there is a season,' says the Book of Ecclesiastes. A 3000-year-old Hebrew inscription concurs. For a text of this antiquity, the Gezer Calendar Stone is strikingly clear – but what does it really mean?

Left: The town of Gezer was given as a gift to King Solomon at the end of the second millennium BC. The Calendar Stone appears to have been fashioned not too long after.

Tel Gezer is mentioned in the Book of Kings: the site was given to Solomon as a dowry when he married the daughter of Egypt's Pharaoh. The Pharaoh (thought to have been Siamun) is said to have taken the city from the Philistines and reduced it to ruins, which means that Solomon did not receive a city, just a smoking site.

Even so, a significant settlement was quickly established here, as boundary-stones found by archeologists confirm. The site was first discovered by the French Consul and amateur antiquarian Charles Clermont-Ganneau in 1871, but it was some thirty years before it was systematically excavated. The Irish archeologist Robert MacAlister directed the work, beginning in 1902, and the remains of an impressive city of the tenth century BC were slowly unearthed. It was not until 1908 that the Gezer Calendar Stone was found. Its inscription sets out the main tasks, in their seasonal sequence, of the agrarian year.

The stela thus offers us an extraordinary insight into life the way it was actually lived at the time. Other ancient inscriptions may impress in their grand sonority or their epic associations: this one has an engagingly down-home quality. It is hard not to be charmed – though it is always as well not to condescend to the past, and our reaction highlights certain difficulties with an inscription that presents more challenges than we may expect.

WHICH HARVEST?

The first is obvious enough: that of working out why there should be so many harvests – those for barley and grapes are specifically identified, but that still leaves two. It has been suggested that the 'harvest' of the first line is for olives. This is followed by a first sowing for cereals (wheat and millet) and a subsequent 'late-planting' for vegetables, such as spring onions and leeks.

Flax was invaluable: its fibres could be made into linen cloth, whilst its seeds were pressed to make linseed oil. As the summer drew on, the fast-growing barley would be reaped first, before the main cereal harvest; after the grapes had been gathered, it was time to pick the 'summer fruit' – anything from apples and watermelons to figs and almonds.

THE BIG QUESTION

The second, and stiffer, challenge is that of reaching an understanding of what the inscription 'meant' in the wider sense; what purpose it served, what it was actually for. It is impossible, after all, to believe that Jewish farmers needed an official aide-memoire for a regime followed by their families for generations. A writing exercise for schoolboys? A folk song or children's jingle? Perhaps, but then why have it so solemnly displayed on public view? The Gezer Calendar Stone reminds us that, however clear we may think an ancient inscription is, it may well keep back from us the meanings that really matter.

Ups and Downs

The archeological evidence suggests that Gezer's heyday was comparatively brief. It was reduced to rubble not long after Solomon's time. This conforms with the written evidence that it was sacked and destroyed by the Pharaoh Shoshenq I (the biblical Shishak) towards the end of the tenth century BC. It was rebuilt and then razed again by the Assyrian ruler Tiglathpileser III in 733 BC. But this was nothing new. We know from the Bible that there was a city at Gezer before the Jews were here. Continuing excavation has uncovered layers of occupation – often violently interrupted – stretching back to the beginning of the third millennium BC. A group of standing stones from the early Bronze Age appears to show Gezer amongst the other cities of its age: is it simply vainglory that the group gives Gezer pride of place?

ON PUBLIC DISPLAY

The Gezer Calendar Stone is in the collection of the Museum of the Ancient Orient in Istanbul.

Above: The Gezer Calendar Stone is inscribed in a spidery Paleo-Hebrew script – one of the earliest examples that we have.

> *Two months for the harvest; Two months for the planting;*
> *Two months for late-planting; One month to cut flax;*
> *One month for the barley-harvest; One month of harvest and festival.*
> *Two months for harvesting grapes; One month for gathering the*
> *summer fruit.*

Lost and Found: The 'Moabite Stone'

The vaunts of Mesha, king of Moab, were recorded on a stela detailing his victories over Israel. Not only does the text shed intriguing light on biblical events, its Moabite is strikingly similar in appearance to early Hebrew script.

When we say that an artefact has been 'discovered', we may mean that it has been dug out of the ground where it has lain, literally lost, for centuries; sometimes, though, a monument may have been hidden in plain sight. So it was with the Mesha Stela – a carved slab of basalt similar in size and shape to the headstone from a modern western grave but designed to serve a very different purpose. It was fashioned in the middle of the ninth century BC on the orders of Mesha, king of Moab at that time. Its purpose was to commemorate Mesha's successful rebellion against Israel and his re-establishment of Moabite independence.

The episode is recorded in the biblical Book of Kings. As Mesha's stela has it, Kemosh, the god of the Moabites, had allowed his kingdom to be conquered by Israel's King Omri and held in continued subjection by his son Ahab, but finally relented and delivered victory to his own people.

A CHANGE OF STATUS
The kingdoms of Moab and Israel alike had long since disappeared, and this was a quiet corner of the Ottoman Empire when the first European archeologists started poking around amongst its ruined sites. But the Mesha Stela still stood – and the ancient stone still had a ritual function for the Arab Palestinians who lived around what is now Dhiban in Jordan. They felt it brought their community luck, even if they did not know why.

So when the Reverend F. A. Klein, a German missionary, 'discovered' the stela in 1868, he stumbled on something that had never actually gone missing. He

Above: In the middle of the ninth century BC, King Mesha made his stand against his Israelite overlord here at Moab. The story was triumphantly recorded on his stela.

was also interfering with a monument that, in the centuries since it was first set up, had taken on an entirely different significance for the people of Palestine. When, with what we now see as the high-handedness of the nineteenth-century colonial, he started making preparations to take the stela away for 'safekeeping' and study, they broke it into pieces to prevent its removal. The result was that, after surviving intact for almost 3000 years, the Mesha Stela had scarcely been 'found' when it really was almost lost.

But its destruction did not produce the desired effect: by this time, the French diplomat and archeologist Charles Clermont-Ganneau had already made a copy of the inscription in papier mâché; in any case, European researchers were happy enough to stick the broken stela together.

Biblical Commentary

Towards the base of the stone, the inscription becomes increasingly unclear: deciphering it becomes more and more a matter of speculation. In recent years, the French scholar André Lemaire caused a stir with his suggestion that a line near the bottom may make direct reference to the House of David: whilst the evidence is inconclusive, his reasoning is not implausible.

ON PUBLIC DISPLAY

The 'Moabite Stone' – successfully pieced together – is now to be seen among the exhibits in the Louvre.

" I am Mesha, the son of Kemosh, King of Moab, from Dibon. My father ruled in Moab for thirty years and I succeeded him. I sanctified this high to Kemosh, because he protected me from all other kings and brought me victory against all enemies. Omri, King of Israel, oppressed Moab for many days, for Kemosh was angry with his people. Then his son succeeded him and said 'I too will oppress Moab'. He said this in my own time. But I held him and his house in contempt. And Israel has been defeated, vanquished in perpetuity... And the King of Israel built Atarot for himself, but I besieged and captured the city, and I slew its inhabitants as a sacrificial offering for Kemosh and for Moab...And Kemosh then told me: 'Go and take Nebo from Israel.' By night I went and I fought from dawn to midday and I captured it and killed all who were in it: seven thousand men and male foreigners and women, female foreigners and slave girls, for I had consecrated the city to Kemosh. And I took the vessels of Yahweh to Kemosh... "

Above: The cracks still show, but the 'Moabite Stone' was successfully put back together by archeological researchers after local people broke it in the nineteenth century.

Tel Dan Inscription

Its tone triumphalist as it tells of Syrian victory and Israeli subjection, the Tel Dan Inscription might have been thought to make uncomfortable reading for modern Jewish scholars. Instead, its discovery sent a thrill of excitement through the world of Hebrew studies.

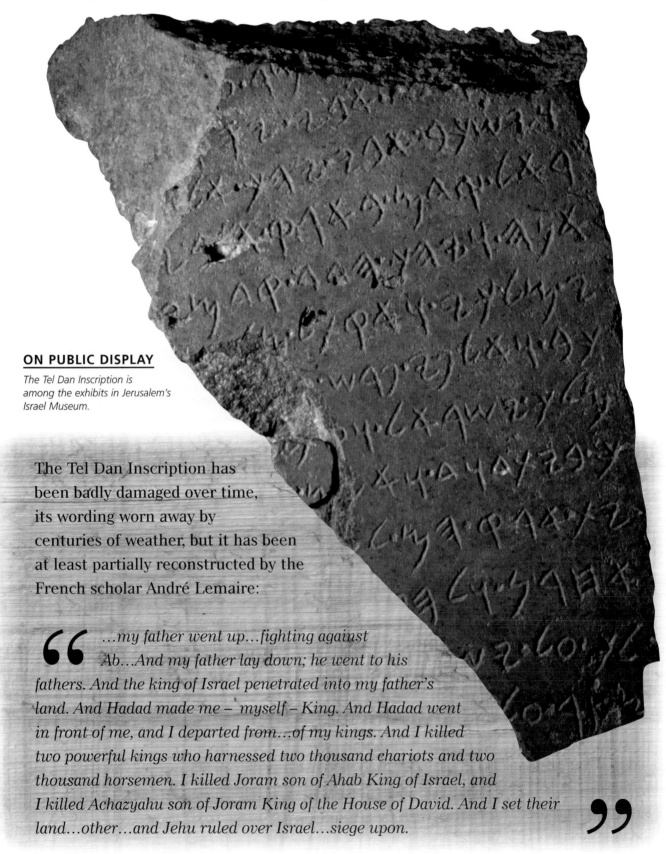

ON PUBLIC DISPLAY

The Tel Dan Inscription is among the exhibits in Jerusalem's Israel Museum.

The Tel Dan Inscription has been badly damaged over time, its wording worn away by centuries of weather, but it has been at least partially reconstructed by the French scholar André Lemaire:

> ❝ *...my father went up...fighting against Ab...And my father lay down; he went to his fathers. And the king of Israel penetrated into my father's land. And Hadad made me – myself – King. And Hadad went in front of me, and I departed from...of my kings. And I killed two powerful kings who harnessed two thousand chariots and two thousand horsemen. I killed Joram son of Ahab King of Israel, and I killed Achazyahu son of Joram King of the House of David. And I set their land...other...and Jehu ruled over Israel...siege upon.* ❞

Dan (literally, 'Judge') was biblical Israel's northernmost city, in what was then – as it is now – a fought-over frontier area. The Golan Heights, in whose vicinity the site stands, were seized from Syria by the Israelis in the Six Day War of 1967; controversially, the Israelis have kept them ever since. Ironically, the Tel Dan Stela shows the tables turned – albeit about 3000 years ago. Its Aramaic inscription records a crushing victory by Syria over Israel. It appears to be written in the voice of the son of the victorious King Benhadad of Damascus; by his own account, the princely narrator played a heroic part in the engagement.

In 1993, archeologists excavating the mound of rubble that was all which remained of Dan dug up part of a large, black, basalt stela. Further fragments were unearthed the following year. Though the stone had been badly knocked about and weathered and the surviving inscription had more gaps than words, there was plenty here to arouse the historians' interest. In the first place, patchy though it was, the account appeared to corroborate what was already known about a time of Syrian supremacy, which lasted through much of the second half of the eighth century BC. The Bible's Second Book of Kings (6, 24) records the following: 'And it came to pass...that Ben-hadad King of Syria gathered all his host, and went up, and besieged Samaria.'

Most exciting of all, however, was the reference in this inscription (if only in passing) to the existence of a royal 'House of David'. Surprising as it may seem, this was the first time that scientific archeology or scholarly research had been able to offer any sort of objective verification for one of the most important strands of the Bible story. Even now, some sceptics suggest that the crucial Hebrew characters

Opposite: Not much is left of the original Tel Dan Inscription, and what there is has not been easy to decipher, but the text has still proved an inspiration for a great many Jewish scholars.

Above: Though much about it remains mysterious, the significance of the Tel Dan Inscription is not in doubt: it takes us straight back to a time of kings and prophets, such as Benhadad II, portrayed in this figurine.

are potentially ambiguous, and that 'House of David' may be a romantically wishful misreading: various alternative interpretations have been offered, though none is especially compelling.

While the debates continue among specialist scholars over its precise wording and what it means, the Tel Dan Inscription stands for the rest of us as a haunting document of biblical times: its dating to that far-off period is certainly not disputed. Exasperating as it may be for the archeologist, the inscription's incompleteness only adds to its allure for the rest of us: maintaining the mystery of the scripture even as it seems to support its truth.

Smothered by his Son

Hazael, who many scholars assume to have been the son who put up the Tel Dan Stela, reigned for 37 years as Benhadad's successor. A great war leader, he won a series of victories over the Jews. A court official before ascending the throne, he appears in the Second Book of Kings (8, 7–14) as the personal emissary of his ailing father to Elisha. The prophet tells him that his father will die, but orders him to let him believe that he will recover. Hazael returns to Damascus and suffocates his father while he sleeps.

The Tale of a Tunnel

Deep beneath the elevated Ophel at the heart of the City of David, in old Jerusalem, a diverted stream runs down a tunnel dug during the reign of Hezekiah. An inscription in the darkness commemorated its completion – though it went undiscovered until the 1830s.

The rest of the deeds of Hezekiah, and all his might, and how he made the pool and the conduit and brought water to the city, are they not written in the Chronicles of the Kings of Judah? So asks the Book of Kings itself, where Hezekiah's doings have indeed just been recorded – though the construction of the Siloam Tunnel also figures in 2 Chronicles (32, 3–4, 30):

'He planned with his officers and his mighty men to stop the water of the springs that were outside the city; and they helped him. A great many people were gathered, and they stopped all the springs and the brook that flowed through the land, saying "Why should the kings of Assyria come and find much water?"…This same Hezekiah

ON PUBLIC DISPLAY

The Siloam Inscription was on display in situ until 1891, when it was stolen. The recovered pieces were sent to Turkey by the Ottoman authorities. Today, they stand in the Istanbul Archeology Museum.

Above: The Siloam Inscription was placed some way inside the tunnel. Forgotten for centuries, it was rediscovered in modern times.

> **"** *And this is the story of the tunnel…while the axes were striking towards each other and while there were still three cubits left to cut through…a man's voice was heard calling to his co-workers, for there was a fault in the rock on the right-hand side…and on the day the tunnel was finally completed, the work-gangs pushed on towards one another, axe towards axe; and at last the water flowed through a channel 1200 cubits long, though there was 100 cubits' worth of rock above the tunnellers' heads.* **"**

closed the upper outlet of the waters of Gihon and directed them down to the west side of the city of David.'

A STRATEGIC STREAM
The Ophel on which the City of David was built was a natural stronghold, readily defended, but the lack of fresh water made it vulnerable to a siege. There was water to be had from the Spring of Gihon, but the topography was unhelpful: if the best use was to be made of the natural contours for defence, it had to be left outside the city walls.

King Hezekiah, who ruled in Judah between about 715 and 687 BC, spent his entire reign in fear of Assyrian invasion, whether under Sargon II or his son Sennacherib. The kingdom was already being forced to pay tribute to Assyria as the price of its relative autonomy, though Hezekiah always nursed the hope of rebelling against this subjection.

It was to this end that he took steps to protect the city's water-supply, building fortified walls around the main water-source, the Spring of Gihon. The stream that flowed from here had always flowed down the hillside beyond the city: he gave orders for the digging of a conduit that would divert it directly underneath the city to the Pool of Siloam. This was a mighty labour: cut straight through the solid rock of the Ophel, the tunnel was to be well over 500m (550 yards) in length and to fall just 30cm (12in).

Right: Running right underneath the Old City, Hezekiah's tunnel brought water from the Spring of Gihon, making Jerusalem more secure against any siege.

A Good Story?

That 'Hezekiah's Tunnel' was built is a matter of demonstrable fact – tourists walk through it daily – but the builder's inscription still has a slight air of fiction. The description it gives of two teams of men hewing their way steadily towards one another is an idealized one. Not that this was anything less than a heroic engineering achievement, but the presence of several 'blind alleys' where the wrong direction was taken suggests rather more haphazardness and trial and error than the inscription implies. Generally speaking, indeed, the tunnel follows a meandering route – significantly longer than it needed to be. Modern scholars suspect that the tunnellers took advantage of a natural fault in the limestone. Even so, there is still a right-angled kink in the middle where the sections meet: this detail would appear to be in keeping with the story.

Shebna the Steward

Could a stone tomb in Silwan, southeast of the city of Jerusalem, be the same one mentioned in the Bible? There, Shebna is castigated for constructing himself a final resting-place too far above his station as a royal steward.

This is the tomb of [Shebna], who was over the household. There is no gold or silver here – only bones. His own and those of the slave-wife who lies here with him. My curse be upon any man who violates this sepulchre.

Above: Tantalizingly, crucial words of this important inscription have been obliterated, so we will never know for sure if this was really Shebna's controversial tomb. It is tempting to assume so, though: the suggestion is by no means far-fetched, even if anything in the way of firm supporting evidence is sadly lacking.

Silwan lies outside Jerusalem, just to the south of the Old City and to the east of the district known as the City of David. Today, this part of the Kidron Valley is very much an Arab district, its residents roused to anger by the construction of the 'West Bank Barrier'. Its Jewish heritage is ancient, though: many finds were made in more peaceful times, but none has been more intriguing than what is widely believed to have been the tomb of Shebna.

PRIDE AND PRESUMPTION

Shebna, who was the steward in the palace of King Hezekiah, fell foul of the Prophet Isaiah by building himself a tomb fit (quite literally) for a king. Whilst the office of steward (or 'comptroller') was an extremely important one, its holder certainly no servant in the normal sense, he had no business being laid to rest in royal style. In the biblical account, he was hounded from office and replaced. Scholars disagree over whether this is the same Shebna who (now reduced in rank and status) is sent as an emissary to the Assyrians in the Second Book of Kings (18, 18).

THE SECRET OF THE STONE

In 1870, the French orientalist Charles Clermont-Ganneau was exploring the ancient necropolis that lined this part of the Silwan hillside when he stumbled on this brief inscription cut into the lintel of a rock-tomb. Clermont-Ganneau was also involved in the discovery and deciphering of the 'Moabite Stone' (*see pp. 78–79*). This inscription proved more intractable, however, so rough was the surface into which the characters had been carved.

Despite the fact that it is written in the standard Hebrew script of the seventh century BC, it was not successfully read until 1953, when it was deciphered by the great Israeli epigraphist Nahman Avigad.

ON PUBLIC DISPLAY

The stone lintel on which the Shebna Inscription was carved was cut away in the nineteenth century and – like so many archeological treasures of the time – ended up in London, in the collection of the British Museum.

Pretensions Punished

'Thus says the Lord God of hosts,' in the words of the Book of Isaiah (22, 15–18): 'Come, go to this steward, to Shebna, who is over the household, and say to him: "What have you to do here and whom have you here, that you have hewn here a tomb for yourself, you who hew a tomb on the height, and carve a habitation for yourself in the rock? Behold, the Lord will hurl you away violently…He will seize firm hold on you, and whirl you round and round, and throw you like a ball into a wide land; there you shall die, and there shall be your splendid chariots, you shame of your master's house. I will thrust you from your office, and you will be cast down from your station. In that day I will call my servant Eli'akim the son of Hilki'ah, and I will clothe him with your robe, and will bind your girdle on him, and will commit your authority to his hand; and he shall be father to the inhabitants of Jerusalem and to the house of Judah…"'

Or rather, it was mostly deciphered: the all-important name of the occupant had been deleted – apparently deliberately. Only its final letters – *'iah* could be seen. This would not of course be consistent with the name of 'Shebna', but it is a form of the name 'Shebnayahu'.

And it is under this name that the same steward appears in the Book of Neremiah (9, 4). All things considered, there may be no conclusive proof that this is the biblical Shebna's tomb, but it is a suggestion that scholars take seriously.

Right: Silwan (ancient Siloam) lies just to the south of the Old City of Jerusalem. This part of the Kidron Valley is today very much an Arab district.

Garment Grievance

Over 2500 years ago, an agricultural worker's grievance against his overseer prompted a petition to his local governor. This official complaint makes clear that even the most downtrodden in ancient Israel still had a strong sense of their rights.

> *May your worship listen and hear your servant's plea. I am a humble labourer, a reaper. I served dutifully at Hasar-Asam, reaping, gathering and storing away the grain all week up to the Sabbath's eve. When my work reaping and storing the grain was finished, however, Hoshab ben-Shobi came: he confiscated my garment, even though I had completed the appointed work. This was days ago that it happened. My fellow-labourers can all vouch for what happened…[the law requires that] if I am found without fault he should restore my garment; if he refuses to, it is your worship's right as governor to order to give it back to me. Be not offended by my plea…*

ON PUBLIC DISPLAY

The Mesad Hashavyahu Ostrakon is among the many fascinating exhibits in the Israel Museum, Jerusalem.

Above: Broken pottery was never in short supply. The shards were kept for recycling as 'notepaper' for use in all but the most formal and prestigious communications.

close to Yavneh-yam, on the coast of modern Israel, is the site of the ancient Jewish fort of Mesad Hashavyahu: this was once the border between Judah and the land of the Philistines. When the fortress was built – believed to have been during the reign of King Josiah (640–609 BC) – Judah was fiercely protecting its independence. Israel had been conquered by the Assyrians in 720 BC, but the southern Jewish kingdom appears to have successfully resisted (*see pp. 30–31*). Nonetheless, it was beleaguered – the problem lying not so much with the Assyrians as with Egyptian plans to expand into the region. Josiah was ultimately to meet his death at Megiddo in battle with the forces of the Pharaoh Necho II – killed by an arrow, according to tradition.

C lose to Yavneh-yam, on the coast of modern Israel, is the site of the ancient Jewish fort of Mesad Hashavyahu: this was once the border between Judah and the land of the Philistines. When the fortress was built – believed to have been during the reign of King Josiah (640–609 BC) – Judah was fiercely protecting its independence. Israel had been conquered by the Assyrians in 720 BC, but the southern Jewish kingdom appears to have successfully resisted (*see pp. 30–31*). Nonetheless, it was beleaguered – the problem lying not so much with the Assyrians as with Egyptian plans to expand into the region. Josiah was ultimately to meet his death at Megiddo in battle with the forces of the Pharaoh Necho II – killed by an arrow, according to tradition.

UNJUSTLY CHARGED

But life went on, in times of peace as in war: there were always fields to till and plant; a harvest to gather. Under the system of *corvée* (enforced labour) then prevailing, however, no peasant could refuse his services when the state demanded. Given that such 'volunteers' were not always willing, the authorities had sanctions at their disposal. Those who failed to comply for whatever reason could

have their possessions confiscated to the value of the labour due, and there were few indeed who could afford to let that happen. Hence the indignation of an unknown reaper at finding that not only has he been forced to do several days' exhausting work to fulfil his duty, but his overseer Hoshab has taken his garment in payment anyway.

So distressed was he that he had an official complaint written for the attention of the 'governor' — almost certainly spending money he could all too ill afford on the services of a scribe to do so. This official may well have been the military commander of Mesad Hashavyahu:

Above: Solomon's wisdom as a judge was legendary but, from the king down to the governor of a little garrison on the frontier, any man in authority was expected to arbitrate disputes.

the lands he had been working were very likely attached to the fort. The complaint was written on an 'ostrakon' – a shard of broken pottery. This may seem strange now, but was perfectly normal in a pre-paper age for all except the most prestigious documents. It was found in 1960, in what had originally been the fortress' guardroom: we have no way of knowing whether the reaper got his garment back.

Taxing Toil

The enforcement of labour by the state as a form of tax is known as *corvée*. The French word is used because in medieval times kings and feudal lords had the right to require this sort of taxation-by-labour of their vassals, but in practice it was widely used the length and breadth of the ancient world. It was a good way for governments to extract fiscal 'value' from those who were clearly too poor to be asked to make money payments, and it had obvious attractions to rulers contemplating major projects of public works. Neither the Pyramids of Egypt nor the incredible highways of the Incas in Peru could have been built without this system. But the ancient economy was labour-intensive throughout: even if there were no roads or buildings to be constructed, there was always a need for people to work the ruler's land.

Stone of Sacrifice

A rough inscription on a piece of stone brings us a striking reminder of an ancient Jewish custom condemned by Christ in a famous episode from Mark's Gospel. It was uncovered in excavations on the Temple Mount.

ON PUBLIC DISPLAY

The Corban Inscription can be seen to this day in the Israel Museum of Jerusalem.

Above: There is something touching about the very crudeness of this inscription, though we can scarcely even guess at the spirit in which it was made.

> " *Given to God* "

The stone is rough – apparently the broken shard of what was once a carved stone vessel – and the inscription almost ridiculously crude. Indeed, it is barely an inscription at all, but has clearly been scratched in haste – and by an utterly inexpert hand at that. And yet, the Hebrew word Corban ('Sacrifice' or 'Given to God') is clearly to be made out; so too are the pair of roughly drawn doves beneath it.

Two doves was the sacrifice ordained by Jewish tradition to thank Yahweh for the firstborn boy. They were offered by Mary and Joseph after the birth of Jesus. Luke's Gospel (2, 22–24) tells us:

'And when the time came for their Purification, according to the law of Moses, they brought him up to Jerusalem to present him to the Lord (as it is written in the law of the Lord, "Every male that opens the womb shall be called holy to the Lord"). And to offer a sacrifice of what is said in the law of the Lord, "a pair of turtledoves or two young pigeons." '

A stone with scratches on is not a pair of doves, of course – but might it have been a voucher or receipt for a cash equivalent, a confirmation that the requisite sum had been paid, whether to a Temple trader who would pay the priests or to the authorities themselves?

We have no way of knowing, though if tokens of this sort were being bought and sold systematically; we might expect them to have been more sophisticated in their manufacture. This artefact has the feel of a one-off – especially as it is the only one of its kind ever found. The Corban Inscription is believed to date from the first century AD – so either at around the same time as or not too long after Christ's ministry.

The adult Jesus notoriously drove the moneychangers from the Temple, along with those traders selling animals for sacrifice – including doves. All the evidence we have is that its sacred precincts continued to be something of a market-place until its destruction by the Romans in AD 70.

Thus the practice of sacrifice ceased only because Judaism had been destroyed, at least in its home country. Though some Jews in the diaspora maintained these customs, most saw little point in offering sacrifices that had, by tradition, to be offered far away in a Temple that no longer existed.

Christ and *Corban*

Jesus gets into a dispute with the Pharisees over the whole question of *Corban*, in the Gospel of Mark (7, 8–13):

'And he said to them, "Well did Isaiah prophesy of you hypocrites, as it is written, 'This people honours me with their lips, but their heart is far from me; in vain do they worship me, teaching as doctrines the precepts of men.' You leave the commandment of God, and hold fast the tradition of men." '

And he said to them, 'You have a fine way of rejecting the commandment of God, in order to keep your tradition! For Moses said, "Honour your father and your mother"; and, "He who speaks evil of father or mother, let him surely die"; but you say, "If a man tells his father or his mother, 'What you would have gained from me is Corban'", then you no longer permit him to do anything for his father or mother, thus making void the word of God through your tradition which you hand on…'

As far as Christ was concerned, the custom of *Corban* allowed the institution to take precedence over people – and to take money which the faithful should really be giving to those who needed it amongst their family and friends.

Left: The Temple Mount in Jeruslaem today. Not long after the Corban *inscription was made, the Romans put down a revolt with such massive violence that Judaism was effectively banished from Judaea.*

Conquering in Christ

Axum was unique: an indigenous Christian civilization in northeast Africa, originator of the Ethiopian Church that still endures. The Ezana Stone records the achievements of the kingdom's most famous ruler, particularly his triumph over the 'Black Pharoahs' of Meroë.

The trading state of Axum arose in what is now the north of Ethiopia and Eritrea, towards the end of the first century AD. Its Semitic founders are thought to have come across the Red Sea as refugees from conflict in southern Arabia, and they gradually built an empire on both shores. Its trading network extended much further, as far as Rome in the west and to Persia and India in the east. Unique among Africa's leading kingdoms, it embraced Christianity in the fourth century, under King Ezana (320–350). The story goes that the Syrian St Frumentius brought the creed to the country: he had been shipped to Africa in boyhood as a slave. The then queen took him into the royal palace as a companion for her son Ezana, who was inspired to follow in the faith of his friend.

Above: Christianity found an on the face of it unlikely breeding-ground in the open hills of Ezana's Axum, in the first and second centuries a strong and expansionist power in northeast Africa.

THE AXUMITE ACHIEVEMENT

However it came about, there is no doubting the wholeheartedness of his conversion: the Axum he built was Christian through and through. And so it was to remain, right down to the present – though, as centuries went on and Islam took an ever firmer hold in the states around it, it became increasingly isolated from Christianity's historical mainstream. But magnificent churches, tombs and richly ornamented stelae more than 20m (70ft) tall bear witness to the richness of Axum's Christian culture at this time.

CHRISTIAN SOLDIERS

Yet Ezana, it might be said, created a Christianity in his own image: his was hardly a cheek-turning, love-thine-enemies faith. His Jesus was an earthly empire-builder, as the inscription on the so-called Ezana Stone testifies. It describes his culminating campaign against the Nubians of Meroë, till then northeast Africa's pre-eminent military and economic power. The languages employed give a sense both of Ezana's power and his ambition: whilst Ge'ez was Ethiopian, Sabaean was the tongue of southern Arabia and Yemen. But the existence of a third, Greek version is evidence of Ezana's desire to see his exploits acclaimed beyond his empire, through the world of the Mediterranean to the north.

The Kingdom of Kush

The 'Black Pharoahs' of Kush or Nubia had been a force along the Upper Nile since the eighth century BC, when they freed themselves from Egyptian domination. The area above the Nile's First Cataract was first conquered in the time of the New Kingdom in the second millennium BC, after which it was treated as a colony. Even when it gained its independence, however, Kush continued to imitate Egypt, its costumes, customs, temples and even pyramids closely following the manner of the old colonial masters. Their conquest of the Upper and Lower Egypts exposed them to the full magnificence of the Egyptian achievement, and only confirmed them in their desire to do things the Egyptian way. After the Assyrian invasion of Egypt in the sixth century, however, they were forced back into their Nubian heartland, and moved their capital further upriver from Kush to Meroë. By the early centuries AD, the power of the 'Black Pharoahs' was in decline – hence the ease of Ezana's victory.

" *With the help of Almighty God, I went to war against the Noba when they rose in rebellion; when they bragged 'He will never cross the Takkaze River' and when they attacked the people of Mangurto, Hasa and Barya...I launched a campaign against them in the power of the Lord of the Earth and met them at Kemalke, the ford on the Takkaze. There they broke and fled, and I harried them for twenty-three days in their flight, killing many and capturing more. My soldiers bore home great booty; I burned their towns, both those built of stone and those built of straw; I carried off their grain, their bronze, their preserved meat and the images from their temples...they hurled themselves into the River Seda, and many died there. I cannot tell how many, but as their boats sank in the flood, many men, women and children were drowned...I reached Kush, at the confluence of the Seda and the Takkaze: I killed many men, and took many prisoners too...And I set up a throne where the rivers Seda and Takkaze meet, facing the stone-built town on the peninsula there.* "

ON PUBLIC DISPLAY

The Ezana Stone still stands amongst the ruins of Axum, in Ethiopia.

Above: Like all such stelae, Ezana's represented his 'pitch' to posterity: here he set out the achievements of his life in the terms in which he wanted them remembered.

Persia

The people we think of as the Persians were comparative latecomers to their country. As late as the second millennium BC, they were nomadic pastoralists, following their flocks across the steppes of Central Asia. The Aryan group of peoples, to which they belonged, began to disperse around 1500 BC, many of its tribes pushing steadily southwards into India. Another group, however, migrated to the southwest. In honour of their own ethnic origins, they called their adopted land 'Iran'. In India, the Aryans were notoriously to set themselves at the head of an elaborate caste system, but the 'Iranians' seemed fated to be put upon by others.

ELAMITE ASCENDANCY

Centuries before this, though, the region had embarked on a long and eventful 'pre-Persian' history. Early on in the third millennium BC, a civilization arose in Khuzestan, in the southwestern corner of the country. Here, the success of Sumer prompted the establishment of a 'copycat' kingdom, Elam, following a Mesopotamian model of agricultural development and state-foundation – and also, it is tempting to say, of writing. However, the similarity between the two scripts is only superficial – a matter of a few symbols. It appears that the scripts of Uruk and Elam evolved simultaneously but independently of one another; if they shared a common ancestry, it is now lost.

Left: Its columns rising tall to end in nothing, its vast halls and staircases open to the sky, the ruins of Persepolis have an almost ghostly grandeur. Darius built this palace at the turn of the fifth century, when the Achaemenid Empire was at its height.

ELAM ITSELF WAS LONG DIVIDED, with rival centres of power at Susa in the north and Anshan in the south. They vied with one another for influence. While the effect of this rivalry must inevitably have been to weaken Elam as a whole, it is hard to imagine even a unified state resisting the expansionist surge of Akkad in the twenty-fourth century. Under Sargon I, 'the Great', the northern kingdom was building a powerful empire, taking in not just Mesopotamia itself but its easterly environs. In the event, Akkadian power declined with Sargon's death, and the Elamites were once more able to assert their independence. But even so, the centuries that followed were to see the imperial advantage see-sawing back and forth between the Elamite state and those of Mesopotamia.

The twenty-first century BC, for example, saw a resurgent Sumer establishing its sway; not until well into the second millennium had the Elamites recovered resilience and strength. Though badly beaten by Hammurabi of Babylon in 1764 BC, they bounced back by the century's end to extend their dominance through much of Mesopotamia.

THE ARYANS ARRIVE

No sooner had its reached this height, however, than Elamite power was ebbing away. Now it found itself facing rivals nearer home. The Kassites, nomadic tribesmen from the Zagros Mountains, are thought to have been relatively recent arrivals, an advance wave of the Aryan immigration. Whatever their origins, their destiny for the moment seemed clear: sweeping down to the plains of Mesopotamia, they raided and conquered at will, eventually setting themselves up as rulers not only of Elam but also of Babylonia.

But the power pendulum had not finished swinging. Elam was to regain its drive and its sense of purpose under the kings of the Igihalkid Dynasty. In the second half of the thirteenth century BC, King Untash-Napirisha brought the north and south together, working hard to

Above: The 'Gate of All Nations', it was called, and it was scarcely an exaggeration. Persepolis was the capital for the greatest empire the world had ever seen, with many scores of different subject peoples.

create a common Elamite identity and pride. Newly united, the Elamites re-emerged as empire-builders. Under King Shutruk-Nahhunte and his Shutrukid successors, Elam attained its zenith, Mesopotamia's pre-eminent power. In 1168 BC, Shutruk-Nahhunte invaded Babylonia, capturing and looting its capital. The prestigious trophies he carried back to Susa included the Code of Hammurabi (*see pp. 18–19*). Then, in 1154 BC, Kutir-Nahhunte invaded again, toppling the last of the Kassite kings, Enlil-nadin-ahi. His troops then carried off Marduk, the Babylonians' main idol.

The great days of Elam were over, though: Babylon revived under Nebuchadnezzar I in the late twelfth century BC. Susa was occupied and the Elamites' plunder taken back. Despite a brief reflowering from about 720 BC, Elamite civilization was once more overwhelmed, first by the renewed rise of the Assyrians and then by Nebuchadnezzar II's Neo-Babylonian Empire.

MEDES AND PERSIANS'

It is from the Assyrian chroniclers that we first learn of the existence of the Medes and the Persians –

both groups came as part of the Aryan migration. The Medes, it seems, made their appearance first. By the end of the second millennium, the Madayu (as the Assyrians called them) were established in what is now northwestern Iran. Through the first half of the first millennium, they became a major power, allying with Nebuchadnezzar II for his campaign against Assyria. The ascendancy of Assur having been brought low, the Medes were able to occupy and extend the Assyrian Empire. By the sixth century BC, under King Cyaxares, they cemented their rule, not only over all except the northern part of Elam (the far southwest of modern-day Iran) but over much of Afghanistan, Azerbaijan and even parts of Pakistan and Anatolia.

But the might of the Medes was not to endure. They were quickly supplanted by another Aryan people: the Parsa or, as we would say, the Persians. This group had settled in two main areas: around Lake Urmia, to the west of the Caspian Sea, and in the southern part of the Zagros Mountains and the plateau of Fars or Parsa, further to the south. Till now they had been

subjects: first of the Elamites, then of the Medes, but by the 550s BC the Persian worm was turning. Under the leadership of Cyrus II, they rose up in revolt against Cyaxares' son Astyages: in 550 BC, they defeated him in battle.

THE ACHAEMENID ADVENT
Cyrus liked to trace his ancestry back to Achaemenes, a Persian ruler of the eighth century BC. If this figure had even existed, he cannot have been too far-reaching in his power: the Persians had then been firmly under the Elamite heel. Bogus pedigrees were practically the norm in the ancient Middle East: the Sargons of both Akkad and Assyria had been barefaced in their mendacity. Cyrus' Achaemenid claims may have been inspired by his embarrassment at the fact that the Astyages against whom he rose was his own grandfather. The Median king had married one of his daughters to the Persian chief Cambyses to secure a political alliance; now her son had led the Persians in rebellion.

Magnanimous in victory, Cyrus was tactful in his handling of the Medes, allowing their lords a special place among his own aristocracy. Taking over their empire in its entirety, he promptly set about expanding it, fighting successful campaigns first in Lydia, Asia Minor, then in Babylonia. His first act on taking the capital was to return the idols its rulers had seized from other states – though he showed respect as

well for Babylon's own traditions. This was to be the Persian way under successive Achaemenid emperors: their instinct was invariably to allow their subjects their cultural autonomy – and, within reason, even political autonomy.

Cyrus' son, Cambyses II, was followed onto the throne by his brother Darius – though not until a bitter struggle had been fought over the succession with a mysterious interloper, Gaumata. Darius the Great raised Persian power to unprecedented heights. He extended the empire to east and west and built a new capital at Persepolis in the south, as well as an additional palace-complex in the old Elamite capital of Susa. Elamite remained one of the official languages of the Persian Empire, and is seen in many inscriptions of the time, along with Babylonian and Old Persian. The existence of many such texts in trilingual versions again

Right: A cuneiform inscription commemorates Artaxerxes III's addition of a staircase to the palace at Persepolis. Thanks to his conquests, Artaxerxes was not only the eleventh Achaemenid emperor but – from 343 BC – the first Pharaoh of Egypt's Thirty-first Dynasty.

Above: The processional friezes at the Persian emperors' palace at Persepolis were one of the artistic glories of the ancient world.

testifies to the easy-going style of Persian rule, which had no trouble tolerating other languages, other cultures. Darius did, however, oversee the development of a new 'Aryan' script, designed especially for use in royal inscriptions.

Unifying Elam

A strangely shaped wall-fitting from the complex of Chogha Zanbil represents a memorial to the monarch who in the fourteenth century BC made Elam the greatest power in the region that became Persia.

Even in its ruined state, it rises high above the surrounding desert, its outline reflecting the row of hills behind. The ziggurat – a type of terraced pyramid – may be the emblematic monument of Mesopotamia, but there is no doubt that it makes an imposing picture here in Khuzestan – well to the east of the alluvial flatlands of the Tigris and Euphrates.

" The Palace of Untash–Napirisha "

A MAGNIFICENT MONUMENT

Dur Untash lies on an upland plateau in the shadow of the Zagros Mountains. In modern times, the site has been known as Chogha Zanbil ('Basket Hill'), because the mound that covered it looked to local people like an upturned basket. The excavated ruins have an altogether less prosaic aspect, and when this construction was first built over 3000 years ago, it must have been awe-inspiring.

Three concentric walls contained the precincts in which the buildings of a magnificent palace-cum-temple complex were grouped around a five-tiered central structure that stands over 50m (160ft) tall. Set at regular intervals in their mud-brick walls were glazed bricks into whose faces sacred inscriptions had been cut. The visitor thus received constant reminders of the different deities in whose honour this had been built – and, of course, of the ruler who had made it possible.

UNIFYING GODS AND PEOPLES

For example, one reads: 'I, Untash-Napirisha, King of Anshan and Susa…built this shrine for my goddess Karirisha, the Lady of Liyan.' The great mother goddess of the Elamites – consort to Humban, who was god of the earth – had for generations had her shrine at Liyan, on

Above: Several of these curious plaques were to be seen around the walls of the palace at Dur Untash, made of glazed ceramic and carefully inscribed.

ON PUBLIC DISPLAY

This remarkable plaque is one of several Elamite items in London's British Museum.

Right: It would look impressive anywhere, but Untash-Napirisha's great construction at Chogha Zanbil seems the more striking here, hundreds of kilometres outside the ziggurat's natural Mesopotamian habitat.

the shores of the Persian Gulf. Since 1800, as the Elamite state had evolved, she had become so closely associated with Pinikir, mother-goddess of the northern uplands, that the two had effectively become a single deity.

Untash-Napirisha's project can, in fact, be seen as an attempt to embody architecturally the oneness – political, cultural and spiritual – of a state too often previously divided between its southern highlands and its northwestern plain. Inevitably, then, it was also about a break with Susa, and the historical 'baggage' carried by the city that had been the capital of Elam since the earliest times. Thought to have been established around 4000 BC, Susa was already 'ancient' by the time Untash-Napirisha came to the throne around 1260 BC.

The new centre had temples to all the important gods of the country's different regions, under the overall aegis of the great 'trinity': Humban, Kiririsha and Inshushinak. Since the last-named had long been known as the patron deity of the city of Susa, the transference of his chief shrine to Chogha Zanbil sent out a significant message to the Elamites at large. His sanctuary was situated at the very top of the sacred ziggurat, perfectly poised between the realms of heaven and of earth.

THE BALANCE OF POWER
Perfectly poised too between the mountains and the river floodplains, between Elamite and Mesopotamian traditions. Its ethnic origins and cultural patrimony may have been distinct, but Elam's destiny had always been closely tied in with those of Sumer and the other Mesopotamian states. The advantage had see-sawed back and forth over hundreds of years, with Elam alternately the conquering power and the occupied territory, but the relationship between them had been more or less constant. By constructing his own ziggurat here, Untash-Napirisha was signalling

his pre-eminence not just here but across the region: Elam was a power both in Khuzestan and Mesopotamia to the west.

In the event, Dur Untash was left uncompleted at his death, but while Susa became the state capital again, this was still a busy and vital shrine. It remained so until the power pendulum swung back towards Mesopotamia once more, and it was sacked by Ashurbanipal's Assyrian army in 640 BC. But Untash-Napirisha had surely got what he wanted: as these curious glazed-ceramic wall-plaques remind us, this was his palace, the monument by which he is remembered to this day.

The Igihalkids

Untash-Napirisha was the sixth king of the Igihalkid Dynasty. Its founder, Igi-Halki, came to power in Elam around the middle of the fourteenth century BC after leading a successful rebellion against the country's Babylonian occupiers. The dynasty's rulers reinforced their position by pursuing a policy of making marriage alliances with the Kassites, then holding sway in Babylon. On those occasions when this marital diplomacy failed, they proved resolute war leaders. Thus, one way or another, they safeguarded Elamite autonomy for many decades. The Igihalkids remained in power until around 1200 when they were replaced by the Shutrukid Dynasty, under whom the power of the Elamite state was to reach its height.

The Sit-Shamsi Shrine

A remarkable sculpture, cast in bronze, conjures up a vivid picture of the ritual life of ancient Elam and looks forward to the later religious history of Persia as a whole. It was itself discovered in a ruined shrine at Susa.

Two naked, shaven-headed male figures, apparently priests, squat facing one another; one holds out a spouted vessel of some kind, whilst the other holds out his hands, their palms upturned – a ritual ablution, presumably, in preparation for some sacrifice or other ritual. Around them on the temple floor lie items whose sacred function we can barely guess at: a pair of rectangular tanks or cisterns; two stepped platforms, like miniature ziggurats; a large *pithos*, or ritual cauldron; what seems to be a stela; and even two little trees or shrubs.

Captured in cast bronze, the scene is extraordinarily evocative – hard though it may be to be sure what it actually evokes. (It is certainly no surprise to learn that, in modern times, the Swiss-Italian sculptor Alberto Giacometti was captivated by this ancient work: gaunt and strange, it spoke his artistic language.) Shilkhak-Inshushinak, the Elamite king who had the work created and inscribed at some time in the twelfth century BC, was generally noted for his piety. His dedication, unfortunately, is of little help in unravelling the meaning of a scene whose significance he would have assumed to be self-evident.

Many cultures have measured out their lives by the rhythms of the sun, its daily comings and goings – and, more alarmingly, its apparent

Left: Susa had long been known as a centre of 'Persian' civilization, but French excavations at the start of the twentieth century uncovered evidence of an earlier, Elamite culture, much influenced by its contacts (in peace and war) with the states of Mesopotamia.

'King of Anshan and Susa'

Anshan and Susa were the two traditional centres of political power and economic influence in Elam: the former was in the south; the latter in the north. The former stood on an isolated plateau amidst the rugged heights of the Zagros Mountains, not far from the modern city of Shiraz. The latter looked out over a gentler, kinder landscape, not altogether unlike that to be found in the Mesopotamian floodplains further west.

Anshan had been the ancestral capital of the Elamites, originally a mountain people, through much of the third millennium BC, and it remained so into the second. For this reason, the first task of any king hoping to establish a unified and successful Elamite state was to impose his will over both these centres, establishing some sort of harmony between them. Over time, however, Susa increased in importance at Anshan's expense: it was so much closer to the centre of the historical action in Mesopotamia. Thus, whether it was a case of Elam being in the ascendant and looking to expand or of the cities of Sumer and Assyria seeking a centre for a conquered province, the northern city of Susa was pivotally positioned.

> **"** *I, Shilkhak-Inshushinak, son of Inshushinak's much-loved servant Shutruk-Nahhunte, realm-enlarging ruler of Anshan and Susa, guardian of Elam, built my own rising-sun ceremony in bronze.* **"**

ON PUBLIC DISPLAY

Of interest as much from an artistic as an archeological point of view, this haunting work is on show in Paris, at the Louvre.

Above: Shilkhak-Inshushinak's inscription may be made out in the top right-hand corner of the sculpture as shown here. It confirms the nature of the ceremony which is on show.

withdrawal during winter. The Elamites appear to have worshipped the sun in its own right in the divine person of Nahhunte, and such a cult sits comfortably enough in the longer sweep of spiritual history in Persia. In later Persian tradition, sun-worship was transformed into a more general reverence for fire: in its turn, fire came to represent enlightenment and moral purification.

The cycle of sunrise and sunset, day and night, light and dark became emblematic of the eternal struggle between good and evil, truth and falsehood, life and death. Zoroaster himself – apparently a priest – may have lived as long ago as 1200 BC, a few generations before this extraordinary model shrine was made. But it was centuries before the religion we know as Zoroastrianism became the guiding creed of Persia.

ELAM'S ZENITH
This extraordinary artefact dates from the period of Elam's imperial height: as Shilkhak-Inshushinak says, his father Shutruk-Nahhunte (named for the sun-god) had extended the kingdom's territories well to the west. He had waged a series of successful campaigns against the Kassites, who then held power in Babylonia, and had brought most of Mesopotamia under Elamite rule.

These conquests were consolidated under his sons Kutir-Nahhunte III and Shilkhak-Inshushinak himself, who followed his older brother on to the throne in 1140 BC.

99

Cyrus Takes Babylon

Nabonidus was king in Babylon from 556 BC, just at the time when Persian power was growing under Cyrus the Great. The so-called Chronicle of Nabonidus records the events of an exciting period that saw the final fall of the Neo-Babylonian Empire.

Nabonidus has been fated to play no more than a minor part in what is supposed to have been his own history. Modern scholars who read the inscription known as Nabonidus' Chronicle are likely to be less interested in what it says about its ostensible subject than in the insights it offers on Cyrus the Great, his Persian conqueror.

ON THE RISE
For all its tantalizing gaps and silences, the text allows us to trace the rise of the first Achaemenid emperor at one remove: we see him making a series of conquests in Mesopotamia and the Middle East, including – crucially – prevailing over the Median ruler, Astyages, in 550 BC. Victories in Akkad (Babylonia) follow, before, in the entry for Year 17 of Nabonidus' reign (539/8 BC), we read of the taking of Babylon itself. The capture of this city, till then the region's pre-eminent power, marked the coming of age of Persia as an empire.

IMPERIAL IMPIETIES
Those researchers not going to the chronicle to further their understanding of Persia's rise are often less concerned with Nabonidus than with his son. The crown prince Bel-sara-asur is believed to have been that same biblical Belshazzar who violated the sacred vessels of the Jewish Temple by using them for a feast in his royal palace in Babylon, and was sent a divine warning in the 'writing on the wall' (Daniel 5). The chronicle does, intriguingly, touch on religious issues, telling us that in 549/8 Nabonidus 'remained in Tema' – famous as a shrine to Sin, the moon-god – while the 'crown prince', his staff and his army stayed in Babylon. Nabonidus did not return for the New Year ceremonies staged in March/April and the rites of Marduk and Nabu, god of wisdom, were both neglected.

Triumph Through Tolerance

It is no great surprise to find Cyrus returning the Akkadian idols to their home cities. He established tolerance as the trademark virtue of the Persian Empire. It was he who, in 539 BC, brought to an end the Babylonian Captivity of the Jews, not only allowing them to return home from their exile but ordering the reconstruction of their Temple in Jerusalem. In general, Cyrus' successors were to prove similarly easy-going rulers. As long as they received the taxes they believed they were owed, they were happy to respect the beliefs and identities of their subject peoples and to devolve considerable authority to 'satraps' – provincial governors – on the ground.

Left: Cyrus receives the homage of a crowd of conquered rulers, as seen through much later European eyes. Everything the historical record tells us about the conduct of his reign suggests that he was an enlightened and in many ways easy-going ruler.

" *In Tasritu [September/October], after King Cyrus had engaged with the Akkadian forces at Opis on the Tigris, the people revolted, but before they knew what was happening Nabonidus had slaughtered them all. On the fifteenth day of the month, the city of Sippar was taken without a blow being struck. Nabonidus fled the field. On the sixteenth day, Gobryas, Governor of Gutium, entered Babylon at the head of Cyrus' army. When Nabonidus dared show his face in the city, he was captured. The Gutians occupied Esagila until the end of the month, but were equipped with only their shields: no one carried weapons within the sacred complex. Neither were the fit times for ceremonies allowed to pass unmarked. On the third day of Arahsamna [October/November], Cyrus himself made his entrance into Babylon. Green branches were scattered before him and peace was established. The King sent his messages of greeting to all in Babylon. Gobryas, as governor, appointed officials to take charge of the city.*

Between Kislimu [November/December] to Addaru [February/March] the Akkadian gods – captured and brought down to Babylon by Nabonidus – were restored to their sacred cities.

Gobryas died on the eleventh night of Arahsamna. In Addaru…the King's wife died. A period of mourning was instituted, from the twenty-seventh day of Addaru to the third day of Nisannu [March/April]. The people wore their hair all unkempt… "

ON PUBLIC DISPLAY

This part of the Nabonidus Chronicle can be seen in the British Museum in London.

A Simple Statement

Not far from the tomb where Cyrus the Great was laid to rest, a lofty column proclaims his importance to all who pass. Even today, it dominates the landscape for many kilometres around, a fitting symbol of the founding emperor's surpassing power.

Cyrus' massive yet modest tomb of stone may still be seen today, though it was stripped of its contents by Alexander's army 23 centuries ago. In some ways more appropriate as an emblem of his power is the great pillar that rises to a height of 13m (42ft). Yet it too is as simple in its conception as it is unadorned in its appearance – as plain and straightforward as its inscription. The most portentous thing about this is that it is given in three languages – Persian, Proto-Elamite and Babylonian. The trilingual text makes more claims about the reach of Cyrus' imperial power than anything in the inscription's explicit wording, which is content simply to name the monarch and offer the (entirely unexceptionable) assertion that he is a 'mighty king'.

A RELAXED RULE

Less was always more for Cyrus, it seems. Compared with other great potentates of ancient times, his

> **"** *Cyrus, the mighty king, an Achaemenid.* **"**

ON PUBLIC DISPLAY

Pasargadae, in Fars, Iran, now enjoys the status of a UNESCO World Heritage Site. It has become a significant tourist attraction.

Left: It impresses by its austerity as much as it intimidates by its sheer size: this pillar at Pasargadae, established as capital by Cyrus the Great in the sixth century, is in keeping with the character of its builder.

An Impressive Tomb

Cyrus died in 530 BC: his tomb was as simple as might have been expected – a sort of hutlike structure atop a mini-pyramid of stepped stone. His epitaph too was modest, if the Greek historian Plutarch is to be believed:

> **66** *Man, whoever you may be and wherever you may come from – for I know that you will come – I am Cyrus who won the Persians their empire. Do not then begrudge me the little bit of earth which covers my remains.* **99**

Right: Monumental modesty appears to have been the keynote quality of Cyrus' rule. His tomb too contrives to be massive yet at the same time somehow unassuming.

style was unassuming; he was famously understanding in his attitude towards the peoples whom he conquered. Claims that he was the world's first champion of human rights are anachronistic, of course: his easy-going manner was born of pragmatism rather than a modern sense of civil liberty. To some extent, scholars who make these claims have been reacting against a longstanding consensus, rooted partly in propagandistic claims by the Greeks – too credulously swallowed – and partly in a modern racism that defined the Persian Wars as pitting European liberalism against Asiatic tyranny.

Even so, there can be no doubt that Cyrus showed a tolerance that was never even dreamt of by the democratic Greeks, willing both to devolve power to local rulers and to allow subject peoples to maintain their traditions. However, those who

rebelled against his rule, or tried to cheat on the taxes to which he considered himself entitled, quickly found themselves up against the limits of that tolerance. Only by acknowledging his authority were they allowed a considerable degree of autonomy, under both Cyrus himself and his Achaemenid successors.

DYNASTIC FOUNDER
If Cyrus has a boast in his inscription here, it is that he is 'an Achaemenid'. Actually, this is his most contentious claim. The original Achaemenes must have lived towards the end of the seventh century BC – that is, if this semi-legendary figure ever existed in the first place. Even if he did, it is unclear what his status was. In those times, there was no Persian kingdom, so Achaemenes could hardly have been much more than a local warlord. He was said to have

established his empire when he took the city of Anshan from the Elamites, though this feat was more likely achieved by Teispes, supposedly his son. Under Cyrus I and Cambyses I, the Achaemenids consolidated their hold over Anshan itself, but it was not until Cyrus II's reign that they could have been said to have an empire. In fact, modern scholars generally regard Cyrus II (or 'Cyrus the Great') as the dynasty's founder, despite the existence of earlier kings of the same line.

Initially, Anshan was a client kingdom of the Median Empire: it was Cyrus II who upset that balance, rising in rebellion in around 553 BC. He won his decisive victory at Pasargadae – which is why he subsequently established his capital on this level plain among the mountains and had himself interred here after his death in 530 BC.

Darius: The Great Inscription

Darius the Great was great indeed. Even allowing for epic exaggeration, the inscription at Behistun makes clear why. But this memorial makes the Persian emperor's most enduring and least conscious contribution to world history, unlocking as it does the mysteries of cuneiform.

A little way outside the city of Jeyhounabad, in western Iran, rise the rocky slopes of Mount Behistun. Around the mountain snakes an ancient road – already a well-established trade route linking the Persian plateau with Mesopotamia when the Achaemenid Dynasty was founded in the sixth century BC. It is easy enough to understand why Darius I, whose reign lasted from 521 to 486 BC, should have chosen to have his achievements advertised here.

Here, beneath a resplendent winged figure of Ahura Mazda, the god of light to whom Darius consecrated his reign, we see the emperor triumphing over an array of conquered kings in carved relief. Beneath is a lengthy inscription – in three languages.

GREAT ACHIEVEMENTS
Darius' was an eventful reign that began in bloodshed. After the death of his brother Cambyses II, who may have been assassinated, he had to fight to claim the throne. The throne passed initially to Smerdis,

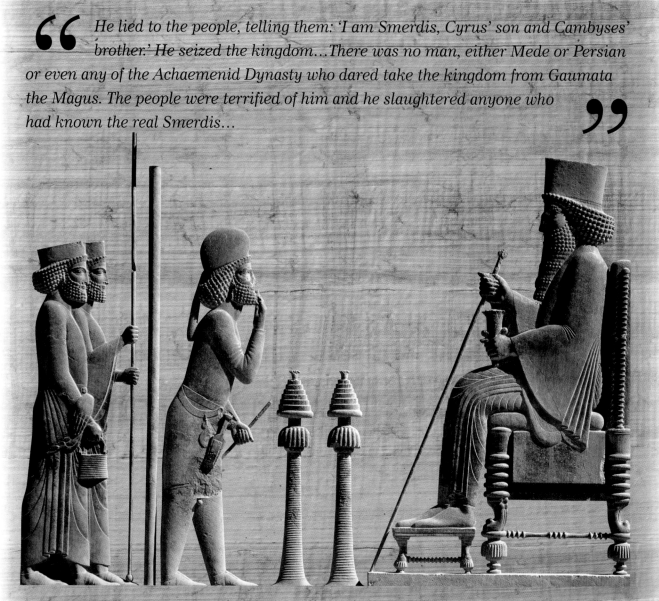

" *He lied to the people, telling them: 'I am Smerdis, Cyrus' son and Cambyses' brother.' He seized the kingdom…There was no man, either Mede or Persian or even any of the Achaemenid Dynasty who dared take the kingdom from Gaumata the Magus. The people were terrified of him and he slaughtered anyone who had known the real Smerdis…* "

Above: Darius receives a deputation from one of his many subject nations. His palace at Persepolis was the centre of a far-reaching network of diplomatic and commercial contacts and such delegations must have been arriving all the time.

another brother of Cambyses and a younger son of Cyrus the Great. He was then apparently usurped by an impostor, Gaumata the Magus (or wizard), who took not just the throne but his name.

Darius was not afraid to tackle Gaumata. He took a small group of friends and comrades and rode out to attack the tyrant in his stronghold. He killed the usurper and his lieutenants, 'and by the grace of Ahura Mazda I became King'. The Achaemenid order restored, the new emperor then worked to put everything to rights, returning the lands that had been stolen, the populations which had been displaced.

Even so, he was to be rewarded for his righteous rule by a bewildering string of rebellions by local rulers, including those of Babylonia, Elam, Media, Armenia, Parthia and elsewhere. Across more than three columns, this blow-by-blow account is rounded off by a brief resumé: the 'Nine Kings' are presented, as it were, 'at a glance'.

The inscription then offers what were clearly meant as concluding remarks on the importance of truth and virtue to Darius' kingship and the need for later rulers to emulate

Below: The inscription at Behistun is accompanied by a relief which shows the emperor asserting his authority over other pretenders to power. Arm raised in admonition, he stands with one foot resting on the prone body of Gaumata, the would-be usurper.

these qualities, before a sort of 'Stop Press' column records events from 521 to 519 BC: a further revolt in Elam and a war against the Scythians of the steppe.

If Darius' self-advertisement seems hyperbolic in its tone today, his reputation is surely as secure as he himself could have wished it in a world so dramatically different from anything he could conceivably have

imagined. But perhaps his greatest gift to posterity was having his inscription (lengthy as it was) inscribed in triplicate: in the respective cuneiform scripts of Old Persian, Babylonian and Elamite. In the mid-nineteenth century, these different versions were of inestimable help to scholars who were just beginning to get to grips with cuneiform script.

> *These are my deeds. I have acted always in the name of Ahura Mazda. Whoever reads this inscription in ages to come, believe my deeds. Do not assume these are lies…I call Ahura Mazda in witness of its truth.*
>
> *With Ahura Mazda's help I accomplished much more which is not recorded here. It is not written here for fear that whoever should read this inscription in ages to come should think it exaggerated and assume it to be lies.*
>
> *For these reasons, Ahura Mazda and all the other gods gave me their support: I was not wicked; I was not dishonest; I was not a tyrant; neither were my family. I have reigned in righteousness, wronging neither the weak nor the strong. Anyone who supported my house I helped; anyone who opposed it I destroyed.*

A Plea from the Past: Persepolis

Darius' foundation tablets, concealed in the fabric of his palace, were finally revealed in the 1930s. A moving message from the past, they called for the protection of a complex reduced to ruins just a century or so after it had been built.

The Greeks announced the arrival of their 'civilization' in the east with one of the most gratuitous acts of vandalism the world has seen. A payback, admittedly, for the Persians' sacking of the Athenian Acropolis a century and a half before, the destruction of Persepolis was still by any standards an act of barbarism. Flames leapt high into the sky over the Persian capital: sparks erupted from the roof as timbers creaked and crashed. Alexander's troops looked on, awed by the destruction they had wrought. Before their very eyes, the might of Persia crumbled into dust. Alexander fired the city at the suggestion of one of his concubines, it is said, though the Macedonian conqueror never did anything he was not minded to. Most likely the story serves to underline the ignominy of the city's end, reduced to ashes on a woman's whim.

REMOVED FROM THE RUBBLE
Well over 2000 years later, in September 1933, Ernst Herzfeld was working in the foundations of the palace, at the heart of the ruins, and found 'two shallow, neatly made stone boxes with sealed lids'. These containers had been secreted at some time during the building process beneath the bases of the wall in the northeast and southeast corners respectively.

The German archeologist had already made marvellous finds, opening up an apadana, or hall, that could accommodate 10,000 for imperial audiences, its walls lined with the most spectacular reliefs. He felt a special excitement, though, as he carefully opened the boxes he had recovered – though he was sure he knew what they contained. Similar caches had been found seven years before at another Persian palace at Hamadan, and Herzfeld had since been searching, with some confidence, for the foundation tablets of the palace.

A PLEA FROM THE PAST
Discoveries across the ancient world, not just at the Persian palace at Hamadan but also at the palace of Sargon II at Khorsabad, had

Another Tablet?

Herzfeld posited the existence of a third tablet, in the northwest corner. Or, at least, its original existence. This part of the palace had been reduced to rubble at the time of Alexander's sacking of Persepolis; any treasures it contained were surely whisked away home to Macedon. It had, the Greek chroniclers enthused, taken no fewer than 10,000 two-mule carts and 5000 camels to shift the loot.

Below: Even in its ruined state, Persepolis is a scene of splendour. The power of the Achaemenids, the scale of their ambition and achievement, can constantly be felt.

> " *Darius the Great, King of Kings, Lord of Nations, son of Hystaspes the Achaemenid. Says Darius: This is all my empire, from the land of the Sakas, this side of Sogdiana, to Kush; from India all the way to Sardis. Ahura Mazda, greatest of the gods, has given me dominion over all these territories. May Ahura Mazda protect me and my royal house.* "

Above: Stunning in its simplicity, Darius' message sets out his imperial stall, but attributes his authority to Ahura Mazda, god of light, and begs for his protection.

ON PUBLIC DISPLAY

Darius' foundation tablet may be seen in the National Museum of Iran, Tehran.

prepared Herzfeld for the probability that the man who built Persepolis in the sixth century BC would have left a dedicatory text in its foundations – no doubt in the course of some special ceremony. And so it turned out: on gold and silver plaques were inscribed the dedicatory message of the Emperor Darius the Great. Like the great inscriptions in the rocks of Naqsh-e Rustam, the same text was given in Old Persian, Elamite and Babylonian.

There was an inescapable melancholy about them now; an irony reflected in the inglorious way by which Persepolis' end came, with the abject rout of the forces of Darius III – descendant of Darius the Great. But then, it was in the nature of this type of time-capsule that it would only ever be opened in the event of the building's complete destruction – in other words, in the event of complete disaster. And if Ahura Mazda had failed to protect his king and his palace, he had safeguarded the dignity of Darius I and punished Alexander, whose great legacy has been shamed by his actions here.

Matters of Weight

We tend to think of the power of Achaemenid Persia as military, thanks in part to Greek propaganda and in part to the boasts of its own emperors. In many respects, however, their reign was remarkably enlightened, with an emphasis upon prosperity and peace.

> *I am Darius, the mighty king, king of all kings, king of all nations, king of the world. I am the son of Hystaspes, the Achaemenid.*

ON PUBLIC DISPLAY

This, and other weights of this kind, may be seen in the National Museum of Iran, Tehran.

Left: Darius wanted his authority to be experienced not just in fear or admiration but in the most mundane and practical affairs of everyday life. This diorite weight represented his commitment to fair trade and commercial probity.

Royal Writing

The writing on this and other weights is unusual in being in 'Aryan script', developed by Darius specifically for use in royal inscriptions. Specialized as it was, it was not often used and had been discarded by the end of the fourth century BC.

Diorite, formed volcanically, was one of the hardest materials to be had in ancient times, gemstones apart: it was difficult to fashion, but could give a lovely lustrous finish. This piece has a wonderfully warm and jadelike tinge of green. It is, unmistakably, a thing of beauty.

IMPERIAL MEASURES
And yet it was a thing of functionality as well: a weight, albeit a particularly prestigious one, kept in the palace at Persepolis. Why should such care and cost have been lavished on the production of something so apparently mundane? The answer tells us much about the Achaemenids' priorities.

Darius the Great makes much of his military prowess in his Great Inscription at Behistun. Understandably: the first duty of a king was to defend his realm. But the main business of Darius' reign was exactly that: business, for he was eager to promote commerce within his empire, to make it a 'single market' along modern European lines. Hence his introduction of a common coinage, and a standardized system of weights and measures to facilitate trade between one part of the empire and another. Like the 'imperial' yard, pound, pint and acre introduced to the far-flung colonies of Britain in the nineteenth century, the new system was not just practical but an everyday reminder of who was in charge.

A BENEFICENT RULE
An inscription like this asserted a sort of proprietorship over these measures, as though Darius were 'King of the World', in some sense 'owning' both weights and measurements. This sort of imperial vainglory did, however, accompany a relatively light ruling touch in the Persia of the Achaemenids.

Government was to a great extent devolved to client rulers or satraps drawn from the different communities, and the peoples of the empire were allowed to maintain their own cultural traditions. Even to the extent that Cyrus, a predecessor of Darius, rebuilt Jerusalem's Temple for the Jews.

Likewise Darius' weights and measures were not rigidly or indiscriminately imposed: people

Above: Darius' forces imposed order across a vast area, allowing trade to flourish and prosperity to grow.

were allowed to go on trading in their old units – and their former currencies. The Achaemenid emperor's aim seems to have been to facilitate economic activity rather than to enforce uniformity across his realm. All the evidence is that he succeeded.

Black Propaganda

Greek mothers terrified their children – and Greek writers thrilled posterity – with talk of the barbaric Persians and the threat they posed to the civilized world. At any moment, they might emerge out of the east again, bringing death and destruction in their wake. These fears were undoubtedly genuine – and, up to a point, justified. There had, after all, been two large-scale invasions in the early fifth century BC.

Not surprisingly, though, the view from Persepolis was rather different. From there, the Greeks were seen as intruders, who had come as colonists to Asia Minor, upsetting the established order. Rather than accepting the authority of the easy-going Achaemenids, they had insisted on taking charge themselves, setting up city-states independent of Persian rule. Seen from this perspective, Persia's hostility towards Greece is readily understood: the emperors saw their attacks as punitive expeditions rather than expansionist invasions.

The Deeds of Shapur I

The carvings at Naqsh-e Rustam were created under two different dynasties, separated by well over a thousand years. But the monument to Shapur I is of especial interest in that it affords fascinating insights into the histories not just of Persia but also of Rome.

The wars between Persia and an emergent Greece in the fifth century BC have become what might be called a 'foundation myth' of western culture. A crass consensus long saw the successive victories of the Greeks as representing the triumph of civilization over oriental barbarism. In one of the great rock reliefs at Naqsh-e Rustam, however, we learn of a less well-remembered brush between Asia and Europe, in which the Sasanid Shapur I prevails over Roman power.

A TWOFOLD TRIUMPH
The frieze records two triumphs in one: the kneeling figure is the Emperor Philip the Arab who capitulated to Shapur in AD 244; the standing man whose arm the Persian emperor holds upraised is believed to be Valerian, whom the Persians took prisoner after the Battle of Edessa in 260.

Above: Shapur, shown here on one of his coins, represents an unfamiliar face of Persia – a power which the mighty Roman Empire found cause to fear.

Shapur's Other Deeds

But Shapur's achievements were many: the Naqsh-e Rustam inscription itself proclaims his extensive conquests in the region, where he promoted the worship of the Persian god Ahura Mazda. From other inscriptions we learn that his exploits in archery were legendary; he is famed as well as the founder of Gundashapur. This city became the cultural and educational hub of the Sasanid civilization – by the sixth century it was the most important medical centre in the known world.

Philip was actually a new arrival on the imperial throne, having marched eastwards with the Emperor Gordian III. He had seized power himself: it is not clear whether Gordian was killed in fighting with the Persians or whether, as many claimed, he was assassinated by Philip and his supporters. Whichever it was, Philip had every reason to want a quick and easy conclusion to the Persian campaign so he could get back to Rome to consolidate his position there.

But if Shapur's claims to have won a heroic victory were in all probability an exaggeration, there was some seriously misleading propaganda on the other side. It defies belief to claim (as the Roman chronicles do) that the Persians had been well beaten but that Shapur had surrendered to them out of sheer villainy.

A CRUEL INDIGNITY
Valerian became Roman emperor in 253, reigning jointly with his son Gallienus. He personally led a campaign to win back Syria and Armenia from the Persians. After early successes, he was defeated by the Persians outside Edessa in 260. It was a crushing blow not only to the prestige of Rome but to Valerian's pride: Shapur was said to have used his captive as a footstool to help him mount his horse.

> " *When at first we ascended the throne, the Emperor Gordian raised an army of Germanic and Gothic troops from throughout the Roman Empire and marched on Assyria and then on Iran and us. A great pitched battle was fought at Misikhe on the borders of Babylonia; Gordian was killed and his army destroyed. The Romans elected Philip Emperor. Philip sued to us for terms: he gave us 500,000 dinars to ransom his men's lives and offered tribute...*
>
> *Then the Emperor broke his word and invaded Armenia. We attacked and defeated a Roman force 60,000 strong at Barbalissus and laid waste to Syria...*
>
> *In the third war, when we besieged Carrhae and Edessa, the Emperor Valerian came against us at the head of an army 70,000 strong...Outside Edessa we fought a great battle with the Emperor. With our own hands we took Valerian prisoner, along with his senior staff and senators. We took them back with us to Persia as captives.* "

Above: Shapur I is just one of several Persian kings commemorated at Naqsh-e Rustam, whose earliest friezes date back to the start of Achaemenid rule, a thousand years before.

ON PUBLIC DISPLAY

Shapur I's testament is to be seen, along with other, earlier Persian royal inscriptions, at Naqsh-e Rustam, near Persepolis, in Fars, southern Iran.

Greece

The earliest evidence we have for the development of civilization in Greece dates from the middle of the third millennium BC. The farmers of this time lived in little village communities: they could make simple ceramic vessels and were skilled in bronze-working, but we have no reason to think that they could read or write. Their Bronze Age culture shows similarities with that of early Anatolia, and it is possible that they had moved into the Aegean from the east. Whether they came overland through Thrace or island-hopped their way across the Aegean, we have no real way of knowing.

THE SEA, THE SEA

It does not, in any case, make much sense to distinguish greatly between Greece and its islands. Even on the mainland, most of the habitable areas were close to the coast. The sea was as much a highway as an obstacle at this time. Granted, it had its hazards: the Aegean is notorious for its storms. When it was at peace, however, travel by sea would have been far easier and more comfortable than trekking overland through some of Europe's most rugged country. The sea remained an important influence on the emergence of a recognizably 'Greek' culture: while primarily agrarian, it placed an ever increasing emphasis on maritime trade.

Left: Archeology is about the layering of each civilization, each generation superimposing itself upon the legacy of the last. At Delphi, the Temple of Apollo designed in the fourth century BC by the brothers Trophonios and Agamedes was built over the ruins of a sixth-century shrine.

THE TRAFFIC IN agricultural produce and luxury goods was to form the basis of the celebrated civilization that flourished in Crete in the second millennium BC. Named for the mythical King Minos, the Minoan culture was already established as early as 1900 BC, when the presumed palace-complex at Knossos was constructed. Archeologists built their own elaborate edifice of wishful supposition on this site, constructing an idealized image of a sophisticated female-dominated society dedicated to the peaceful pursuit of pleasure.

TEMPLE ECONOMIES

It was always too good to be true, of course. All the evidence is now that, far from being given over to heedless sybaritism, Minoan society was industrious and extremely tightly run. There was a ruling elite of priests (or priestesses – the notion of matriarchy may not have been entirely mythical), and it oversaw an elaborate economic system in which agricultural tribute was traded for raw materials to manufacture into high-value, luxury products. A written script seems to have been developed to facilitate the smooth running of this 'temple economy'. Initially a hieroglyphic script, it became a sound-based script, now called 'Linear A'.

By the middle of the millennium, however, Minoan civilization was gone – destroyed by some cataclysm at which we can only guess. Its legacy lived on, however: the next important Greek civilization, which emerged on the mainland some time around the thirteenth century BC, employed a script that shows marked similarities to Linear A. The Mycenaean culture, so-called because it was first identified at the site of Mycenae, was, like the Minoan, fanatically bureaucratic, its priests or clerks keeping near obsessive records in what is known as 'Linear B'.

How much else the two cultures had in common is far from clear: it hardly helps that both were seen in such stereotypical terms by their first researchers. If Arthur Evans saw Knossos as a paradise of love and beauty, Heinrich Schliemann saw Mycenae as a warriors' stronghold, a place where men were men. Today, as scholars learn more and more about them, these visions seem suspect. The two societies may well have been much more similar than was thought.

THE RISE OF THE POLIS

Vanishing as abruptly as it had appeared, the Mycenaean culture collapsed some time towards the end of the thirteenth century BC: the great site at Pylos shows signs of having been destroyed by fire. We can only speculate about the fate that befell it: was it sacked and burned in a raid by the mysterious 'Sea Peoples', who were ravaging the coasts of the eastern Mediterranean at this time (*see pp. 58–59*).

The centuries that followed have been known as the 'Dark Ages' – for no better reason than that we know so little about the time. The picture

Above: Aristotle's philosophy was among the many glories of a Greek civilization which bequeathed a rich and varied cultural heritage including everything from politics and tragedy to wrestling.

we have is of an anarchic scene in Greece, with local warlords carving out little territories for themselves and ruling them from fortified strongholds on strategic hilltops or rocky outcrops. Around them clustered little communities: their warriors and personal attendants and a peasantry that depended on them for protection and which paid them tribute in return.

As time went on, and the ruling military elite grew in wealth and power, it developed a taste for imported luxuries and prestigious craftworks. Merchants brought in the goods they sought, whilst a new class of artisans also took shape: society was growing in complexity. The new 'middle classes' may have been no threat to the warrior-aristocracy, but they could not be pushed around quite as easily as the peasantry. 'Democracy' – government by the people – was as yet a long way off, but Greece's communities were beginning to move in that direction.

Urban settlements were springing up where before there had only been glorified hill-forts. The lord's stronghold endured on its raised 'acropolis', but this was increasingly seen as belonging to the whole city – a place of refuge in the event of attack but also, ever more importantly, a spiritual sanctuary and a pedestal for prestigious public buildings.

Civic consciousness grew and, with it, a more general Greek identity – albeit, paradoxically, one that found itself affirmed most obviously through conflict. The poleis were more or less constantly at war with one another, though competition of a more peaceful kind was available from 776 BC, when Greece's athletes came together for the first Olympic Games.

GREATER GREECE

The more prosperity grew, the greater the demand for luxuries and the motivation for trade with the world outside. By the eighth century BC, with the population growing fast and cultivable land in scant supply, the Greek cities began sending out settlers to other shores. 'Greek'

settlements sprang up across the Aegean in Anatolia, but also in Sicily, Sardinia and mainland Italy. Other expeditions ventured farther afield: soon there were trading colonies from the Crimea to the coasts of Egypt and the south of France. Some of these colonies became so established that they sent out colonizing expeditions themselves, propagating further the culture of what is known in Latin as Magna Graecia ('Greater Greece').

Back home, meanwhile, Athens was starting to come to the fore among the city-states, introducing democratic reforms in the early years of the sixth century BC. As archon, or chief magistrate, Solon cancelled all existing debts and gave the different classes a voice in government. There was no smooth and seamless progression towards freedom: in 560 BC, power was seized by the tyrant Peisistratos; he was ousted in 552 BC but was back in power 11 years later. His sons succeeded him after his death in 528 BC.

Not until 510 BC did the Athenians get their city back. They acted immediately to foreclose the possibility of another tyrant: under the leadership of Cleisthenes, they introduced government of the people, by the people, for the people. Or rather, of the citizens, by the citizens, for the citizens – a body that included neither women nor foreigners nor slaves. That said, it was an extraordinarily radical

reform: thousands were given a genuine stake in everyday decision-making and in the administration of civil and criminal justice.

Democratic Athens enjoyed a 'Golden Age' in the fifth century: from 461 to 439 BC, it was under the charismatic spell of the statesman Pericles. It was on his urging that the Acropolis was beautified with buildings like the Parthenon, and with statues and other works of art. Pericles also extended the scope of Athenian popular government still further.

RIVALRY WITH SPARTA

In Greece as a whole, the reforms were controversial. Some cities took steps to emulate Athens; others were appalled. The conservative camp was led by Sparta, a traditionally militaristic society that believed in the military virtues of rigid hierarchy and unquestioning obedience. But when, in 490, the citizen-army of Athens won its memorable victory over the Persian invasion force of Darius I (no thanks to the late-arriving Spartans), the prestige of the city amongst its peers soared. That said, Athenian democracy stopped firmly at the city limits: there was nothing equitable about the way Athens conducted the affairs of the Delian League, a supposed alliance that was actually little more than a large-scale protection racket.

Had they managed things more justly, the Athenians might have

Above: Greece exported its civilization far and wide, as can be seen from this inscription on the wall of an amphitheatre at Patara, on Turkey's Lycian coast.

been able to call upon more faithful support when – inevitably – conflict came with Sparta and its allies of the Peloponnesian League. Breaking out in 431 BC, the Peloponnesian War ended in 404 BC with Athens on its knees.

Greek civilization – classical Greek civilization, at least – was now in terminal decline. Athens was finished, and the democratic moment had definitively passed. When Philip of Macedon came south in the fourth century BC, he did so as a conquering tyrant; and his son Alexander was to rule in the same spirit. He may have extended Greek rule over much of the known world, but it was not the sort of Greek rule that Solon, Cleisthenes or Pericles would have recognized.

After Alexander's death in 323 BC, fighting erupted amongst his generals over the division of the spoils. Antipater emerged as the ruler of Greece itself. It was hardly the prize he had hoped for: Greece already seemed to be a backwater in its own empire.

The real wealth and power were to be found in Seleucid Asia and Ptolemaic Egypt. In the century or so that followed, Greece was to stagnate still further, economically and culturally: in 187 BC, it was taken under Roman rule.

Minoan Mysteries

Perhaps as much as 2000 years before the Golden Age of Athens, a Bronze Age civilization was flourishing in Crete. The Minoan culture was made famous by the discoveries of Arthur Evans, but the truth was more elusive – and more interesting – than he knew.

The story of King Minos is one of the most famous of Greek myths, unforgettable for the Minotaur – half man, half bull – lurking in a labyrinth deep beneath the royal palace. Imagine the astonishment of the world when, at the very end of the nineteenth century, an English archeologist announced that he had found Minos' capital. Working at a site at Knossos, northern Crete, he had begun unearthing what appeared to be a truly spectacular royal residence. Its labyrinthine passages were a storehouse of rich food and drink, the basis for a lifestyle of the highest imaginable luxury and refinement.

PEACE AND LOVE

Knossos appeared to have had no walls – the threat of war was apparently absent here. And, despite the ubiquitous bull-symbolism (clear confirmation for Evans of the Minos connection), this was a strikingly feminized culture. It was a society apparently run by bare-breasted women, and fine ceramics showed a deep and abiding love of nature. Meanwhile, sumptuous wall-paintings showed male and female athletes vaulting over the backs of bulls, grace and skill triumphing over brute violence and strength.

Evans' discovery came at the fin de siècle – a time notorious for its aestheticism and its decadence, the age of the symbolist poets and of Oscar Wilde. Was 'Minoan Culture' anything more than a Victorian Englishman's idea of an ancient dolce vita? Without quite falsifying the archeological record, Evans appears to have taken a fair few liberties. More recent scholars have looked at the evidence more sceptically. Did women generally go topless or was this true only of certain priestesses for special ceremonies? Did the Minoans love nature – or just specific nature deities? And, as an island power, Knossos may have had no need of walls: it is possible that the Minoans defended themselves at sea. The discovery in the 1980s that human sacrifice and cannibalism were practised was the ultimate shock to those still clinging to Evans' idealization.

A TEMPLE OF TRADE

In recent years, the picture has been emerging of a more prosaic – but equally fascinating – society;

Right: Arthur Evans did not just excavate Knossos when he worked here in the 1900s: he partially reconstructed what he believed had once stood there. The resulting structures – and many of the wall-paintings within – arguably owe as much to his own romanticizing imagination as they do to archeological fact: some scholars would go so far as to dismiss the supposed ruin as a confection.

Evans may well have been right, though, about the role of women. Ritually, at any rate, the most important figures do appear to have been the priestesses of Potnia, the earth-goddess – though this does not necessarily tell us much about the position of ordinary women in society at large.

Life revolved around what is called a 'temple economy'; the so-called 'palace' may actually have been an extensive temple, with endless passages and chambers for storing tribute. Agricultural produce – wool, wine, grain – were sent in from the countryside as tax and exchanged with overseas traders for precious commodities.

Copper from Cyprus and the Aegean islands; semi-precious stones from southern Greece; ivory from Syria; ostrich eggs and alabaster from Egypt – all these items were imported, and turned into valuable artefacts by armies of craftsmen based in Knossos. This trade was described by a large army of scribes.

It was to keep track of all this commercial to-ing and fro-ing that, some time towards 1900 BC, they developed their own hieroglyphic script – still undeciphered. In the centuries that followed, a new script evolved, now known as Linear A. This too is poorly understood: the Minoan language seems to have had little in common with Greek. As far as we know, though, it was limited in expressiveness and designed almost exclusively for record-keeping. From it, we may glean such facts that a single sheep might yield 1.5kg (3lb) of wool, a figure not matched again until modern times.

Minoan civilization vanished suddenly midway through the second millennium BC, perhaps destroyed by the enduring 'winter' caused by floating ash from the eruption of Thera (Santorini) around 1500 BC.

ON PUBLIC DISPLAY

The Phaistos Disc can be found in the Archeological Museum of Heraklion, on the island of Crete.

The Phaistos Disc

Discovered in 1908, in a Minoan palace in southern Crete, the Phaistos Disc has so far defied all attempts at interpretation. Many have tried, of course – and several have claimed success – but serious scholars confess their bafflement. Like the Linear A tablets and several important Etruscan inscriptions, it is hard to interpret 'neat' noun-symbols in the absence of any clear grammar or narrative structure. It does not help that these particular symbols have nothing obvious in common with those of Linear A or of any other contemporary language. One striking feature of the Phaistos Disc is that its characters were not 'written' as such but stamped in the wet clay before this ceramic disc was fired: it is, some have suggested, the first 'typewritten' text.

Above: The characters stamped into the Phaistos Disc have so far defeated the best efforts of the scholars, though the artefact was evidently created in Minoan times.

117

The Mycenaean Moment

Another civilization, another script. The Linear B of the Mycenaeans, however, can at least be recognized as representing an early form of Greek. It was deciphered in the 1950s, but still holds many secrets, mostly because of the terse economy of its use by ancient scribes.

What Arthur Evans was to Knossos, Heinrich Schliemann was to Mycenae – but the two men could hardly have been more different in temperament or interests. Where the former looked at Crete and saw a society of gentle pleasure-seekers, the latter was in search of a heroic, Homeric past. He had already discovered the site of Troy; now he was looking for the place from which the Greek fleet had set out for that epic war. He believed he had found it when he arrived at Mycenae in the northern Peloponnese in 1874. Its massive masonry and its famous 'Lion Gate', restored some 30 years before by Greek archeologist Kyriakos Pittakis, were enough to convince him that this was the seat of some great warrior society.

A BUREAUCRATIC ARMY
In fact, the force that kept Mycenae on the march was the army of scribes that supervised every area of economic life. With a meticulousness that might have taken the Minoans aback, they recorded every coming and going in their own script, the so-called Linear B. This bore striking resemblances to the Minoan script, but had obvious differences as well. Its mysteries were eventually fathomed in the 1950s, at which point it became clear that the Mycenaean language could be recognized as an early form of Greek. But, although this script can now be read, it seems to have been used for only the baldest sort of record-keeping: beyond the most terse of check-lists, no significant texts have ever been found.

REGIMENTED RULE
The Mycenaean state arose around the beginning of the thirteenth century BC – not long after the collapse of Minoan civilization, in other words.

Above: Experts wrestled with the ins and outs of Linear B for years before it could be proved that it represented an early form of Greek.

An Ancient Irony

Much of what we know about Mycenae comes from the Pylos tablets, though these were never meant to be a lasting record. The evidence is that these were soft-clay 'jotters' for daily note-taking and that their contents were intended to be written up later in more permanent form – probably on papyrus 'paper' imported from Egypt. Once transcribed, the tablets would have been wiped clean and used again. In the event, though, these tablets were baked into permanency – by the same fire that destroyed the Pylos complex.

Above: Apparently a descendant of the Linear A used a little earlier by the Minoans, Linear B formed the basis for a complex bureaucratic culture at Mycenae.

ON PUBLIC DISPLAY

Fascinating items of Mycenaean art and sculpture are to be seen in the National Archeological Museum of Athens, including examples of Linear B.

When the Cretan culture fell, it seems that a mainland state simply took over its economic system – and adapted its written script to its own ends. Insights into how this functioned come from a collection of inscribed ceramic tablets found at another Mycenaean city, Pylos, in southwestern Greece. Pylos was a regional capital, presiding over the administration of two provinces – the 'near' and 'farther', subdivided into nine and seven districts respectively. Nothing moved anywhere within that area without being recorded by the scribes of Pylos, whether it were a single sheep sent by a small farmer or a consignment of bronze sufficient to make 500,000 arrowheads (or, as the record scrupulously notes, 2300 swords).

A SOCIETY OF SPECIALISTS

This was a society organized to within an inch of its life: payroll tablets show that skill-specialization was the rule. Of the 270 bronzesmiths registered for Pylos alone, one group devoted itself entirely to the task of producing chariot wheels.

Along with goldsmiths, silversmiths and jewellers, one man was recorded as being employed exclusively in the occupation of producing 'blue-glass paste'. Less prestigious trades were covered just as carefully: as well as entries for perfumers and ivory-carvers there are details of shepherds, goatherds, cattle-drovers, woodcutters and huntsmen.

Women's work was not forgotten: Pylos had no fewer than 37 female baths attendants (whose fig and wheat rations were all recorded). Other women served the state as corn-grinders, linen-makers and spinners.

GAIN OVER GLORY

In the end, we are left with the impression that, behind the belligerent facade presented by the 'Lion Gate' and those massive walls, Mycenae was more a mercantile than a militarist society. It did have an army, as those meticulously recorded weapons-orders show, but it was far too busy making and trading to have time for putting to sea and attacking Troy.

Sacrifice for a Centaur

A rough-hewn column of chiselled stone uncovered in Campania recalls the days when this region of southern Italy was settled by the Greeks, a part of that far-flung colonial empire which came to be known as Magna Graecia.

Poseidonia, the city of the sea-god Poseidon – or Paestum, as the Romans came to call it – stood on the coast 80km (50 miles) southeast of Naples in the present-day province of Salerno. It was founded at the end of the seventh century BC, a sub-colony of Sybaris, itself an Italian outpost of the Greek city of Helice. By the mid-sixth century, it was flourishing: so much so that its prosperity came close to rivalling its famously successful mother-city, further to the south. Around 550 BC, work began on the construction of a magnificent temple to Hera, Zeus' wife and queen of Olympus.

OLD-FASHIONED

Still stunning, even in its ruined state, this is among the earliest known constructions of the 'classical' type, all colonnaded elegance, though its thick-set pillars give a sense of squatness absent from such iconic constructions as the Parthenon. Built about a hundred years later, but right next door to Hera's temple, is the shrine to Poseidon himself, the city's proprietary deity. It has a similarly sturdy look with its bulging columns, suggesting that it was designed as a companion to its early neighbour.

Even by those standards, however, the Chiron Cippus discovered during excavations here has a crude and even primitive look not generally associated with the ancient Greeks. Its shaft – just over 1m (40in) high – is markedly irregular in form. If it were not for the inscription, indeed, we might almost imagine it was a standing stone from the Neolithic era. In fact, the dedication does little to lend any appreciable air of sophistication: the lettering seems ham-fisted in its execution, the dedication skimpy in its terseness.

Right: Incense or other offerings are believed to have been burned on top of the Chiron Cippus, which was created around the middle of the sixth century BC.

PRIMITIVISM

This pillar seems to have constituted – or belonged to – a *cippus*, a stand on top of which incense or other offerings were burned in honour of the named deity. Experts date its carving to about 550 BC. How a culture capable of producing Poseidonia's Temple of Hera came to create so apparently awkward an item, we can only speculate. Sheer haste? Or a deliberate harking back to rituals of the distant past?

There was always something primitive about the Greek tradition of the centaur – an unsettling hybrid, half-human, half-horse. Behaving with a violent, drunken recklessness, these mythological creatures were a reminder to the classical consciousness of how close beneath the civilized surface lurks something more dangerous and more disturbing. Fighting, boozing, rutting, they reminded Greeks of the fragility of human culture, which can break down at any moment into lawlessness and chaos.

A SPECIAL CENTAUR

Chiron, in fairness, was marked out from the rest of his race by differences not only of character but of origins. While the others were the offspring of the rain and sun, he had been conceived when the Titan Cronos took on the form of a horse to rape the water-nymph Philyra. Ancient artists often pointed up

ON PUBLIC DISPLAY

The Chiron Cippus is among the prize possessions of the National Archeological Museum of Paestum, Italy.

" *To Chiron.* "

Above: Poseidonia's Temple of Poseidon and, beyond it in the background, that of Hera: it is hard to believe that the same culture created the Chiron Cippus.

these distinct antecedents: like other centaurs, Chiron is shown to have the head and torso of a man (frequently clothed), but his lower half is also that of a man, while the trunk and hind legs of a horse are attached behind. This set him apart from the ruck of centaurs, who were generally shown with just the upper half of a man set upon the body of a horse.

Chiron's humane actions also set him apart: he brought up the infant Achilles, who had been abandoned by his mother, Thetis (giving him the warm blood of freshly hunted hares in place of mother's milk). He was also held to have reared Asclepius, whose mother, Coronis, was killed by Apollo: the infant god of medicine was snatched from her body as it burned on a pyre. Chiron taught the boy, who was destined to be the god of surgery and medicine, all that he himself knew about the healing arts.

Death of an Immortal

If sacrifices were offered to Chiron, this was perhaps no more than the centaur's due, such had been his sacrifice on behalf of humankind. After Prometheus incurred the wrath of Zeus by stealing the secret of fire for the good of all, he was punished by being chained to a crag in the pit of hell (Tartarus). Every day, an eagle came to rip open his abdomen to tear out the liver, which had just enough time to replenish itself before his next visit. The only possibility of release from this eternal torture, said Zeus, was for an immortal to agree to take his place. This seemed unlikely: who would submit to unspeakable torture and, by descending into Tartarus, renounce immortality? It was Chiron who made this ultimate sacrifice, partly because it suited him. Heracles had accidentally wounded him with a poisoned arrow, and he was desperate to escape its ravages into the realm of death.

An Olympic Champion

Found at the site of a former Greek colony in Calabria, Italy, a bronze tablet commemorates an ancient athletic triumph. The inscription shows how widely dispersed the Greek world was in the sixth century BC, and how seriously the games at Olympia were taken.

> *Kleombrotos son of Dexilaos, having won at Olympia and promised the prize to Athena, dedicated a tithe.*

ON PUBLIC DISPLAY

Kleombrotos' dedicatory plaque may be seen today in the Sybaritide National Archeological Museum, Calabria.

Above: An athlete's gratitude is recorded here, apparently in fulfilment of a vow – his Olympic victory would have made Kleombrotos for life.

So wealthy was the city of Sybaris, so luxurious the conditions in which its leading citizens could live, that it gave us our modern word 'sybarite' – one who lives for pleasure. One who must have set himself a more unsparing regime was Kleombrotos, a successful athlete, who lived in the city some time in the sixth century BC. Though located in Italy, at the northwestern corner of the Gulf of Taranto, in what is now Cosenza, Sybaris was considered part of Magna Graecia ('Greater Greece'). Hence the existence of a shrine to the goddess Athena; hence too the participation of the town's top athlete in the Olympic Games across the sea in Greece.

A VICTOR'S THANKS

Kleombrotos returned a winner, and it appears to have been in thanks for her support in the competition that he had a plaque put up in Athena's honour in her temple. Made of bronze, it is crudely lettered in an archaic form of Greek, the lines straying slightly out of true, appearing to spiral upward from right to left. But the goddess was no doubt grateful for the acknowledgement, just as her priests were no doubt appreciative of the cash gift the victorious athlete mentions having also made.

GREATER GREECE

The plaque is a fascinating reminder of how different the cultural map of the Mediterranean looked in the days before the rise of Rome – and even of classical Greece. One of the more surprising (and, indeed, seemingly counterintuitive) aspects of the history of the Greek cities is that their colonial period pre-dated their emergence as major states. Britain, Germany, the United States: these were powers first and empire-builders second. The Greek cities actually built their economic prosperity through trade with overseas colonies that they themselves had established between 800 and 600 BC. From southern Spain to the Crimean coast, from western Turkey to North Africa, hundreds of such trading-settlements were founded. There was a particular concentration around the coast of southern Italy and Sicily: rich lands, just a short hop from Greece itself. The colonies seem to have been homes from home: architectural evidence and ceramic finds suggest a continuing closeness with the home cities back in Greece.

A SPECIAL CITY

Sybaris was founded relatively early, around 720 BC, by settlers who ventured out from the city of Helice, in Achaea, on the northern coast of the Peloponnese. It stood out among all the Greek colonies, having prospered to a remarkable degree and made itself a dominant

Above: The Olympic Games showcased the strength and prowess of Greek youth, and every city wanted to do well. Participating athletes knew they were competing not just for their own personal honour but for the pride and prestige of the community that had sent them.

power among the other colonies of the region. Despite its size and wealth, little trace of Sybaris has survived. In 1963, however, an excavation on the Timpone Motta, a hill that once would have overlooked the city, forming its 'acropolis', uncovered the remains of what had clearly once been the Sanctuary of Athena. It was here that Kleombrotos' tablet was rediscovered, some twenty-six centuries after it was first placed in dedication.

Amateur Status?

One of the most intriguing aspects of the Francavilla plaque is the undertaking of Kleombrotos to dedicate a tithe (or tenth) of his prize to Athena. What prize? How could any athlete meaningfully offer a tenth of his glory to the goddess? What would be the point of giving her a tenth of a laurel crown? The conventional wisdom has always been that the ancient Olympics were – very strictly – an amateur event, but there is evidence that 'encouragement' was offered by the athletes' home cities, in some cases at least. By the beginning of the sixth century, Athens was giving its medal-winners a sum of 500 drachmas; Isthmia gave victorious contestants 100 drachmas. The Athenian prize in particular is remarkable, on a par with anything a modern professional might earn: Olympic historian David C. Young has estimated that it is the equivalent of a million dollars or more – and for a single victory.

The Satirist

An Ionic column marks the grave of a Greek poet, the sort of monument that might become a military hero. Archilochus did have a soldierly side, but he was more complex – and more interesting – than this shrine to patriotism and valour would suggest.

You could tell Archilochus' grave, according to one tradition, by the cloud of wasps buzzing round above it, paying tribute to the sting of its occupant's satiric wit. A more solid memorial, which turned the grave into a shrine, was placed here a century after his death, by which time his reputation had subtly shifted and he was starting to be seen – at least by his compatriots – as a more solid character.

ONE OF THE FIRST
Archilochus was a poetic pioneer: one of the earliest writers of verse we know by name and celebrated in antiquity for his satire. He was not, of course, the first Greek poet: Homer's heroic epics are believed to have been composed some time in the ninth century BC; Hesiod's formal pastorals and philosophical verses followed towards 700 BC. But, born around 680 BC, Archilochus is widely credited with

having brought a more personal voice, a less formal tone, to the craft of verse – in short, to being one of the first lyric poets.

AN IRREVERENT EDGE
If the word 'lyrical' suggests something soft and romantic, this was not in fact Archilochus' forte: he was most famous – or notorious – for the quality of his invective. (The iambic metre he was held to have invented, though destined to be

> *Archilochus of Paros lies here; this monument was dedicated by Dokimos son of Neokreon.*

ON PUBLIC DISPLAY

Archilochus' heroon may be seen, along with other finds from ancient Paros, at the Archeological Museum in Parikia.

Left: Dokimos placed his monument to Archilochus over a century after the poet's death: he raised his own standing by commemorating this Parian hero.

Right: Irredeemably irreverent in his verse, Archilochus was too cynical for soldiering, it might be assumed; in fact he seems to have loved the life – until he met his death in battle.

associated with poise and even serenity in the poetry of modern times, was in the classical world a medium of abuse.) About a hundred fragments of his work have endured, thanks to their quotation in the writings of later classical commentators: they vary considerably in subject matter. Along with withering satire, there are poems of love and eroticism (though these too tend towards the irreverent and sometimes scabrous). Archilochus has the distinction of having written the first known fable featuring animals. Epigrammatic as ever, it reads:

> *The fox has innumerable tricks;*
> *The hedgehog only has one – but*
> *it's a good one.*

His surviving body of work contains poems of war and fighting as well, though even on this noblest of themes Archilochus tends to display a seriously cynical streak. But he was a man with many creative caps, and on occasion he did voice some unimpeachably pious, patriotic sentiments; it was for these that his countrymen chose to remember him in later times.

THE PATRIOT OF PAROS

He died in about 645 BC, but the placing of an Ionic pillar and a marble slab in 510 BC made a simple grave into a *heroon* – a hero's shrine. The monument marked his institutionalization as an object of patriotic devotion: a 'Bard of Paros' in whom the island's people could take pride. The memorial makes no attempt to deny Archilochus' bohemian side (a marble slab shows him reclining as though at a banquet with a woman beside him and a wine-bearer in attendance), but its overall effect is his enshrinement as a hero. Archilochus' character was multi-faceted, of course, and did up to a point include a persona as a pious patriot. From a modern perspective, though, it is difficult to resist a feeling that so august a monument is sending up the satirist.

Mightier than the Sword

The story goes that Archilochus was the illegitimate son of a nobleman, Telisicles; his mother was a slave-woman from his household. When Archilochus was a young man, Telisicles was prompted by the Delphic Oracle to lead an expedition from Paros to colonize the island of Thasos, far to the north off the coast of Thrace. Archilochus had no intention of accompanying him: he had been promised the hand of Neoubulé, daughter of Lycambe, one of Paros' leading nobles. When Lycambe reneged on his agreement, Archilochus retaliated by persecuting him and his daughter with a series of legendary satires – and, it is said, ultimately driving them to suicide. Archilochus then took up the life of a wandering mercenary. When he fell in battle, the man who killed him was cursed by Apollo.

The Heart of Ancient Athens

Another city might have had some great building as its centre; a military stronghold, a temple or a palace. But the world's first democracy had an open space, a place of public assembly: the Agora was the heart of Athenian life.

Rough-hewn, rectangular *horoi*, or boundary-stones, marked the entrance to the Agora in its southwestern corner. It was important to know that you were entering this sacred space. Those convicted of what might be called crimes of honour – 'draft-dodging' or desertion from the military, blasphemy or abuse of parents – were not even allowed to enter, and for others there appear to have been special rules. We know for certain that, from the fourth century, there were basins for the ritual washing of hands before entry, and there is every likelihood that these stood there before.

THE ATHENIAN IDEA
It says much about the significance attached by the Athenians to public assembly that the Agora was a place of quasi-religious importance. After all, in modern terms, it

was simply a place where men met and talked. Athens was not short of sacred sites: Pericles had built a splendid new temple-complex dedicated to Athena on the Acropolis. But if the Parthenon and its companion-buildings proclaimed the Athenian civic virtues to the world, for the Athenians themselves those virtues had their centre and shrine in the Agora.

The Agora was basically an open area, though around its edges were covered colonnades, or *stoai*, where idlers could walk and talk out of the sun and rain. We should not imagine cloistered quietness, though: the place would typically

have been thronged. And not just with high-minded citizen-statesmen talking about democracy: there were barber-shops and taverns here as well as hawkers, hustlers, acrobats and entertainers of every kind. Beyond, in the area around the Agora, were the courts and council-chambers and other important public buildings.

THE NIGHT OF THE HERMS
At its northwestern corner, the Agora was delimited by boundary-stones of a different sort, called *hermai*. These were named for Hermes, the messenger of the gods, who was also god of boundaries (the logic perhaps being that his winged sandals carried him easily across them). The *hermai* were strange stelae, rectangular in shape and

Above: The Temple of Athena Parthenos ('Athena the Maiden'), known to the modern world as the Parthenon, is the most glorious creation of Pericles' 'Golden Age'.

Monument to a Tyrant?

So central a place did the Agora occupy in the life of democratic Athens that its citizens came to imagine it had always been there. In fact, as late as the seventh century, this site seems to have been partly a burial ground and partly a residential area. And though the Athenians themselves assumed that it had originally and always been a place sanctified to democracy, the Agora had been set out by the tyrant Peisistratos. The despots who ruled in pre-democratic Athens were not 'tyrants' in the modern, blood-soaked sense, but Peisistratos had certainly been a one-man ruler. Like the dictator who makes the trains run on time, though, he had been good at getting things done, beautifying the city by his building projects. One of these appears to have been the creation of the Agora – albeit as a parade- or processional-ground rather than a symbolic civic space.

flat, apart from carved male genitals at the appropriate height and the god's head at the top.

On a single night in 415 BC, during the Peloponnesian War, these *hermai* were mysteriously vandalized. It happened just before an important military force was due to depart for Sicily. The blame fell on Alcibiades, a leading statesman – and, indeed, the man behind the Sicilian expedition. Rather than being allowed to defend himself, he had to lead the expedition – then was summoned back from Sicily to face trial. He escaped with his supporters, having realized that he was going to be condemned on trumped-up charges. Without his leadership, the Sicilian venture foundered. Worse was to come for Athens: Alcibiades defected to Sparta, and became an important general in the enemy's cause.

" I am the boundary of the Agora. "

ON PUBLIC DISPLAY

This boundary-stone is still to be seen at the edge of the Agora, in Athens.

Right: This horos, or boundary-stone, would have had a special significance for the Athenians: strict rules governed entrance to the sacred space of the Agora.

Living by the Law: Gortyn

The entire legal code of Gortyn, a city-state in southern Crete, was etched onto a wall for all citizens to see. Much has been lost, but the 600 lines that remain afford a fascinating glimpse of the everyday concerns of classical life.

Above: Some of the Gortyn Code was lost; other sections were pieced together by archeologists from slabs used nearby as building-stone.

ON PUBLIC DISPLAY

Parts of the Gortyn wall have been reconstructed so sections of the code may be seen in situ, at Gortyn in southern Crete.

Whoever commits rape upon a free man or woman must pay a fine of 100 staters [1 stater = 4 drachmas]…a slave who rapes a free woman should pay double… Someone who forces a female house-slave should pay two staters, but if she is no longer a virgin just one obol if he does it by day, two obols if he does it by night…

Anyone caught committing adultery with a free woman in the house of her husband, father or brother will be liable to a fine of 100 staters. If the act takes place in someone else's house, the fine is fifty staters; if the woman is the wife of an apetairos [a free man without citizenship] the charge is ten staters…

If a slave going to a free woman should marry her, the children will be born free; but if the free woman goes to the slave, their children will be slaves. And if the same mother has both free and slave children, if she should then die her property would go to the free children.

A woman who gives birth to a child after leaving her husband having been divorced, she must have it taken to the husband's house before three witnesses. If he will not accept the child, it will be her right to decide whether to bring it up or expose it…

Classical stereotypes may mislead. Not all Greek city-states had the sort of fully developed democracy to be found in the Athens of the fifth century BC. Yet, at the same time, it is striking just how far what we might call the civic spirit seems to have spread through the various parts of the Greek world at this time. Gortyn, an otherwise unexceptional polis in the south of Crete, is a perfect example. Here, the laws of the city were written up on walls for all to see.

The code we have was carved – apparently by a single hand – across the wall of a building beside the agora, the open public space at the city's heart. Given the inscription's content, it seems logical that the building would have been the *bouleterion*, or courthouse, but really we have no way of knowing for certain. Its stones were pillaged by later Greek builders before ending up as part of the fabric of a Roman *odeion*, or concert arena. But what remained of the script was clear enough to be relatively easily pieced together.

DORIC DIALECT

Written not in the Greek of Athens but in the Doric dialect of Crete and the other southern islands, the resulting inscription extends across an area of wall 9m (30ft) long and approximately 1.5m (5ft) from top to bottom. In all, it comprises 600 lines of text: aspects of commercial and contract law are addressed, but most of the provisions here deal

Above: Though much is missing, the Gortyn Code gives us the fullest single source we have for the law of Greece's Golden Age. The sections we have focus mainly on marital and domestic questions.

with domestic issues. (Inscriptions on criminal law have presumably been lost.)

On all subjects – from adultery to adoption, from the rules of inheritance to the rights of slaves – the law of the city has its position. The Greeks were only too well aware that there was more to democracy than freedom: if good fences make good neighbours, strong laws save misunderstandings and unfortunate disputes. As codified in Gortyn, Greek law prepared for every eventuality.

As the Ox Ploughs

One curious feature of the Gortyn Code is that it is written in *boustrophedon* fashion: literally, this means 'turning like an ox'. In early Greek writing, as in many other scripts, the writer started out working from left to right. On completing the line, however, rather than jumping back to the left-hand side to start again in the same direction, he simply dropped a line and wrote his way back from right to left. This, of course, was how a ploughing ox would turn when it reached the end of a furrow, hence the name by which this fashion of writing came to be known.

Trial by Jury

Athenian democracy did not just extend over the government of the state; it covered the administration of justice too. Every Athenian could expect his case to be heard before a jury of his peers: the procedures were taken very seriously indeed.

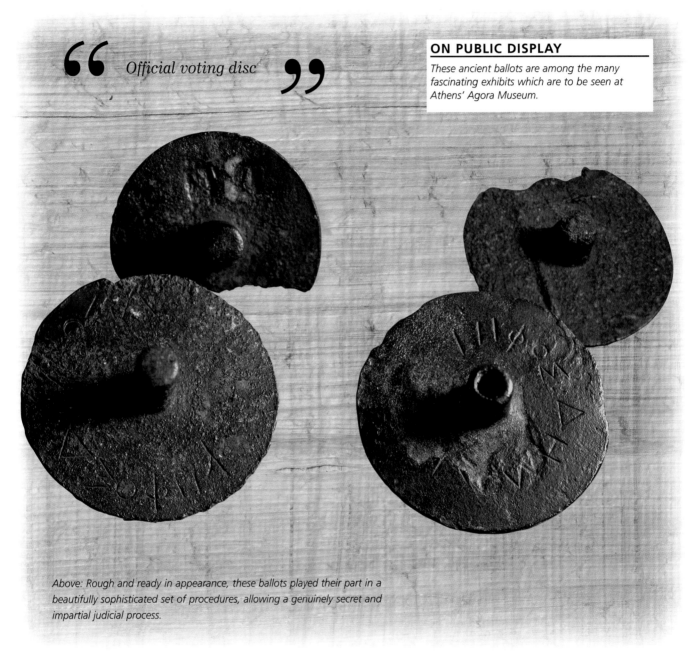

" *Official voting disc* "

ON PUBLIC DISPLAY

These ancient ballots are among the many fascinating exhibits which are to be seen at Athens' Agora Museum.

Above: Rough and ready in appearance, these ballots played their part in a beautifully sophisticated set of procedures, allowing a genuinely secret and impartial judicial process.

The inscription is starkly functional, but the real significance here lies not in what is written but in the form of the raised boss or hub at the disc's centre. A solid bump meant a vote for the defendant – a 'not guilty' decision in a criminal case. Where the axle was hollow, like a little tube, it was a vote for the plaintiff or prosecutor. Once the case had been heard, the jury (which might number 200 men or more) filed out of the courtroom. As they left, they passed a pair of urns. Into one each juror cast his chosen ballot; into the other, the one he was rejecting. Once everyone had voted, the ballots in the first urn were counted and a verdict reached.

The beauty of the scheme was that the ballot was anonymous. The secrecy of the vote could be assured. The discs were designed to be held in the palm of the hand, one finger keeping the bump at the centre covered: it was impossible to tell which way a juror planned to vote by looking. Though the difference between the two types of ballot could not be mistaken when it came to counting, they were similar enough to be readily mass-produced.

Democracy, we are often reminded, brings not just rights but also responsibilities. Athenian democracy was certainly no exception. Between the functioning of the political system and the conduct of the law, it was astonishingly labour-intensive by modern standards. (Hence, of course, the importance of Athens' considerable population of non-citizens: the foreigners and slaves – and women – whose work kept the economy going while the citizen classes debated legislation and heard legal cases.)

Aristophanes' comedy *The Wasps* (422 BC) concerns an old man who, with a great deal too much time on his hands, takes every possible opportunity to go on jury service. Most citizens were less eager to perform their democratic duty.

Rotas had to be introduced to ensure that everybody took their turn.

To this end, blocks of 2000 citizens at a time were chosen, representing all Athens' ten electoral 'tribes'. They were required to make themselves available, if called upon, for a certain length of time.

Chosen by Machine

It was important that the final selection of the jury should be completely random, so that there should be no suggestion of unfairness of any kind. An ingenious solution was found: every citizen eligible to serve as a juror was given special tickets, or *pinakia*. These were small, thin tablets of bronze, each inscribed with the person's name and tribe. On presenting himself for service, the juror gave his ticket to the official operating the *kleroterion*, or allotment machine.

The *kleroterion* was an upright slab of stone, with hundreds of slots arranged in horizontal and vertical rows. The latter represented the voting tribes, and the jurors' names were fed into the *kleroterion* in such a way that every horizontal row had the names of ten potential jurors, one from each of Athens' electoral tribes.

Down the side of the *kleroterion* ran a metal tube: at the top was an open funnel; at the bottom was a cranking handle. Bronze balls coloured black and white were poured into the funnel at the top, where they were jumbled up. When the handle at the bottom was turned, a ball popped out: if it was black, the bottom row of *pinakia* was removed and restored to their owners, who were told they had been discharged from duty for that day. If the ball was white, on the other hand, the men would be directed to the court and required to serve on that day's jury. The crank on the machine was then turned again, and the process continued until the selection process had been completed.

Above: The workings of Athenian democracy were ingenious and complex. These inscribed pinakia *and the bronze ball were used in the* kleroterion *jury-selecting machine.*

Driven Out by Democracy

It took only a moment to scratch a man's name upon an Athenian 'ostrakon', but it could have enormous consequences for that man's life. No case illustrates that more clearly than that of Themistocles, the Athenian leader who was eventually exiled by his own countrymen.

" *Themistokles Prearrhus.* "

A man's destiny depended on these bits of broken pot, inscribed as they were by angry voters with the name of Themistocles. He had saved the city once, but a leader in democratic Athens alienated his electorate at his peril. Themistocles was to end his life in exile.

ON PUBLIC DISPLAY

So unpopular was Themistocles that ostraka bearing his name are by no means rare. These examples are from the Agora Museum in Athens.

Modern democracy's many shortcomings stem mainly from the fact that it is not very democratic. Elections are held once every several years. Each elector gets to cast a single vote, aggregated in with those of millions of other men and women, after which the victorious party has a free hand. A modern administration will take thousands of decisions, great and small, on the basis of this 'mandate' from the polls.

The limitations of Athenian democracy have frequently been pointed out: it was founded on the ownership of slaves and excluded women. And yet almost as startling is how truly representative it was – how closely and immediately it could reflect the people's will.

THE SAVIOUR OF HIS CITY
Take the case of Themistocles. He had been the dominant personality in Athenian politics since the 490s. A sort of Athenian Churchill, he urged his countrymen to maintain their guard against Darius I's Persians, even after their victory at Marathon in 490. Others wanted to sit back and enjoy Athens' moment in the sun, but Themistocles maintained the state on a war-footing. What's more, he refused to relax his vigilance when Darius died in 486. More controversially still, when a new seam of silver was discovered at the state mine at Laureion, he argued for the money to go on warships rather than on public buildings.

Against their instincts, the Athenians were convinced by Themistocles' case. Just as well, because Darius' son Xerxes launched an invasion with 100,000 men. And again, Themistocles had held his nerve. As the Persians swept south into Attica, he instructed the Athenians to abandon their city.

They lay low in the port of Piraeus while the Persians rampaged through their city. But Themistocles had set a trap for the Persian fleet. Lured into the strait of Salamis, Xerxes' ships were smashed by the triremes built by Themistocles. Without logistical support, the Persian army had no alternative but to withdraw.

AN ENEMY OF THE PEOPLE

Themistocles' stock should have soared. However, he tried people's patience with his caution and his preoccupation with defence. He continued to plough funds into shipbuilding and constructed the 'Long Wall' that linked Athens with its port, Piraeus.

In so doing, he dramatically changed the psychological orientation of the city, making what had been an inland capital the

Below: Ostracism was worse than a death-sentence, as far as patriotic Athenians were concerned. As imagined here by a nineteenth-century painter, it involved leaving behind not just city but family and friends.

centre of a maritime state. Rather than rebuild the temples and citadels of the Acropolis, which had been reduced to rubble by the Persians, Themistocles wanted the ruins left as they were as a reminder of both Asian savagery and the need to be alert.

This was all too cheerless for a society in the mood for a celebration. He might have been a hero, but Themistocles was getting on the nerves of the citizens. And they were easily swayed by the arguments of those who called for Themistocles to be expelled. (Many are believed to have been sympathizers of Sparta, which was threatened by the rise of Athens.)

AN IRONIC END

Ostracism must have been a painful penalty for anyone to face. For someone as proud as Themistocles, it must have been excruciating. The rules normally allowed the exile to return with no stain on his character, but the campaign against Themistocles continued. In the end, it was Xerxes' son Artaxerxes I who came to his rescue, giving him the governorship of Magnesia in Asia Minor. There he was worshipped as a god by the province's inhabitants, and seems to have been a loyal servant of the emperor. He finally died in 459 BC.

No Defence

There was no defence against ostracism – indeed, no specific charge had to be brought. If it was the 'will of the people' that a man be expelled, then so be it. There were two steps. First, a ballot was held to see whether citizens wanted to hold an ostracism. This was a straightforward poll to establish 'yes' or 'no'. If the answer was affirmative, the poll was staged a few weeks later. Each voter scratched the name of the man he wanted to expel on a ceramic shard (which the Athenians used where we might use scraps of paper). Beneath, he wrote the deme, or electoral tribe – Themistocles belonged to the Prearrhus constituency. If more than 6000 votes were cast, all were counted, and the 'winner' established. Within ten days, he had to leave Athens, with no right of appeal. And he had to remain in exile for ten years, on pain of death.

The New Athenians

The Athenians saw citizenship as a privilege not lightly to be granted, but the Peloponnesian War was a time of crisis. In 403 BC, they extended the rights of citizens to the Samians, who had stood by them through the darkest moments of the war.

Left: Hera, seen here with her husband Zeus, was the patron deity of the Samians. In taking Athenian citizenship they aligned themselves with Athena, with whom Hera had not always seen eye to eye.

This decree is carved into a stela beneath a pictorial relief in which the goddess Athena offers the hand of friendship to Hera, proprietary goddess of the Samians. It is, observes Alastair Blanshard, a historian who has studied this inscription, a deceptively straightforward handshake: if only diplomacy could really be this easy!

DEMOCRACY RESTORED...
The decision to bestow Athenian citizenship on the Samians had originally been reached in 405 BC: this is what the inscription means by 'all that was earlier decreed'. Yet this agreement had summarily been cancelled by the 'Thirty Tyrants', the Spartan-dominated oligarchy that had come to power in Athens in the aftermath of the final defeat of 404 BC. The tyranny had been overthrown – though not before hundreds of influential democrats had been forced to drink hemlock or sent into exile – and democracy had been restored by Thrasybulus' coup of 403 BC.

...BUT NOT GREATNESS
The new Athenian citizenship was not quite what it had been, it goes without saying. Though free again, Athens was very much a state on the back foot. In time, Thrasybulus would lead his people in open rebellion against Sparta; for the moment, though, the forms of negotiation had to be maintained. (Had the Athenians been negotiating from a position of strength, they would never have dreamt of conceding citizenship, no matter how deserving the Samians might have been.)

Blanshard's close reading demonstrates that the 403 decree betrays a sense of the unsatisfactory circumstances of its inscription. The embarrassed look over the shoulder to the earlier decree reminds us that two years could be an awfully long time in Athenian politics; there is an air of defeated resignation as well about the concessions being made to the Samians over the negotiation process.

Hearth and Home

The 'Pyrtaneion', in which the Samian Decree proposes a state reception for Athens' friends, takes its name from the Greek word *pyr*, meaning 'fire'. Here, priestesses tended the eternal flame that symbolized the city's enduring life. Like the Temple of Vesta in Rome, the *pyrtaneion* was the 'hearth' of the city – and by the same token, its symbolic 'home'. There was also a dining-hall here, in which Athenians could relax between meetings of the state council in the *bouleterion* next door and in which visiting delegations could be entertained.

Stalwart Samos

The glory days of classical Athens were brought to a bloody and undignified end when the Peloponnesian War broke out in 431 BC. This pitted Athens and its 'allies' (actually subject-states) of the so-called Delian League against the might of Sparta and its Peloponnesian League. Through decades of stop-and-start fighting, the balance between the two sides tipped back and forth, but Sparta finally prevailed with Persian help, in 404 BC. The Battle of Aegostami the previous year had proved decisive: despite Samian support for the Athenian fleet, the Spartan general Lysander scored a crushing triumph. Athens, traditional ruler of the Aegean waves, was lost without this power, cut off from grain imports and from contact with its colonies and allies overseas. Samos, which had provided a safe harbour for the Athenian ships before the fighting, remained loyal even in the aftermath of defeat. As Lysander's land-forces cut a swathe through Athens' former territories, their advance was checked by heroic resistance from the Samians.

ΚΗΦΙΣΟΦΩΝΠΑΙΑΝΙΕΥΣ
ΕΓΡΑΜΜΑΤΕΥΕ
ΣΑΜΙΟΙΣΟΣΟΙΜΕΤΑΤΟΔΗΜΟΤΟΑΘΗΝΑΙ
ΩΝΕΓΕΝΟΝΤΟ

> " *This resolution passed by the council and the people…All praise to the Samians, who have shown themselves good men towards the Athenians; all that was earlier decreed for the people of Samos by the Athenians shall once more hold, it has been agreed. The Samians may, as they demand, send whatever representatives they themselves should choose to Sparta. Since on top of this they ask the Athenians to join in their negotiations, they may select further envoys who will negotiate alongside the Samians to secure whatever benefits they can for both parties, and will consider their decisions together with them…. Bring the Samian delegates before the people to do business if they ask for anything, and also invite them to dinner in the Pyrtaneion tomorrow…* "

Above: There is an element of bluster – even, perhaps, of wishful thinking – behind the portentous rhetoric of the Samian Decree. The citizenship the Athenians were granting was not all that it might have been had Athena's city fared better in the Peloponnesian War. Even so, the Samians seem to have been happy enough to become Athenian – still, apparently, a covetable status.

ON PUBLIC DISPLAY

The Samian Decree is on display in the Acropolis Museum, Athens.

Dry Delphi

Delphi is famous today for its shrine to Apollo and its oracle, but in ancient times it was also sacred as a sporting venue. On a stadium wall, a sombre inscription reminds spectators that they will be held to the strictest standards of sobriety.

> *Wine is forbidden anywhere near the track. Any man who breaks this rule will have to make amends to Apollo by pouring a libation, offering a sacrifice and paying a 110-drachma fine, half of it to the god himself, and half to the man who has informed on him.*

Above: The prohibition notice was literally built into the fabric of the stadium, an indication of the seriousness with which it was intended to be taken, in an arena which had been consecrated to Apollo.

ON PUBLIC DISPLAY

The inscription still stands in the stadium wall in the arena in Delphi, Greece.

After the Olympics, the Pythian Games – held every four years – were the most important athletic event in the Greek sporting calendar. The stadium at Delphi was fittingly impressive. First built in the fifth century BC, it made cunning use of the local topography: the rock of the hillside formed natural terracing, out of which seating for spectators could be carved.

Some time after 300 BC, this central stadium was expanded, given further seating, and made the heart of a larger complex, including a bath, an open-air gym and a hippodrome (horse-racing arena). Much of this work appears to have been paid for by a wealthy Athenian, Herodes Atticus, who also funded improvements at Olympia.

Both these sporting venues and a nearby theatre appear to have been sacred to the god Apollo – the proprietary deity of Delphi as a whole. It was with the sun god that the Delphic Oracle was presumed to be in communication; his shrine lay not far from here, surrounded by a *peribolos*, or sacred court. The exact nature of the relationship between the games and the god is not fully understood: the Pythian Games were certainly viewed as a sacred tribute to Apollo, but they were at

Above: The original terracing, to the north of the arena at Delphi, was cut out of the native rock in the fifth century. Another stand was subsequently built.

The Panhellenic Games

The Pythian Games were one of four great sporting tournaments in which all the cities of Greece competed regularly: the others were the Olympics, the Nemean (held in Nemea, in the northeastern Peloponnese) and the Isthmian (held in Corinth). Of these, the Olympics and the Nemean Games were both sacred to Zeus, whilst the Isthmian Games were consecrated to Poseidon, the sea-god. Each four-year cycle was known as an Olympiad – the Olympics were definitely the most important games; the Pythian Games also came four-yearly, timed to come midway between Olympic competitions. The Isthmian and Nemean Games came every two years, but were timed to avoid any clash with the other great festivals. Athletes' existences were naturally measured out in Olympiads, which offered a never-ending round of competition. To some extent, though, everyone's life was shaped by the rhythms of the Olympiad cycle, the mainspring of ancient Greece's cultural calendar.

the same time very much a serious sporting tournament. Successful athletes are individualists, and ancient Greek competitors appear to have been no exception: they were in to win, for themselves and then for their cities.

CROWD CONDUCT

Then, as now, sport was not just for participants but also for spectators: how much thought they gave to Apollo (or how much that mattered) we can only wonder. With competitors coming here from across the entire Greek world, a great deal of local patriotism must have been at stake, and this must have lent an extra edge to events that would already have been hotly contested. Was the wine prohibition just a religious taboo, or should we conclude (as some historians have done) that ancient Delphi experienced crowd trouble of the sort that has plagued soccer and other sports in modern times?

Much has been invested in emphasizing the purity of ancient Greek games, an ideal that damns the cynical commercialism held to afflict sport today. The need for a prohibition on wine among spectators at these meetings does, however, suggest that ancient athletics was not quite as unimpeachably high-minded as we were once encouraged to assume.

Competitive Music

One of Apollo's most important cultural functions was as the patron god of music. Delphi's *Mousikos Agon* ('Musical Contest') was seen as analogous to games. Despite the existence of prestigious events like Moscow's Tchaikovsky International Competition, the idea that musical performance might be a competitive event seems odd to most of us in the modern world. But the competitive impulse ran right through Greek culture: the great tragedies of Aeschylus, Sophocles and Euripides received their first performances at Athens as entrants in the drama competitions held in honour of Dionysos. At Delphi, the *cithara* competition – which involved singing, whilst accompanying oneself on the lyre – was as important in its way as the sports events. Also closely fought was the 'flute' event – actually, its double reed made the Greek pipe much more like a modern oboe; one pipe was played in each hand, thus redoubling the effect. There was no *Mousikos Agon* at Olympia, as such, but the winner at Delphi played his pipe to accompany the pentathlon at the Olympic Games, so there was a degree of cultural cross-fertilization between both disciplines and competitions.

Sold to Apollo

Large areas of the wall within the Temple of Apollo at Delphi were covered in graffiti – over a thousand messages in all. These recorded the freeing of slaves, following a curious quasi-legal formula in which they were symbolically 'sold' to the god himself.

Above: Letters of liberation – a simple declaration that a deal had been done with the god Apollo was all it took to make the manumission valid.

ON PUBLIC DISPLAY

Many of these manumission messages can still be plainly seen, scratched into the Polygonal Wall in Apollo's Temple, at Delphi.

> *At a price of three silver minas, Pythian Apollo bought a Roman-born woman slave named Nicaea from Sosibius, with a view to securing her liberty. The seller under the law was Eumnastos of Amphissa. He has received his money and the purchase was carried out in the name of Apollo, so the slave could have her freedom…*
>
> *Telon and Cleto, with the agreement of their son Straton, sold Pythian Apollo a male slave named Sosus, a Cappadocian by birth, at a price of 3 silver minas. Sosus commissioned the god to handle the sale on the condition that he should have his freedom guaranteed, so that no one might be able to claim ownership of him for all time…*

Without question, it makes an inspiring sight: a wall of massive masonry, scrawled all over with little messages of liberation. Each of these rude inscriptions, scratched in the stone, stood for freedom for some man or woman twenty-odd centuries ago: we can read their names and imagine their joy at their deliverance. But the temptation to see these graffiti as representing some sort of ancient 'Schindler's List' is to be avoided: at very least, the 'small print' must be read. Those who 'manumitted' their slaves may on occasion have done so in a spirit of gratitude for some heroic act or for a lifetime's devoted service, but most were more hard-bitten in their reasoning. It went without saying that Apollo's price would have to be paid by the former slave from his or her earnings.

Many slaves who had their manumission written up at Delphi – perhaps the majority – were actually to secure only a partial liberty. Whilst their owners renounced their claims to ownership, they did so only on the condition that the slave committed his or her service through the former owner's lifetime. So it was with 'a male Galatian slave named Maiphatas and a female Illyrian slave called Ammia'. They were granted their freedom by their master, Critodamus, but were to:

'stay with Critodamus for as long as he should live, doing whatever he should order them; if they should leave him or refuse to do his bidding, this sale will be considered cancelled.'

A CAREFUL CALCULATION

From the master's point of view, such an arrangement had the advantage of giving the slave the best possible incentive for good behaviour. It also spared the owner's family the expense of continuing to keep the slave through his or her own old age. A cruel trick? This system, known as paramone, may strike us as such, but a slave in ancient times knew better than to expect miracles. The assurance of freedom after their master's death would have given them something to look forward to, even if it was to come only after many more years of servitude and toil.

Above: A slave-woman waits upon her elderly master in a scene from a Greek vase-painting. Most manumitted slaves could expect to be genuinely free only when their original owners died.

An Accepted Fact

That their liberty-loving culture was built on a foundation of chattel slavery was an irony utterly lost on the Greeks themselves. Like others in the ancient world, they took their right to own others for granted. Prisoners-of-war and their descendants had long been kept as possessions, and there was a stream of fresh arrivals brought from overseas by foreign traders. In sheer numerical terms, democratic Athens was the worst offender. A census taken towards the end of the fourth century BC came up with a figure of 400,000 slaves for Athens and Attica – about 20 slaves for every citizen. Leaving aside the mixed motives of those who manumitted their slaves at Delphi and at similar shrines, slaves who gained their freedom this way were very much in the minority. The number freed in Roman times appears to have risen sharply, though here too a strong element of calculation appears to have been present. The habit of keeping slaves was deeply ingrained, enduring well into the early centuries AD, its ethics unquestioned even in Christian times.

The Philosopher's Stone

Few men ever had the privilege of learning at the feet of so great a teacher – but then few teachers ever got to educate so great a king. A fragmentary inscription bears witness to the bond between two of the outstanding figures of ancient times.

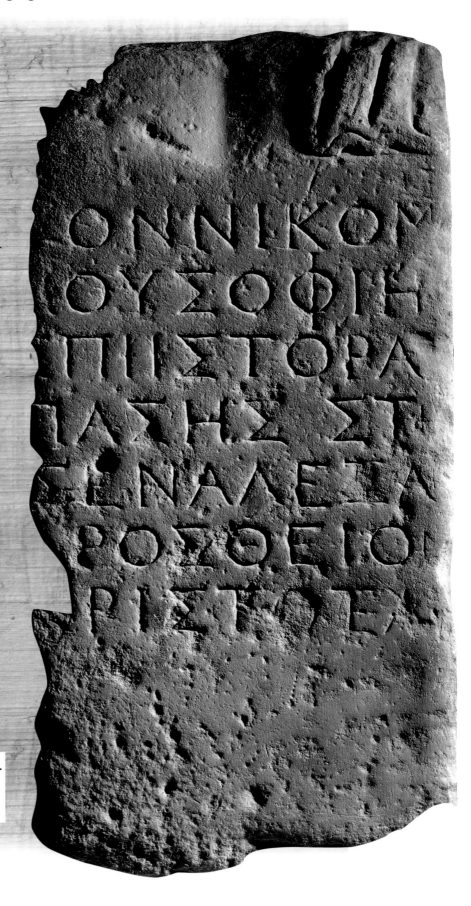

> 66 *Alexander set up this portrait of the divine Aristotle, son of Nichomachos, fountain of all wisdom...* 99

Right: The wording makes it clear that this slab was once the base of a herma, surmounted by a sculptured head of the great sage. Aristotle's importance was already clear in his own age.

ON PUBLIC DISPLAY

The Aristotle Herma is now housed in the Agora Museum, which occupies the reconstructed Stoa of Attalos.

Only the inscription – and that is incomplete – survives of what appears originally to have taken the form of a *herma*, with the philosopher's head displayed atop this blank stone slab. It was discovered during excavations of Athens' Stoa of Attalos, on the Agora's eastern side, though it must have pre-dated that second-century construction by well over a hundred years. Alexander, born in 356, began his campaign of conquest in 336. He must have dedicated this monument some time before he set off.

FAMILY TIES

Aristotle's connection with Alexander had been longstanding. The future philosopher was born in Macedon, the son of the court doctor to King Amyntas, who was the father of Philip II and thus the grandfather of the conqueror of Asia. For many years, though, it seemed as though Aristotle had left his birthplace behind. As a teenager he went to Athens. There he stayed for twenty years, first as student and then as teacher, developing his distinctive intellectual approach.

Plato's teacher, Socrates, was forced to commit suicide in 399 BC – charged with corrupting Athenian youth by his ideas. The student who so carefully recorded Socrates' thought also continued his teaching activities, and then, at some time around 387, he set up a special Academy outside the city centre. In Plato's accounts it is difficult to be sure where the voice of Socrates leaves off, to be replaced by the voice of Plato. It is clear, though, that Plato thought 'reality' was no more than the imperfect embodiment of ideal forms: the thinker's task was to see past immediate perceptions to the truth beyond.

Aristotle disagreed: rather than speculating on how things should be, he argued that we should concern ourselves with how they were. His 'empiricist' view was that we can know only what we can see and test by observation.

Though Aristotle had yet to grasp the full implications of this view, it became the basis for the whole system of modern scientific thought. And it was a view that can be applied equally (as Aristotle himself later realized) across the whole range of intellectual activities, from psychology to drama and the law.

A BOLT-HOLE

Around 346 BC, an enemy laid a charge of impiety against Aristotle – the memory of Socrates' fate must still have been raw. With Athens unsafe, where else would he go but home? He returned to Macedon, where he was welcomed at the court of the new King Philip. He was entrusted with the education of Alexander, and seems to have been his tutor for six or seven years. After that, Athens beckoned; the charge against Aristotle had been forgotten. On

Above: Heads of Aristotle were popular in Roman times, though they may well have been based on earlier models. Some such sculpture originally stood atop the herma in the Agora.

his return, he shunned the noise of the city, establishing himself among the leafy walks of the Lyceum outside the city.

The Spirit of the Stoa

It is fitting that Aristotle should have been memorialized here, even if he did teach mainly at the Lyceum, a little way outside the city centre. It is no exaggeration to say that Western thought was born in and around the Athenian Agora. A place of general resort for all the men of the city, it had been the natural place for Socrates to set up shop. Amidst the bustle of the *stoai*, he peddled his instruction in rhetoric and reasoning even as other vendors sold snacks or trinkets or performed feats of conjuring or acrobatics. Though his pupil Plato transferred his activities to the Academy and Aristotle ultimately based himself outside the city at the Lyceum, the *stoai* remained important in the intellectual life of Athens. One school of thought, proclaimed by Zeno of Citium at the end of the third century BC, became known as 'Stoicism' because it had first been expounded in the 'Stoa Poikile' ('Painted Stoa'). And even at the Lyceum, the spirit of the *stoa* survived in the way Aristotle walked with his students as he talked – hence the name 'peripatetic' (literally 'walking about'), which was given to the tradition of philosophy he founded.

From Alexander to Athena

The most perfect architectural gem of one of the ancient world's most perfect cities was endowed in 334 BC by Alexander the Great. His present to Priene was made in gratitude to the goddess Athena for his first victories over the Persians.

" *King Alexander dedicated the temple to Athena Polias.* "

Above: Alexander's endowment of a temple to Athena may have had the appearance of piety, but the cult it really furthered was his own.

The young Alexander famously lamented the fact that his father, Philip II of Macedon, had not left him enough world to conquer. No sooner had he succeeded to the throne than he crossed the Dardanelles: hurling a spear into the Asian shore, he proclaimed the Persian Empire his. An almost laughably presumptuous claim, but it was Alexander's unique genius to make hyperbolic boasts – and then not just to deliver on them but to better them.

A POLITICAL CAMPAIGN
He started out unspectacularly: in May 334, on the banks of the River Granicus, his army outmanoeuvred a small advance force of Darius' men. By the standards of the glories to come, it was an insignificant victory, but Alexander was ready to milk it to the maximum. In the

ON PUBLIC DISPLAY

Shipped to London in the nineteenth century, this inscription is now on show in the British Museum.

Stiffed?

Did Alexander's munificence fall short of its flamboyant promise? Stylistic evidence suggests that parts of the temple were not completed till the second century BC. The obvious implication would be that Alexander's actual investment did not measure up to the generosity of his gesture. It seems that in ancient as in modern times, cost overruns in prestige projects were frequent, and for this particular temple no expense was spared.

Right: Priene was hit by a series of disasters in the centuries after its construction, yet even in its ruined state it is a spectacular site.

months that followed, he made his way through the old Greek colonies of western Anatolia, rooting out the Persian garrisons there, and taking pains to present himself as a Greek and a liberator.

He was, of course, a Macedonian; the son of a military strongman – and a dictatorial ruler in his own right. But he had enough awareness to see where his political advantage lay. He could certainly see the benefits of an involvement in the Ionian city of Priene, where what amounted to an ideal Greek city was being built.

A NEW PRIENE

Priene had been a seaport, but the estuary it was built on had silted up over centuries and the site had become increasingly unhealthy. It was therefore in the process of being rebuilt on a more elevated site some way inland, according to the self-consciously rational 'grid' system originally devised by the architect and town-planner Hippodamus of Miletus. Prior to this, the most famous 'Hippodamian City' had been Piraeus, the port of Athens, rebuilt on Pericles' orders after the Persian Wars. The renewal of the old; the affirmation of Greekness; the defiance of Persian power; the desire to associate himself with democratic Athens – all these things would have been in Alexander's mind when he made his endowment to the temple. Athena Polias ('Athena of the City') was not just the goddess of Athens but the goddess of the Greek polis,

the city-state and all it stood for. The new temple was to be built by Pytheos, famous for his work on the splendid tomb of King Mausolus – the original Mausoleum and later to be designated one of the Seven Wonders of the World. Pytheos was also distinguished as a pioneer of the Ionic order of columns – a feature of the Temple of Athena here.

The structure stood on a rocky terrace that raised it above the rest of the city, though its east–west orientation melded neatly with the overall grid-plan. Seen from outside, it was a masterpiece of symmetry; the interior was dominated by a half-

sized copy of Pheidas' famous cult-statue of Athena in the Parthenon. The original Athena Parthenos is believed to have been about 13m (42ft) tall, so Priene's would still have cut an impressive figure.

Alexander was, of course, to move on to greater things, but the Temple of Athena Polias at Priene remains a monument both to his military prowess and to his political acumen. Though the temple was flattened by an earthquake and further damaged by fire, the pieces have been partially reassembled: we can at least imagine the grace and beauty that used to be.

Roman Rededication

At some point during the reign of the Roman Emperor Augustus (27 BC–AD 14) the temple was rededicated, as an inscription upon an architrave (now fallen) clearly shows.

'The people dedicated this to Athena Polias and to the divine Augustus, son of God.'

'The people' may technically have had a choice, but they will certainly have known what was good for them in a region now very firmly under Roman rule.

The Parian Marble

From the island of Paros comes a remarkable slab of marble, inscribed with a chronological table covering more than a thousand years. Idiosyncratic in approach, it presents proven history alongside myth: in a spirit of playfulness, or of credulity?

So accustomed are we to hearing that the Greeks are our intellectual ancestors that it can come as a shock at times to be reminded how different they really were. One such jog comes from the so-called Parian Marble, now in the Ashmolean Museum in Oxford, England. Or, rather, mostly in the Ashmolean Museum: a chunk of the top was lost when it was brought back to Britain in the seventeenth century, while the bottom was discovered only in 1897. That remains in the museum on Paros, the Greek island where the marble was originally found, and after which it has been popularly named.

CHRONOLOGICAL CURIOSITIES
The inscription upon the marble is a chronological table, covering the whole of Greek history – up until the moment when it was carved, around 299 BC. While many of the dates given for key events confirm what is

Below: Greek history passes before us in procession in the chronology of the Parian Marble. But then, so too does all manner of myth and legend.

known from other sources (including Peisistratos' coup, in 561; the Battle of Marathon, in 490), some deal with episodes that are less well known. And some, the modern reader might think, are pretty much unknowable, yet are included along with the rest, apparently on equal terms. Deucalion's flood, for instance – the equivalent of Noah's biblical deluge in the Greek myths – is dated

precisely to 1529 BC. Meanwhile, the invention of the flute is confidently pinpointed to an exact year, 1500. Also mentioned is the invasion of Attica by the Amazon warrior-women, in 1255; and the War of Troy, fought – apparently – from 1218 to 1209.

Opposite: One of the first Greek artefacts ever to be acquired by a collector, the Parian Marble remains one of the oddest.

The Antiquarians

The Parian Marble was bought in Smyrna, Turkey, by an agent of the English antiquarian Thomas Howard, the Earl of Arundel. Howard was famous – or notorious – for what at that time seemed an eccentric passion. He had a large collection of classical stones, largely statuary, which became known as the Arundel Marbles. Brought back to London in 1627, the Parian Marble appears to have been the first ancient Greek inscription ever seen in England. Howard's friend, the lawyer John Selden, a scholar celebrated for his genius as a linguist, produced a full translation (including, fortunately, the top section, which has since been lost). It was another amateur scholar, John Evelyn (famous today for the liveliness of his diaries), who, in 1667, persuaded Howard's grandson to donate the Parian Marble to Oxford's Ashmolean Museum.

ON PUBLIC DISPLAY

The Parian Marble has been in Oxford since 1667, and is one of the greatest treasures of the Ashmolean Museum.

" *1582 Cecrops I is King in Athens.*

1521 King Hellen I of Phtiosis gives the name Hellenes to the Greek people and inaugurates the Panathenaian Games.

1500 Hyagnis, father of Marsyas, invented the flute...

1259 Theseus became King of Athens and brought the 12 townships into one, giving them government and democracy...

1218 The Trojan War begins...

1209 The Fall of Troy...

c. 790 Archias, son of Eagetus, the tenth in line of descent from Temenus, led a party of colonists from Corinth to found Syracuse...when Aeschylus, King of Athens, was in the 21st year of his reign...

683 The annual archonship [office of chief magistrate] was set up...

644 Terpander of Lesbos,

son of Derdenes, found a new way of playing the lyre, and modified the old style. Dropides was archon of Athens...

604 Alyattes became King of Lycia...

581 The competition for the wreath was reintroduced at Delphi.

560 Peisistratos the Tyrant seized power in Athens.

490 The Athenians fought the Persians at Marathon...and won the battle. "

Delphic Delusions?

The oracle at Delphi was famous for being cryptic, but not for being economical with the truth. In 279 BC, however, when Brennos and his Celts sacked the celebrated shrine, the general reaction seems to have been one of complete denial.

Delphi is in central Greece, just to the north of the Gulf of Corinth. To the Greeks, it was therefore the centre of the world. A symbolically shaped stone here was regarded as the *omphalos*, the navel of the earth. From beneath it came the pronouncements of the Pythia. People flocked from far and wide to seek her prophetic counsel. At certain times of year, she descended into a natural underground chamber. Those who came to consult the oracle heard her cryptic utterances echoing up through a cleft in the rocks as if from the earth itself.

THE SHAMAN'S TRANCE

The Pythia was priestess at Delphi's Temple of Apollo, but she may well have represented an earlier tradition. Several scholars have pointed out that the rituals surrounding her prophetic utterances bear a striking resemblance to those of shamanistic religions. Now most often associated with 'primitive' tribes in Central Asia and the Americas, shamanism was once widely spread. The shamans (often women) take spiritual flight, during which they can speak with the ancestors and other spirits and bring back messages for their communities.

They make these journeys in a state of trance, to a frenzied backing of chanting and drumming. Their euphoria is frequently helped on by 'entheogenic' drugs. In Siberia, for example, the *Amanita muscaria* (fly agaric) toadstool is typically used; Navaho shamans used the peyote cactus. It has been suggested that emanations from the mineral springs beneath the Pythia's underground chamber may have had a comparable psychoactive effect.

IN DENIAL

But where did the Pythia's euphoria end and the delusions of Greece as a whole begin? In the third century BC, under the leadership of Brennos, a huge army swept down through Thrace into the peninsula of Greece. Most historians agree that this force sacked the shrine at Delphi. Among the Greeks themselves, though, we find only denial. The gods intervened to save the sacred place, say inscriptions like the one put up in thanks by the grateful citizens of Cos.

It is hard to know what really happened. The ancient testimony is contradictory, and subsequent seismic activity in the region has left the archeological record in disarray. It is hard to resist the suspicion, though, that history was rewritten here. The impulse is understandable: Greece as a whole was genuinely delivered from the Celtic invader, so it must have made irresistible symbolic sense to say that the shrine at Delphi, this most ancient of religious sites, had also been saved.

Off the Record

No inscriptions survive to give the Celtic side of this or any other story. They are believed to have had a religious taboo against writing. Their art testifies to the sophistication of their culture (as do the oral epics collected by monks in the Christian era), but in the written record of their time they have been condemned to play the barbarians' part. A Greek culture so complacent in seeing Delphi as the navel of the world was hardly going to exert itself to find the civilized side of the warlike Celts. Neither did the Romans, whose capital had been sacked by a Celtic warband in 391 BC and who found themselves fighting Celtic tribes in their campaigns across western Europe.

Left: Little now remains of Delphi's Temple of Apollo but, set high up on a steep mountainside, the site still has a very special atmosphere.

> 66 *Of the barbarians who launched an invasion of Greece and attacked the Shrine at Delphi, we hear that those who attacked the Temple were punished both by the gods and the men of that place, who came to save the Shrine when they realized that it was under assault. The Temple has been saved and decorated with the captured weapons of its attackers, the rest having been destroyed in further fighting with the Greeks. This is to show the rejoicing of the people at this great victory and the sacrifices they have offered to the god in thanks for his intervention in saving the Temple, its precincts and indeed the whole of Greece.* 99

Above: Delphi was sacred to all the Greeks, so it was only natural that the citizens of Cos should want to show their gratitude to the god Apollo for delivering his city.

ON PUBLIC DISPLAY

This inscription is still to be seen in the ruined Temple of Apollo and Asclepius in Cos.

The Phoenicians and the Etruscans

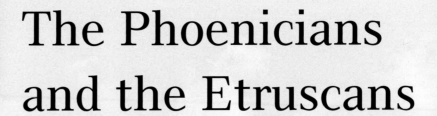

Ancient societies were often almost obsessive in their record-keeping: armies of scribes maintained careful track of everything. The result is that we now know far more than we might ever have imagined about the most obscure details of the Egyptian ritual calendar, Greek law and Roman fiscal administration. It can come as something of a surprise, therefore, to be reminded that there are also ancient cultures about which next to nothing is known for sure.

The 'Sea Peoples' (*see pp 58–59*), for example, flit in and out of ancient history, making their mark from Mycenae to the coast of Egypt. Yet we have no real idea who they were. Bloodthirsty raiders of some sort, clearly: the general consensus has been that they played a wholly destructive part in the dramas of antiquity. In the absence of evidence, though, just what should we believe?

Left: Tyre, in present-day Lebanon, was a thriving port in classical and Byzantine times, but it earned its place in history long before as a home of the mysterious Phoenicians.

WHAT OF THE CELTS, for half a millennium a decisive influence on the affairs of Europe and beyond? Their warrior elite extended their cultural influence outward from Alpine Europe from the sixth century BC. Sumptuous treasures testify to their craftsmanship, their joy in beauty, whilst the epics later written down by Irish monks make clear that lack of literacy need be no obstacle to poetry. But the Celts had a religious taboo against writing, which means that we never get to hear from them 'in their own words'. Rather, we have the testimony of a series of more or less unsympathetic Greek and Roman commentators. At their most tolerant, these authorities gave the Celts credit for a sort of wild nobility; often, though, they put them down as mere savages. It is surely reasonable to suggest that, had the Celts themselves told their own story, posterity might now view them differently.

MERCHANT ADVENTURERS

If the identity of the 'Sea Peoples' (*see pp. 58–59*) is lost in time, we do at least know something of another sea people: the Phoenicians. From about the middle of the second millennium BC, these merchant-mariners set out from the ports of Tyre and Sidon and other ports along the coast of Lebanon, to trade up and down the Mediterranean and beyond. They were clearly of Semitic origin: their language, though by no means entirely understood, shows unmistakable signs of kinship with Canaanite and early Hebrew. But just who they were – and even how far they saw themselves as a 'people' – is uncertain, despite the best efforts of archeologists and historians. The name 'Phoenicians' was given to them by the Greeks and early Romans with whom they traded; as used today, it is potentially misleading. It endows with a collective identity what may well have been disparate groups: though from roughly the same ethnic background and geographical area, they may have set out independently of one another.

Their sheer seamanship is easily forgotten: this was a time when ships and navigational techniques were far less sophisticated than they would become. At Tyre, the Phoenicians built what may well have been the world's first artificial harbour. They developed a way of rigging their ships to make way against the wind; and they learned to navigate at night by the stars.

The Greek historian Herodotus claims that, at the start of the sixth century BC, a Phoenician crew was commissioned by the Pharaoh Necho II to explore the waters of the Red Sea. Later, towards the middle of the fifth century BC, the Phoenician navigator, Hanno, is reported to have made his way through the Strait of Gibraltar and sailed down Africa's Atlantic coast.

ENTREPRENEURS TO ANTIQUITY

The Phoenicians sailed as traders, taking with them the famous purple dye of Tyre, sought after by royal elites throughout the ancient world, as well as cedar wood and special sand from their coast, much prized by the glassmakers of their day. But they were merchants first and last, content to act as middlemen dealing in others' products: they loaded up their ships with silks and spices, ivory and gemstones, finely worked bronze and beautiful ceramics, as well as less prestigious commodities such as wine, salt and dried fish.

To secure supplies of metals – gold, silver and tin – they travelled the length and breadth of the Mediterranean, establishing a long-term presence in Iberia. They also set up colonies in southern France (at Massilia, or Marseilles) and in Sicily, Sardinia and North Africa: the cities of Sabratha and Carthage both began as Phoenician bases.

Typically, the major colonies quickly went their own separate ways: they retained their Levantine cultural and religious traditions, but pursued political and economic agendas of their own. Situated not far from modern Tunis, Carthage was to become especially influential. Taking possession of key ports and parts of the hinterland around the western Mediterranean, it was eventually to find itself in conflict with the might of Rome.

THE ETRUSCAN ENIGMA

For the moment, though, the Phoenicians' contacts on the Italian mainland were harmonious enough. They appear to have had a good relationship with the Etruscans, for example. That is one of the comparatively few things we know for certain about one of Europe's most intriguing but elusive peoples. For a long time it was thought, indeed, that the Etruscans were actually immigrants from Asia themselves – so unaccountable were their origins, so clear the 'oriental' influences in their culture (*see pp. 164–165*). Their early history remains obscure, but most scholars

Left: Italy's Etruscans were among the most important trading-partners of the Phoenicians. They made this vase some time during the seventh century BC.

now assume that their civilization evolved out of the indigenous Villanovan culture (*see pp. 162–163*), which flourished in Italy in the eighth century BC, and that the eastern influences were imported over subsequent centuries of trade.

The Etruscan heartland lay in Etruria, a region to the north of Rome corresponding very roughly with the Tuscany of today. There was rich and fertile soil here, abundant rainfall and plenty of warm sunshine, making the conditions extremely favourable for agriculture. Cereals, olives, grapes and hazelnuts all grew well. Of especial interest to the Phoenicians, though, were the area's mineral reserves: these were immense, with important seams of tin, lead, copper, silver and iron ore. There were further reserves of iron ore on the island of Elba, a little way offshore in the Tyrrhenian Sea. The thick forests that clothed Etruria's hills also provided a ready supply of wood, vital as fuel for the smelting of these metals.

ETRUSCAN WEALTH

The Etruscan elite grew very wealthy – as the treasures of their splendid tombs so clearly testify. They carried out a flourishing trade with the other peoples of central Italy. They also extended their sphere of influence steadily southwards, as far as the modern region of Campania. Yet it is misleading to talk of the Etruscans as a single power, or as conscious empire-builders: to begin with, they were – like the Greeks – no more than a group of separate city-states, sharing cultural traditions but pursuing their own separate political and economic goals.

It was not until about 600 BC, so the later Roman chroniclers tell us, that some sort of overarching Etruscan state structure emerged with the formation of the League of the Twelve Cities. This was part political, part religious in conception. It held annual gatherings at which the princes or kings of the different cities came together to conduct ritual observances and hold discussions as

to the direction of the alliance in the year to come.

As the Etruscans' area of control expanded, they came first into contact, then into conflict with the Greeks, who had colonies around Italy's southern coasts. The Greeks called the Etruscans the *Tyrrhenoi* ('Pirates') – a blatant slander born of envy and of rivalry. They were scandalized too by the way the Etruscans allowed their women to attend their feasts; to recline beside them on their dining couches and to eat, drink and dance with them. Etruscan women were often highly educated and independent-minded; many owned property and took a leading role in public life.

But the Greeks were not too proud to trade with the Etruscans – at least, at first. There is even evidence that Greek potters, goldsmiths and other artisans set up shop in Etruscan towns, where they influenced the work of native craftsmen. The Etruscans' taste for Greek luxury goods was unabashed; they also adopted the Greek alphabet for writing down their own script. To this day, scholars seeking to study Etruscan texts find themselves in the paradoxical position of being able to read every word whilst for the most part being unable to fathom what they mean.

The Etruscans were no mean artists or artisans themselves. The wall-paintings in their tombs are

Above: The Phoenicians developed their own elegant and, crucially, alphabetical script, as seen in this inscription from the Sanctuary of Jupiter Ammon, in Tripoli.

among antiquity's most stunning masterpieces. Their black Bucchero ceramics and beautiful bronzes – cast or engraved – were exported all around the Mediterranean. As time went on, the Etruscans grew in confidence and their cultural 'cringe' before the Greeks gave way to mere respect, and eventually to open defiance and hostility. In about 540 BC, the League of the Twelve Cities agreed a military alliance with the Phoenicians to keep the Greek colonists out of Corsica. Though this was initially successful, the Twelve Cities sustained a body-blow in 510 BC when the Romans overthrew the Etruscan ruler of their city. And then, in 474 BC, a Greek fleet led by Hieron of Syracuse smashed the Etruscan navy off the Campanian coast.

The period that followed saw the expansion of Rome and the establishment of its hegemony across Italy. The Etruscan cities were conquered, their physical infrastructure obliterated, their cultural identity erased. This highly sophisticated people endured in the historical record as no more than a gang of tyrants that had to be toppled for Republican Rome to achieve its destiny.

Alphabetical Adventurers

The Phoenicians were not the first people to develop an alphabetical script. Even so, their achievement is of special interest. These merchant-adventurers' most important export was their way of writing which opened the door to literacy for the modern West.

> *Aleph...*
> *Beth...*
> *Gimel...*
> *Daleth...*
> *He...*
> *Waw...*
> *Zayin...*
> *Heth...*
> *Teth...*
> *Yod...*
> *Kaph...*
>
> *Lamed...*
> *Mem...*
> *Nun...*
> *Samekh...*
> *Ayin...*
> *Pe...*
> *Sade...*
> *Qoph...*
> *Res...*
> *Sin...*
> *Taw...*

Right: The people of Ugarit appear to have devised their alphabet before the Phoenicians did – but they did not have the Phoenicians' contacts in the West.

ON PUBLIC DISPLAY

Examples of the Ugarit alphabet are to be seen, along with other treasures from the Ugarit site, at the National Museum in Damascus, Syria.

They travelled to the four corners of the ancient Mediterranean, and perhaps well beyond; they established thriving colonies in North Africa, Sicily and Spain. Too little is still known of their cultural achievements, considerable as these surely were, and much about their civilization remains a mystery. Every day in modern life, however, we keep alive one crucial innovation of the Phoenicians: the alphabet that enables us to read and write.

ORIGINATING THE ALPHABET
Theirs was not the first alphabet, of course: there had arguably been an alphabetical element in Egyptian hieroglyphics since early in the third millennium BC, certain symbols standing consistently for certain sounds.

The Egyptians never made the jump to a wholly alphabetically based system, however – why would they need to, when their hieroglyphic system served them so well for a set of clerical needs that had changed very little over many centuries?

It was not until the middle of the second millennium that the people of Ugarit developed what scholars believe to have been the first true alphabet (*see pp. 20–21*). The

Phoenicians' came a little later, but by the beginning of the first millennium BC their script was in use throughout their Mediterranean trading empire.

THE SAME...YET DIFFERENT

This was the alphabet that was adopted and adapted by the Greeks, providing the foundation for subsequent Western scripts. Thus, it helped bring about the emergence of what we now call Western civilization. And though the signs may seem very different, with letter-names like Beth, Daleth, Kaph, and so forth, we are in a familiar phonetic territory with Phoenician script.

Some of the apparent similarities are actually deceptive: Aleph, though recognizably the ancestor of the Greek Alpha or the Latin letter A, was at this stage actually no more than a glottal stop. In fact, the Phoenician alphabet had no vowels: it presumably functioned rather like modern-day 'txt msgng', the writing more a mnemonic reminder of meaning than a fully explicit setting-out of meaning. It is a system that does have drawbacks, with obvious potential for ambiguity or lack of clarity.

COMMERCE

However, such brevity does also have advantages. It certainly offers far more flexibility than any pictographic script. It is no coincidence that, like the alphabet of Ugarit, the Phoenician alphabet was developed by a people engaged in maritime commerce. Forever on the move, they were constantly trading with and employing people whose understanding of their language was only partial: they had to have a quick and easy way of writing things down.

COMMUNICATION

Commerce was key to the dissemination of this alphabet, and, by the same token, to its ultimate endurance. Just as a language lives by being spoken and heard, an alphabet can endure only in so far as it is written down. Nothing made this script intrinsically superior in any obvious way to that of Ugarit – indeed, many scholars suspect that both may have evolved from a single proto-Canaanite alphabet that has now been lost.

But, transmitted as it was across the Phoenicians' trading network, this particular script was broadcast far and wide and taken up enthusiastically by other peoples in the region, including the Etruscans and the Greeks.

Whilst the former were destined for the same historical near oblivion as the Phoenicians themselves, the Greeks laid the foundations for the intellectual and cultural history of the West – and could not have done so without the alphabet.

Right: Far more flexible and easy to use than any pictogram-based system, the alphabet was an inestimable advance in human culture. It was through the Phoenician version that the idea was introduced to the West.

Born to the Purple

The identity of the Phoenicians remains obscure – or, rather, what marked them out as a people. Ethnically and linguistically, they were clearly Canaanites, from coastal Lebanon. What is less well understood is how they came to strike out as seafarers, to a large extent turning their backs on their Levantine origins. We know them today under the name by which they became known to the wider world – as the Punici (Latin) or Phoinikes (Greek), the Purple People. Of all the rich commodities they brought with them to foreign ports – including gold, ivory, ceramics, cedar wood and spices – none was more sought after than the rich purple dye, traditionally manufactured in their home port of Tyre. This natural pigment was secreted by a shellfish – the *Murex brandaris* – and it produced fine fabrics of a deep and lustrous purple hue.

153

King Kilamuwa

Discovered at Zinjirli, southeastern Turkey, in 1902, was the palace of Kilamuwa, the Phoenician king of Ya'diya or Sam'al. At the entrance, he stands in carved relief alongside a funerary inscription in which he hails his own achievements – at his ancestors' expense.

Left: Though generally associated with the Egyptians, sphinxes (often winged) are a feature of Phoenician art, as they were of earlier Canaanite cultures in the Middle East.

Vaunting arrogance and touching pathos come together in the Inscription of Kilamuwa: he himself has a regal bearing but a faintly worried air. With his right hand, he points commandingly to the insignia of key Canaanite gods, but his left hangs down and holds a drooping lotus blossom. The sad flower, whether cut or wilting, was the recognized symbol of royal death, in several ancient cultures, including the Semitic ones.

A COLLECTION OF COLONIES

For all its boastful tone, the accompanying inscription gives us a revealing insight into the realities of kingship in Phoenician-ruled Cilicia in the ninth century BC. Despite the unifying label placed upon them by history, and despite a common cultural and linguistic inheritance, the 'Phoenicians' were never actually a single people. Starting out from separate cities, most notably Tyre and Sidon, they struck out on their own account on trading and colonizing ventures; in their turn, these colonies went their own way.

Carthage is by far the most famous of these, but other states were set up much closer to home amidst the ruins of what had been the Hittite Empire. Kilamuwa's kingdom of Ya'diya was just one of these 'Syro-Hittite' states: aggressive competitors, they vied with one another economically and – as Kilamuwa testifies – on the field of battle.

A Different Perspective

To hear Kilamuwa tell it, the king of Ya'diya had simply to snap his fingers and the Assyrians came meekly to do his bidding. Since Assyria in the ninth century BC was a superpower in the Middle East, it is no surprise to find that the episode was remembered rather differently in Kalhu. If, that is, it was remembered at all: Shalmaneser III's inscription makes no mention at all of Kilamuwa. What he does claim, in his account of his eleventh year (848), is that:

'Rimmon-idri of Damascus and twelve of the Kings of the Hittites with one another's forces strengthened themselves. A destruction of them I made.'

It may well be that the Danunian threat to Ya'diya gave the Assyrian king a convenient pretext for an attack on the Danunian state.

Azitawadd of Adana

'May the name of Azitawadd stand out eternally, like those of the sun and of the moon,' reads the royal inscription in the city of Karatepe in the Taurus Mountains. Another Canaanite, the King of the Danunians, had established himself in this far southeastern corner of the Anatolian peninsula about a century before Kilamuwa came to power in Ya'diya, in the mountains to the north. The capital, Karatepe, was itself in the hills, but Adana was for the most part a lowland kingdom, a convenient corridor for trade between Anatolia and the heartlands of Canaan. It is hardly to be wondered at that so strategically sited a state should have grown so strong in economic and military power, or that it should have presented Kilamuwa with his stiffest challenge.

> **"** I am Kilamuwa,
> the son of King Haya.
> King Gabar reigned over Ya'diya
> but achieved nothing.
> Then came Bamah, and he
> achieved nothing.
> My own father, Haya', did nothing
> with his reign.
> My brother, Sha'il, also did nothing.
> It was I, Kilamuwa…who managed
> to do what none of my ancestors had.
> My father's kingdom was beset by
> powerful, predatory kings, all holding
> out their hands, demanding to be fed.
> But I raged amongst them like a fire,
> burning their beards and consuming
> their outstretched hands.
> Only the Danunian kings
> overmastered me; I had to call on
> the King of Assyria to assist me…
> I, Kilamuwa, the son of Haya',
> ascended my father's throne.
> Under their previous kings, the
> [people] had howled like dogs,
> But I was a father, a mother and a
> brother to them.
> I gave gold, silver and cattle to men who had never so much
> as seen the face of a sheep before.
> Those who had never even seen linen all their lives I clothed
> in byssus-cloth from head to foot.
> I took the [people] by the hand and in their souls they
> looked to me just as the orphan looks to his mother.
>
> Whoever of my sons comes after me and interferes with this inscription, may he be
> dishonoured among the people…
> And if anyone should damage this inscription,
> Let Gabar's god Ba'al-Samad destroy his head,
> And let Bamah's god Ba'al-Hamon destroy his head… **"**

Above: The Kilamuwa Stela makes clear the majesty of the colonial kingdoms founded by the Phoenicians in the Near East, in what had until recently been Hittite territory.

ON PUBLIC DISPLAY

The Kilamuwa Stela is now to be seen in Berlin, in the Vorderasiatisches Museum.

A Street in Carthage

Carthage was a blasted site for so many centuries that its history as a busy, bustling city is easily forgotten. An inscription records the dedication of the street amidst whose ruins was found a poignant reminder of this living past.

Above: The Carthaginians were the descendants of the first Phoenician traders – hence the name the Romans gave them, Punici. Hence too their use of the Phoenician alphabet, which was modified only slightly over time.

ON PUBLIC DISPLAY

Many other fascinating artefacts like this one may be seen at the National Archeological Museum of Carthage, Tunis.

> " *This street in the direction of the square before the new gate in the southern wall of the city was built and opened by the people of Carthage in the year of the Suffetecy of Shafat and Adonibaal and of the magistracy of Adonibaal, son of Eshmunkhilletz…Abdmelqart…Bodmelqart, son of Baalhanno, son of Bodmelqart was serving as chief highways engineer; Yehawwielon, his brother, saw to the quarrying of the stone. All the merchants, porters…of the city also contributed, both those without money and those with – the goldsmiths, potters, firers and sandalmakers. Anyone found defacing this inscription will be liable to a fine of 1000 silver shekels, plus 10 mina to pay for a new inscription.* "

*D*elenda est Carthago – 'Carthage must be destroyed!' The words of Cato the Elder to the Roman Senate have proved immortal. So conscientiously did the legions complete this task in 146 BC that they razed the city and its walls to their foundations.

It is hardly surprising: the Phoenician colony on the coast of North Africa was now the Mediterranean's most important maritime trader and naval power, but for centuries already Rome had considered it as its great rival and most important threat. Carthage's colonies around the southern coast of Italy had been an ever present menace to the power of Rome and its security.

WAR TO THE DEATH

Ultimately, there were three 'Punic Wars' (from the Latin *Punici*, 'Phoenicians'). In 264 BC, when it first went to war with Carthage, Rome had not been ready for naval conflict, its expansionist ambitions as yet confined to mainland Italy and its offshore islands. Indeed, to design its own fleet, it had to start from scratch, copying Carthaginian vessels. Some twenty-three years of strenuous conflict followed before Rome finally prevailed.

It had been most fortunate to survive the second war (218–202 BC), in which the brilliant young general Hannibal marched his army and its elephants up through Spain and over the Alps into Italy. He was defeated but only after many years and at great cost. And Carthage soon built up its power again. Hence the cry of Cato in 157 BC and hence the outbreak of the Third Punic War when, in 149 BC, a great Roman army invaded Africa.

THE PERFECT PORT

So strong has the Roman hold been on the modern imagination that Carthage's destruction has loomed far larger than its life. It was a colony founded by Phoenician traders from Tyre and Sidon, traditionally in 814 BC. By that time, the Phoenicians had already been trading through the Mediterranean for a century or more. They traded in everything, but had a special expertise in the minerals market, dealing in copper, tin, gold and silver. The site, just north of today's Tunis, offered access to the African interior; it was roughly at the halfway mark between the Phoenician home ports of Tyre and Sidon and the Spanish ore-fields. Its situation could hardly have been bettered: Carthage stood on a rocky outcrop between two perfect natural harbours, later to be connected by a canal. The perfect port, it was the perfect base for trading up and down the region and for building a successful economy.

CARTHAGINIAN CONSCIOUSNESS

It is this prosperous merchant city that is represented in an inscribed black limestone tablet found during excavations of its ruins. The dedication for a newly built street, it testifies to the energy and enterprise of third-century Carthage and the civic sense that inspired every class of artisan and tradesmen together for the common good. The *suffetes* it refers to were judges charged with the responsibilities of public administration, not unlike the consuls of contemporary Rome.

A Sinister Side

It is, of course, regrettable that the Romans' sacking of Carthage was so thorough in its vindictiveness. Much of inestimable value has been lost. We know comparatively little of the Phoenicians' culture – especially when compared with those of Greece and Rome – and finds like this tablet are always tantalizing in their incompleteness. In at least one respect, however, ignorance has been bliss. It was not until 1921 that the discovery of a special cemetery, the Tophet, confirmed ancient claims of child-sacrifice by the Carthaginians. Hundreds of infants were found, their throats apparently slit in rituals designed to appease the gods at times of crisis. Many more remains of this sort have since been found throughout the Phoenician world.

Above: The Romans razed Carthage. Now, 2000 years later, their own city lies in ruins.

Melqart of Malta

An inscription found in Malta, written in both Greek and Phoenician, opens a window onto one of the ancient world's least understood cultures and languages. Much remains mysterious about its origins and significance, but it is believed to date from the second century BC.

Found at Marsaxlokk, southeastern Malta, in 1697, the twin marble shafts into whose pedestals these words were carved were long assumed to be the stems of broken candelabra. Only more recently have scholars offered the view that these were *cippi*, ceremonial stands for the burning of funereal incense and other offerings. This suggestion seems far more convincing, though it cannot be definitive: the continuing confusion highlights the uncertainty still surrounding so many aspects of a Phoenician culture known to have extended across much of the Mediterranean region.

A TRADING NATION

This civilization was very much a maritime one, founded primarily on long-distance trade. The Phoenicians were a Semitic people who came from what is now Lebanon: Tyre and Sidon were their great home ports. They are known to have been trading in the eastern Mediterranean and the Aegean as long ago as the tenth century BC. By the ninth century, they had established trading colonies in North Africa. Carthage, the most famous of these, was traditionally founded in 814 BC. It quickly carved out an empire of its own. Soon it had supplanted the Levantine centres, creating its own colonies elsewhere in North Africa as well as in Corsica, Sicily, Sardinia, southern Spain – and Malta.

MYSTERIOUS MELQART

Melqart was, as the brothers' dedication suggests, a semi-legendary Lord of Tyre; his very name, *Milq Qart*, means 'King of the City'. The Greeks identified him with their hero-god Heracles: why they should have done so is unclear, since no stories of great exploits have survived, but the connection is consistently maintained in the ancient sources. Such apparent 'evidence' as we have for the identification tends to be of a circular sort: sculptors showed Melqart performing Herculean feats precisely because they associated him with the Greek hero. The similarity between the two may have been no more than that they were both mortal humans who were designated gods after their deaths – but even of this we cannot be sure in Melqart's case.

He appears to have been associated with the sun – but which Asiatic god was not? When he shook his head and hair, one story said, the rain showered down. Recent research in Carthage suggests that large-scale child-sacrifice was practised: was this carried out in Melqart's honour? For the moment, at least, we have far more questions than answers about this deity – and, for that matter, about the Phoenicians.

A Shrine for All Seasons

Above: There is little left to show for it now, but Astarte's Sanctuary at Marsaxlokk, Malta, was a major religious centre in ancient times.

Despite their explicit dedication to Melqart, the *cippi* were unearthed at Tas Silg, a hill above Marsaxlokk, celebrated for Astarte's ancient shrine. This Middle Eastern deity was the Phoenician equivalent of the Mesopotamian Ishtar, patroness of fertility, love and war. As such, she seems to have been the inspiration for the Greek goddess of love, and for the Roman Venus (whose planet had been sacred to Ishtar in Babylonian times). But it was with another Greek goddess, Hera, wife of Zeus, that she was identified here, as suggested by joint dedications from the third century BC onwards. Under Roman rule, the sanctuary passed to the proprietorship of Hera's Roman equivalent, Juno. Could it have been just a coincidence that, when a Christian church was built here in the fourth century AD, it was consecrated to another female figure, the Blessed Virgin Mary?

> " *To Melqart, our master and lord of Tyre, Abdesar and Aserkemor, his brother, the sons of Asirxehor, himself the son of Abdesar, made this solemn offering for heeding their prayer and giving them his blessing.* "

Above: It took time, patience – and much scholarly experience – to decipher the inscriptions of the cippi *in their rugged stone, but the effort paid off, yielding fascinating insights.*

ON PUBLIC DISPLAY

Of the two cippi, *one is now in the National Archeological Museum in Valletta; the other (Rohan-Polduc's gift to Louis) is in the Louvre.*

Spoils of War and Revolution

Found in 1697 at Marsaxlokk, the *cippi* came into the possession of the Rohan-Polduc family, entrusted with the rule of Malta by the French Crown. In 1780, Emmanuel de Rohan-Polduc gave one as a gift to King Louis XVI – just a few years before the French Revolution brought him down. Rohan-Polduc's first loyalty was not to France, however; he was attempting to re-establish the rule of the Knights of St John of Malta, the soldier-priests headquartered here since the Crusades. This stance was frankly quixotic, given the steep decline of the Ottoman Empire on the one hand and the rise of revolution and modern power politics on the other. The island was taken first by France and then by Britain, under whose 'protection' it was to remain until the 1960s. Even so, the *cippi* survived.

Etruscan Earth Goddess

A simple strip of bronze found in a sanctuary near Orvieto bears the name of a little-known Etruscan goddess. Could she be the same deity as is depicted in an extraordinary statue known (inevitably but, perhaps, misleadingly) as the 'Venus of Cannicella'?

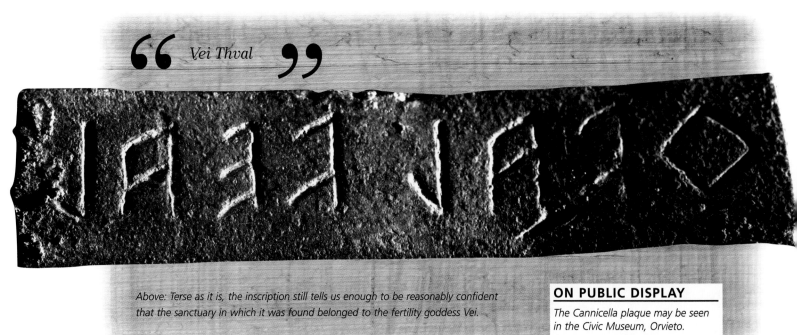

" *Vei Thval* "

Above: Terse as it is, the inscription still tells us enough to be reasonably confident that the sanctuary in which it was found belonged to the fertility goddess Vei.

ON PUBLIC DISPLAY

The Cannicella plaque may be seen in the Civic Museum, Orvieto.

This plaque was found in what had clearly been a temple in the ancient necropolis at Cannicella, outside Orvieto, at the heart of the area once occupied by the Etruscans. Even now, we are a very long way from any extensive understanding of Etruscan, but it seems safe to assume that this bronze-foil plaque represents a dedication to the goddess Vei. What goes for the Etruscan language holds too for Etruscan culture: not much is known of this particular deity. A statue found in the same sanctuary may shed some light – though, out here at the very limits of our modern archeological understanding, any attempt to solve the mysteries must be made with caution.

OUT OF THE ORDINARY
A large – though not life-sized – female figure, this statue stands out in several ways, certainly by the standards of Etruscan art. It is unusual, if not unique, in representing a nude woman; almost as odd, though, is its execution in marble. There are few precedents for this: Etruscan craftsmen seldom worked in this unyielding stone. Some scholars believe the figure must have been imported from Greece – or, more likely, from one of southern Italy's Greek colonies. Stranger still, two distinct marbles have been used: the breasts in particular appear to have been made separately and

Death and Fertility

On the face of it, a cemetery seems an odd place to find a statue representing a fertility goddess. What could be farther from new life than death? In the cyclical terms in which the ancients saw these things, however, the connection was a close one – much like death and resurrection in the Christian scheme. Egypt's Osiris, god of the underworld, was god of fertility as well: 'Osiris beds' – special human-shaped frames filled with earth and containing seeds – were placed in Pharaonic tombs to suggest the idea of subsequent rebirth. Demeter, meanwhile, was connected with the underworld by the loss of her daughter, allowed to return to the world above for just half of the year. For the ancients, the planting of the seed in the earth was analogous to the burial of the body: both, it was hoped, would burst forth in new life after the dark and chill of winter.

added to the finished figure (one breast, indeed, was lost and has never been found).

WHAT MANNER OF WOMAN?

As a nude female figure, the statue was promptly named the 'Venus of Cannicella' on its discovery in 1884, but this label may well be a misleading one. The nearest equivalent to the Greco-Roman goddess Aphrodite/Venus in the Etruscan pantheon was called Turan (literally, 'the mistress' or 'ruler', in reference to the compelling power of erotic love), though she was generally represented with the wings of a swan.

Besides, there are reasons to think that the 'Cannicella Venus' is not all that she seems. For a start, there is reason to believe that the statue may originally have represented a man – hence the later addition of the breasts. Her long-legged, snake-hipped appearance may conform to modern criteria of 'size-zero' beauty, but may yet be further evidence that the statue has changed its sex. Why should this be?

Did a hard-pressed sculptor simply find himself short of one female figure, or was there some ritual reason for his choice? It does not seem that the intention was to create an androgynous figure. On the contrary, the statue's gender is made explicit by a grooved incision suggesting the labia. This would have been unusual in any figure, Greek or Etruscan, when this statue was carved in the late sixth century BC – a case of overkill, of a sculptor 'protesting too much'?

The way the statue stands certainly suggests that she is designed to play the erotic, 'Venus' role, however. While one arm has gone altogether and the other is half-missing, the indications are that she once stood in what art-historians call the 'pudica pose'. That is, with one hand coyly concealing her genital area and the other across her breasts in a way that actually drew attention to these zones.

VENUS OR VEI?

But the presence of the plaque – and the funereal context in which

the figure was found, in a shrine in a cemetery – arguably hints at a darker, more complex role for this strange statue. Vei, a version of Demeter, Greek goddess of the earth, crops and fertility, stood for sex as procreation rather than as erotic play. She saw women through pregnancy and childbirth: at other Etruscan shrines, archeologists have found ceramic offerings in the stylized shape of deflated wombs, inscribed with the name 'Vei'.

The evidence is inconclusive: other ancient cultures endowed their fertility goddesses with buxom curves and 'childbearing hips' – very different from those of the 'Venus of Cannicella'. On the other hand, the context in which this figure was found – not to mention the inscription – suggests that this was indeed the goddess Vei.

Below: The Etruscans appear to have regarded the hereafter as, literally, a continuation of the here and now. Hence the efforts they made to make the dead feel 'at home' – even to the extent of building house-shaped tombs.

Etruscan Ashes

The overarching irony of Etruscan archeology is that Italy's first advanced civilization lives most enduringly in a rich and exotic funerary culture. Discovered inside an elaborate tomb, a beautifully inscribed urn sheds at least a glimmer of light on the Etruscan way of death.

I t is not, of course, unusual for ancient peoples to be known to archeologists primarily through their burial sites, but with the Etruscans the discrepancy is especially striking. Little is known of their life and culture except what may be viewed through the prism of death. Their (presumably) wood-built cities have vanished virtually without trace, their sites covered over by later urban developments or ploughed up over centuries of agriculture; only their cemeteries have survived.

PHANTOM CITIES
But what cemeteries! The Etruscan graveyard could with justification be called a necropolis – literally, a 'city of the dead'. The logic can hardly be faulted: the Etruscans expected to spend far longer in their tombs than in their homes, so they made them magnificent and lasting. The necropolises at Tarquinia and Cerveteri had

hundreds of round turf-topped dwellings cut out of the soft tufa rock for the departed, laid out in streets as in any city of the living. Once, presumably, these burial grounds served neighbouring urban centres, but those living cities have now been lost.

Each 'house' had its own carved doors and windows and its interior was laid out like any home, with

> *I am the urn of Larth Calisna Sepu and his wife Cursni.*

Right: Their ashes mingled in a single urn, a noble couple embark on the afterlife. The Etruscans enjoyed equal, companionate marriages by ancient standards, to an extent that scandalized the Greeks and Romans.

ON PUBLIC DISPLAY

The urn from the Calisna Sepu Tomb takes pride of place in the Archeological Museum in Colle di Val d'Elsa, Tuscany.

carved couches and other furnishings: those of the most important magnates had sumptuous wall-paintings showing hunting, sporting or banqueting scenes. Often the dead themselves were represented, whether in wall-paintings or sculpted in stone or ceramic. Typically they were shown reclining on couches as though the hereafter were a never-ending feast, at which – in death as, apparently, in life – Etruscan women associated freely with men. One of the most famous Etruscan artefacts, found at Cerveteri, is the stunning terracotta sarcophagus in which a married couple were interred. Their coffin forms the couch on which the beautifully modelled figures of man and wife recline together as though at a convivial feast with their family and friends.

AN IMPORTANT FAMILY

The grandest tombs, which are naturally the best-known today, were the resting-places of the rich, of course. Those further down the social scale had more modest huts of stone, while many must have had no tombs at all. In the northern part of Etruria, meanwhile, where the native rock was less forgiving, imposing tombs could be built for the elite only. One such was discovered at Malacena,

outside Monteriggioni, in 1893. Here a regular, rectangular chamber has been dug out of the rock, its roof supported by a central column. Stone slabs construct an imposing external porch, or 'dromos', allowing for entry to the tomb. It was found packed with treasures, including many luxuries of Greek manufacture and ceramics decorated with a distinctive blue-black glaze now known as 'Malacena'. A number of ornate urns were also found: the inscription on the most magnificent of these revealed that this was the tomb of the important Calisna Sepu family, which appears to have flourished some time between the sixth and fourth centuries BC.

Above: Outdoor scenes bedeck the wall of an Etruscan tomb: the wealthy went to their rest in sumptuous luxury in what amounted to mansions of the dead.

Vanished Villanova

Greek colonists who arrived on the western coast of Italy in the eighth century BC found a prosperous civilization already well established. As was the Greek way, they dismissed these indigenous Italians as savage pirates, but they needed their mineral resources (including tin, copper, lead, silver and iron). Enriched by their trade with the outsiders, a rich Iron Age culture quickly developed, now known as 'Villanovan', from the site where archeologists first identified it in the nineteenth century. Along with mining, agriculture prospered: soils were rich here, and the climate favourable, and by the sixth century a distinct Etruscan civilization had emerged. Despite the hostility of the Greeks, the Etruscans were evidently enamoured of Greek luxuries – and also of the items brought in by Greek traders from centres farther afield in Asia Minor. Hence the enormous artistic variety of the finds made in Etruscan tombs – and hence too the tales of the Estruscans' 'oriental' origins.

When in Rome...

...do as the Etruscans do. The Roman achievement was largely built on Etruscan foundations. Literally, in the case of the 'Cloaca Maxima', the great sewer-cum-drain that made the boggy Tiber Valley habitable. This crucial construction was undertaken by the Etruscans, around 600 BC. As the city that sprang up here expanded, signs of earlier Etruscan settlement were obliterated, even as the rising Roman culture did its best to brand the Etruscans as tyrannous and barbaric. In fact, the Romans adopted many Etruscan customs and institutions, from architectural techniques to religious rites and social practices (like the use of couches for dining). But since the Etruscans' written language has remained, to all intents and purposes, indecipherable, history has, quite literally, been written by the victors.

The Pyrgi Plaques

Beautiful yet baffling, these golden tablets communicate their meaning because their text is inscribed not only in Etruscan but also in Phoenician. Their message being short, however, they are no 'Rosetta Stone'; in fact, they provide few clues to how the Etruscan language works.

Found at Pyrgi, central Italy, in an excavation of 1964, these shimmering leaves of gold speak to us in spite of, rather than through, their Etruscan text. Scholars have just enough Etruscan to feel confident that, with the help of the Phoenician version, they have unlocked its sense – even though the two texts paraphrase rather than translate one another's meaning.

ON PUBLIC DISPLAY

The Pyrgi Plaques are among the many beautiful artefacts on show at the National Etruscan Museum, in the Villa Giulia, Rome.

> *To the Lady Uni-Astre/Astarte. This holy place was established and endowed by Tiberius Velanias, King of Caere. In the month of the Sun-sacrifice, as a gift to the temple, he added a little shrine. He did this in gratitude to the Lady Astarte, who with her own hand had raised him up to kingship and allowed him to rule three years…the statue of the goddess shall remain in place in the shrine as long as the stars stay in the heavens.*

Left: Intractable the text may be, but one message is unmistakable: the Pyrgi Plaques speak of stupendous wealth and luxury. Etruria was rich in resources, and the Etruscans traded with a range of different partners.

The Oriental Etruscans?

The Etruscans are the great outsiders of antiquity: scholars have struggled to assimilate them into any meaningful historical scheme; their linguistic impenetrability is only the most obvious aspect of a more general mystery.

Their culture seemed strikingly alien to the Greeks – and not just because they were mercantile, and ultimately military, competitors, a fact that must surely have helped to shape their perceptions. Ancient historians came up with elaborate theories for their origins, including invasions from Asia Minor in long-forgotten times. For a long time, modern scholars were persuaded by these explanations: how else to explain the exotica that turned up in excavations of Etruscan tombs? Ostrich eggs; ivory; jewellery and ornaments strangely fashioned from gold and silver – surely no Italians had made these things. Indeed, they had not – but only because these were imports brought to Etruria by the Phoenicians from the Middle East and from their North African colonies. One thing the Phoenicians do not seem to have brought the Etruscans, however, is their language: that mystery remains all the Etruscans' own.

ASIA IN ITALY

Of course, an inscription can reveal as much 'between the lines' as in its explicit content; the questions it prompts, moreover, may represent insights in themselves. The obvious question here is this: What was a king in Italy doing offering sacrifices, and dedicating a shrine, to an Asian deity? Astarte was the great Middle Eastern goddess of love and war, a part of Mesopotamian tradition for centuries. As the matriarch of the Phoenician pantheon, she had major shrines in Tyre and Sidon and her cult was also well established in Carthage. Cyprus and Cythera were important centres: it is no accident that both these islands should subsequently have laid claim to being the birthplace of the Greco-Roman love goddess Aphrodite/Venus.

That Astarte should have had a following in Italy seems strange from a modern perspective in which Italy's essential 'Europeanness' seems utterly stable and definitive. This is largely because, in modern times, history has been viewed from a strongly Eurocentric point of view.

That Eurocentrism has been many centuries in the making; it would not have made much sense to the Greeks or Romans – and would have been still less adequate to describe ancient times. Then the Mediterranean was at once the heart and the highway of the world – as the Phoenician inscription on the Pyrgi Tablets reminds us.

ALLIES

At the time when the tablets were made, around 500 BC, Pyrgi was a port serving Caere, the Etruscan antecedent to the city now known as Cerveteri. What could have been more natural than that it would have been included among the ports of call of the Phoenicians, whose trading vessels plied back and forth across the Mediterranean from Tyre and Sidon to Spain? There were Phoenician centres not far away in Malta, Sardinia and Sicily; and, of course, a Neo-Phoenician capital across the sea at Carthage. By the sixth century BC, the Etruscans had actually formed an alliance with the Carthaginians to resist Greek colonization in the central parts of Italy.

Above: The Etruscans were accomplished craftsmen, with a specialization in beautiful bronze-work. They imported techniques and styles as eagerly as they did actual artefacts from the Middle East. So much so that scholars long suspected an Asiatic origin.

The Ficoroni Cista

Named after Francesco Ficoroni, the Italian connoisseur who came by this stunning objet d'art in the eighteenth century, the Ficoroni Cista belongs chronologically to the Roman Republic. It was, moreover, made in Rome: its creator's inscription (in Latin) could hardly be more clear. Why, then, do we hesitate to call this a work of 'Roman' art?

> *Novios Plutius made me in Rome.*
> *Dindia Macolnia gave me to her daughter.*

Right: Stunning as it is, the Ficoroni Cista's function is unclear. Whilst cistae of this sort have been found in a number of Etruscan tombs, we are no nearer working out what they were or why they were placed there.

ON PUBLIC DISPLAY

The cista is in the National Etruscan Museum in the Villa Giulia, Rome.

Chiefly because, artistically, it belongs in an Etruscan tradition: cistae had always been a feature of Etruscan tombs. Cylindrical vessels in bronze, with lids and feet, and generally with ornate handles and fine bronze chains (for lifting, presumably), they were evidently prestige items, often beautifully made.

Their function, however, remains unclear: they may have been used to hold luxuries, like ointments or cosmetics, for use by the deceased in the afterlife. That said, the Ficoroni Cista seems too big for such a purpose, standing 75cm (30in) tall. By this time, of course, it is possible that the cista may have been included mainly as a matter of ritual. This was one of several *cistae* found in the necropolis in Praeneste, southeast of Rome, in an area where Etruscan influences are known to have persisted well into Roman times.

IMMORTAL TWINS

Beautifully executed in the bronze of the *cista*'s drum are scenes from the expedition of Jason and the Argonauts, in search of the coveted Golden Fleece. Pollux's victory over the bullying centaur, Amycus, is also illustrated.

Pollux was celebrated in classical times as one of the twin sons of Leda. She was raped by Zeus, who took the form of a swan for this purpose, and Pollux was the product of this union. At the time of the rape, however, she had also been pregnant by Tyndaraeus: his son, Castor, grew up as Pollux's twin. Inseparable in life, they were parted when Castor died, but the gods took pity on the grief-stricken Pollux. Both youths were transformed into the two-star constellation that is still named after them, an ever present symbol of a love transcending death. Hence the popularity of the twins as a motif in funerary art. (By tradition, the twins sailed with Jason on the *Argo*, and Pollux's triumph over Amycus was another symbolic victory over death.)

If the *cista* form is Etruscan, its decorative theme is impeccably classical. It is believed that Plutius

Above: Etruria seemed to hanker after the alien and the exotic even when Roman rule appeared thoroughly established. It was here at Palestrina that the famous 'Nile Mosaic' was made around 100 BC.

modelled his picture of Pollux and Amycus on a painting by the Greek artist Micon. The Greek traveller Pausanias described seeing a picture strikingly similar in the Temple of Hephaestus, in Athens. But since no such picture has survived since Pausanias wrote his account in the second century AD, this must remain a matter of speculation.

At Home in the City of the Dead

The word 'necropolis' literally means 'city of the dead', but it commonly means no more than 'cemetery'. In the Etruscan case, though, it must be taken more literally. Stone-built tombs, boxlike in construction, were set out along little streets; inside, they had a strikingly domestic feel, enhanced in the most opulent examples by richly painted banqueting and other scenes. One famous tomb at Caere contains a sarcophagus on which sit figures of the couple who occupied it, husband and wife taking their ease together, their coffin a couch. The impression we have is of an afterlife lived pretty much along the lines of this one; hence the idea that the *cistae* might have held toiletries or similar items.

Artificial Offal: The 'Liver of Piacenza'

One of the oddest inscriptions to have survived from the Etruscan era has come down to us not on a stone wall or a golden plaque but on a lump of bronze carefully fashioned into the shape of a sheep's liver.

The 'Liver of Piacenza' is, as its name suggests, a liver – or at least a life-sized model of one in bronze. But while one side has the smooth and bulbous external contours of the organ, the other is largely flat, as though cut open. This surface has been meticulously divided up into separate fields or zones, each with the name of a different Etruscan god. Sixteen separate zones surround the edge of the liver. These may correspond to different sections of the sky. Of the twenty-

Indistinct Deities

Though the inscriptions on the Piacenza Liver are not especially unclear, Etruscan is still only very imperfectly understood. Two names scratched on to the outside, near the centre, are thought to be *usil*, or 'sun', and *tivr*, 'moon'. Among those deities who appear to be named on the open face are Selva (god of woodland and of boundaries), Fufluns (god of plants and of joy), Cilens (god of night), and Nethuns (the Roman Neptune).

Left: Few finds have seemed quite so astonishing as the 'Liver of Piacenza', an artefact which really makes very little sense in modern terms. Whilst experts agree that it was very likely a sort of training manual or teaching model for apprentice soothsayers, they have made little progress in explaining how it should be interpreted.

ON PUBLIC DISPLAY

This item is among the exhibits at the Municipal Museum of Piacenza.

Above: Nature loomed large in the consciousness of Etruscans. They believed that the hills and rivers had their own spirits. Despite their superficial similarities with Roman deities, the Etruscan gods and goddesses can be seen as clearly representing elemental forces, where their Roman equivalents were quasi-human characters.

four 'inner zones', some radiate out from the centre at the elongated end; others are more tightly grouped towards the wider end with its various protrusions.

'READING' THE ENTRAILS

No one in ancient times began a major undertaking without seeking a soothsayer's view on how propitious the times were for the venture they envisaged. In several cultures, and this obviously included the Etruscans, this necessitated the sacrifice of an animal and the consultation of its entrails. Sheep-livers were among the organs most widely used in the art of 'haruspicy' – the divination of the future through the study of animals' organs.

So any man about to marry, build a house, or even close a business deal; anybody anxious about the prognosis for a sick spouse or child or other relative; any farmer concerned about his harvest – anyone, in short, who had a need to know the future, would consult the haruspex, or priest.

The priest began by offering a sheep in sacrifice on that person's behalf. Having slaughtered the animal, he opened up the liver and scrutinized it carefully, checking the colour and texture – and, especially, the proportional size – of the different zones. The overall shape of the liver and its position in the body relative to the other organs may also have been considered; as, perhaps, were the relation of all these factors to the movements of the sun and stars.

The exact details remain obscure: there is no doubt, though, that on the basis of data derived from the liver, the priest felt able to offer his forecast for the outcome of events. The divinatory system used was analogous to those that followed the tracks of lightning-bolts or the paths of birds in the sky (a practice known as augury) – both techniques that were widely employed in ancient times.

HARUSPICY FOR BEGINNERS

While all this may explain why an Etruscan priest might have consulted the liver of a sacrificed sheep, it does not account for the existence of the bronze liver. The most obvious explanation, most modern scholars are agreed, is that it represented a manual for learners – a sort of haruspicy 'how-to guide'.

Out of the East?

The 'Liver of Piacenza' is not, in fact, as unusual as we might assume: artefacts resembling it have been found by archeologists in Babylonia – albeit of clay and of much earlier date. A variety of ancient sources testify to the popularity of the practice of haruspicy in Mesopotamia, the Hittite Empire and elsewhere in the early Middle East. Some scholars believe this to indicate that the Etruscans themselves originally emerged from Asia.

An Etruscan Estate

The so-called Tabula Cortonensis is one of the longest and fullest Etruscan documents discovered, a legal agreement governing the transfer of an estate from one family to another. It is believed to have been drawn up some time around 200 BC.

Left: Etruria was blessed by the gods, fertile farmland with favourable climatic conditions: a well-managed holding here was a very valuable property.

Discovered outside Cortona, Umbria, in 1992, the so-called Tabula Cortonensis is a bronze plaque, originally about 50cm (20in) high and 30cm (12 in) across. A relatively heavy and substantial sheet of metal, some 3mm (⅒in) thick, it was found in pieces. It may have been cut up for the bronze to be melted down, and since then one of the resulting eight sections has been lost.

At the top of the tablet is what was once identified as a 'hanger'. Now, though, it is thought more likely to have been a place for attaching an identifying tag (as on a modern office file), allowing it to be picked out easily from a set of similar tablets held together. Experts believe that this may have been a standardized 'form' document. Some of the proper names seem less distinct, and may have been added later.

TOO MANY NAMES

The number of proper names has proved something of a problem for modern scholars: the full text is positively thick with them, limiting its usefulness as a tool of linguistic investigation. With well over 200 words, the *tabula* should have been an invaluable resource for scholars of a still highly mysterious Etruscan tongue, but once the names of the various parties, witnesses and notaries are excluded, the text seems a great deal shorter.

REVELATORY

Even so, as Etruscan documents go, the Tabula Cortonensis is comparatively clear. The estate being transferred seems to have been in the countryside to the east of Cortona: the 'lake' referred to is Lake Trasimeno, in 217 BC the scene of a battle in the Punic Wars. The language may be legalistic and dull, the subject-matter mundane: so little do we know, though, of the Etruscans and their lives that such scraps of everyday insight come with the force of revelation.

Cast Characters

One striking feature of the Tabula Cortonensis is that the writing does not appear to have been engraved; rather, the whole has been cast (though proper names may have been added later). The 'lost wax' method would have been used: the text is first inscribed in wet clay, then molten beeswax is poured over it and allowed to set. This wax form is coated in liquid clay and then a layer of coarser clay added around it, completely encasing the wax. Channels are left for molten bronze to be poured in – and for the gases from the vaporized wax to escape. It is a difficult technique to master, but exquisite results can be achieved: the workmanship on display in the Tabula Cortonensis is outstanding.

" *The following items are acknowledged as being the property of Petru Sceves: the olive groves, the vineyard, the house – with an estimated value of ten talents. Meanwhile the property of the Cusu family, descendants of Laris, by the lake…comes to some six talents and ten.*

This property, plus four measures [of gold?] make up the full value of the estates of the Cusu family and Petru Sceves taken together.

As witnessed by the following: Larth Petruni, Arunth Pini, Larth Vipi Lusce, Laris Salini of Vetna, Larth Velara of Larth, Larth Velara of Aule, Vel Pumpu Pruciu, Aule Celatina of Setumna, Arnza Felsni of Velthina, Vel Luisna Lusco, Vel Vsina of Nufre, Laru Slanzu, Larzla Lartle Vel Aule, Arnth Petru Raufe.

The arrangement being accepted by Vulca Cusu of Laris and sons, Laris Casu, descendants of Laris, Larin, son of Laris, Petru Scevas and his wife Arntlei…

This agreement now having been formally issued on behalf of the Cusunu family and lodged in accordance with the law…two copies have been left with the Cusu family, descendants of Laris, and with Petru Sceves…

These proceedings have been witnessed and certified by Larth Cucrina of Lausu and the priest Zilath Mechl Rasnal… "

Above: Though the Tabula Cortonensis is one of the longest Etruscan inscriptions yet discovered, it has proved less helpful than hoped for in assisting Etruscan language-scholars: much of its word-length is accounted for by the names of its various signatories and witnesses.

Rome

O f the various traditions surrounding the emergence of the city that became the capital of the ancient world, we are on the safest ground with the one that it 'was not built in a day'. The legend of Romulus and Remus (*see pp. 178–179*) may be more colourful; the story that Rome's Republicans rose up to throw off the yoke of their Etruscan overlords, the tyrannical Tarquins, may be more stirring – but neither narrative can be relied upon. In fact, without the Etruscans, there could never have been an urban settlement here: it was they who built the 'Cloaca Maxima' – Rome's main sewer, still in use today. It was originally designed for drainage, making what had till then been a boggy valley available for agriculture and, increasingly, human habitation.

PLOUGHSHARES INTO SWORDS

Another tradition, that of Rome's foundation in 735 BC, may be more or less correct, but the development of an important urban centre here must have been slow. The Latin tribes who first came together to establish a city here were shepherds and farming folk, rather than empire-builders. The rustic attitudes of these proto-Romans were never entirely to disappear – especially in the rural regions. They were certainly alive and well in the fourth century BC, when priests placed their warning inscription at the edge of the Grove of Spoleto (*see pp. 176–177*). More generally, though, the Romans were to undergo a more or less total transformation in social values and priorities.

Left: The Romans 'made a single city of the world', wrote the poet, extending their imperial reach from Scotland to Syria. And to Leptis Magna, Libya, shown here.

To GET A SENSE of the scale of the shift in emphasis involved, we have only to look to the evidence that Mars, now famous as the Romans' god of war, was first worshipped as an agricultural deity.

FREEDOM – FOR THE FEW

The year 509 BC is the conventionally accepted date for the expulsion of the Tarquins. Quite how it happened, we do not know, but it does seem that Etruscan domination was cast off and the Roman Republic founded towards the end of the sixth century BC. Rome had its freedom, then – or at least its *patres*, or patricians, did. The common people, or *plebs*, had no say in who would serve on the Senate, an assembly of aristocrats. And it was the senators who chose which of their number were to be the two consuls. Elected annually, these were the real decision-makers in the city.

For all the impassioned eloquence lavished on the theme of freedom by its orators, Rome's idea of liberty was rather more limited than that of Athens (which was embracing democracy at about this time). Political representation was confined to the rich and already distinguished; social mobility was positively discouraged, marriage

Above: There is no shortage of Roman inscriptions for ancient historians to study. They dedicated just about everything, it seems – like this monument to the Emperor Antoninus.

mésalliances not merely frowned on but forbidden. Commoners could have access to some of the power of the patricians by binding themselves to particular patrons as 'clients', serving and supporting them in return for favours.

A 'class-struggle' of sorts took place in the course of the fifth century BC: as in Greece, a prosperous 'middle class' of merchants and craftsmen came to the fore. People's Tribunes were introduced, to represent the masses, though this was widely seen as a token measure. Though the 'Twelve Tables' of Roman law, introduced in 450 BC, did include some provisions protecting members of the *plebs* against arbitrary coercion or confiscations by the patriciate, it was only in 367 BC that the Senate opened its doors to the lower-class members, and only in 342 BC that a requirement was introduced that one of the city's consuls should always be plebeian.

WAR AS A WAY OF LIFE

By this time, Rome had already embarked on the course that was to take it to greatness: that of military expansionism. In fairness, it initially fought to survive. As leader of the Latin League (an alliance of Latin cities against the Etruscans), it was at war through most of the fifth century BC.

In 396 BC, matters reached a turning point with the defeat of Veii, an important Etruscan city; by 351 BC, Tarquinii and Falerii had also fallen. Once victory over the Etruscans had been assured, however, the Romans turned on their former allies in the Latin League, including the Samnites and the Umbrians, and made themselves the masters of central Italy.

Above: The Romans had a template for civilization, which they exported wherever they went. This particular mini-Rome was at Palmyra, in what is now Syria.

By extending their sphere of influence into southern Italy, the Romans came into conflict with Greek settlers in the region. Their enmity towards the colonists did not, however, prevent their appreciating the refinement of Greek art and culture. 'The Greeks conquered their conquerors rude,' the Roman poet Horace was to put it glibly, but not inaccurately. Repelling the invasion of Pyrrhus of Epirus, the Romans set about making themselves masters of the south. Appius Claudius started the process in 312 BC, when work began on the Appian Way.

THE PUNIC WARS
The new road led to Roman dominance in the south, all the way to the 'toe' of Italy, from where it was just a short hop to Sicily and Sardinia. There, however, in 264 BC, the Romans found themselves at odds with another set of colonists, the Carthaginians – or Punici. The Romans were peculiarly ill-equipped for fighting a war that would have to be settled at sea, since they had no experience whatsoever of maritime combat. They even had to copy captured Carthaginian vessels to construct their own first warships. Even so, after twenty-three long, hard years, they won the First Punic War in 241.

The Second Punic War began in 218 BC, when Hannibal led a large army (elephants and all) far to the west, to the Strait of Gibraltar, before sweeping up through Spain and southern France and then down over the Alps into northern Italy. He very nearly prevailed, carrying all before him and scoring signal successes at the Trebbia River and Lake Trasimeno – and finally at Cannae in 216 BC. This last defeat should have been the end of Rome, whose forces were comprehensively smashed – as many as 45,000 legionaries may have been killed in that one battle. However, the Romans' resilience was remarkable. By 212 BC, they had fought their way back into contention and Hannibal had been cornered. Badly outnumbered, he had no alternative but to flee for home. The war came

to its formal end in 202 BC, when Scipio 'Africanus' defeated him at Zama, not far from Carthage.

A READY-MADE EMPIRE
Its status as the pre-eminent power in the Italian peninsula now unassailable, Rome was also able to help itself to Carthage's imperial possessions. Not just the Mediterranean islands but also much of Spain fell to the Romans. Launching punitive attacks on former allies of Carthage in Macedon and Asia Minor, they were able to acquire new territories. When Carthage rose up again in 146 BC, the Romans were ruthless in their response, destroying the city and adding the province of Africa to a growing empire.

For the moment, at any rate, this was an empire without an emperor, but the drift towards such rule was already under way. Inevitably, perhaps, in so uncompromisingly militaristic a society, there was an instinctive respect for decision and an impatience with discussion: a succession of strongmen succeeded in sidelining the Senate. Julius Caesar, the conqueror of Gaul, enjoyed all but monarchical powers at the time of his assassination in 44 BC. This dramatic action only postponed the inevitable: Caesar's adopted son Octavian won the civil war that followed and, in 27 BC, was appointed *Princeps* – 'Emperor' – and given the title *Augustus*.

UPS AND DOWNS
The Empire was already close to its greatest extent, stretching from Scotland to Syria, from Germany to Egypt. Hadrian (reigned AD 117–138) was to call a halt, and start fortifying the frontier. But it would be wrong to assume, with the imperial noon now past, that matters would slide downhill all the way. For all the talk of 'Decline and Fall', it is easy to forget how enduring the Empire was.

If Rome had not been built in a day, neither would it fall in too much of a hurry: a good three centuries of stability and, for the most part, prosperity followed

Above: This altar, carefully inscribed, comes from the city of Dougga (Thugga) in Tunisia. Civilization without writing would have been unthinkable by Roman times.

Augustus' elevation. There were economic and fiscal crises, of course, and even the occasional military reversal. There was political intriguing and there were palace coups. Perhaps the most striking thing that a study of the surviving inscriptions shows, however, is the extent to which there was a genuine *Pax Romana* ('Roman Peace') – at least for most of the Empire, most of the time. Men went about their business; women worked in shops and bars; dignitaries campaigned for political office; they worshipped their gods – or, sometimes, new ones, imported from the Empire. The most intriguing of these inscriptions describe not important imperial decrees or military triumphs but, rather, ordinary lives, moving by their sheer mundanity.

Sacred to Jupiter

The lettering is crude, but the menace in the message unmistakable. This is a sacred wood where special rules apply. The Lex Luci Spoletina ('Law of the Grove of Spoleto') was issued in the fourth century BC to protect a grove dedicated to the ancient rites of Jupiter.

> *Let no one violate this sacred grove. Do not take or cut away what belongs to the wood...Whoever breaks this law will have to offer Jupiter an ox in propitiation. Anyone who does it deliberately and with malice aforethought will have to pay a fine of 300 assi as well as sacrificing a propitiatory ox.*

ON PUBLIC DISPLAY

Two stones bearing this warning message – one from each side of the wood – are to be seen in the National Archeological Museum of Spoleto.

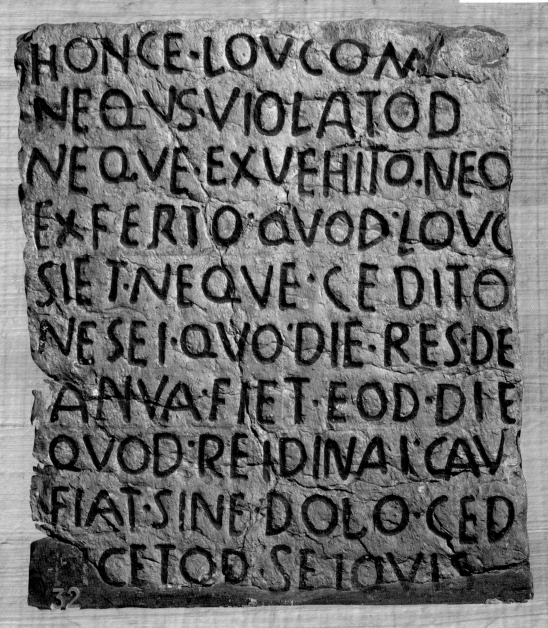

Above: A warning to the unwary – or the simply heedless – the notice from Spoleto threatens stringent punishment for the grove's violation: an ox would have been an expensive sacrifice.

Even today, the wood outside Spoleto, central Italy, has a special atmosphere. It became a favourite haunt of St Francis of Assisi, who sought out its silent glades to pray in peace. In Roman times, this had been actually been a sacred grove, dedicated to the rites of Jupiter, to whom the holm oak was consecrated as a sacred tree. Two stelae with a warning inscription stood for centuries at either edge of the wood. The stones to be seen today are modern copies, but the originals are on display in Spoleto's National Archeological Museum. They make an intriguing addition to the town's Roman heritage, which includes a theatre from the first century AD.

PRE-ROMAN

Seen in this context, however, it is easy to forget how exceptional they are. The Lex Luci Spoletina ('Law of the Grove of Spoleto') is believed to have been proclaimed in 315 BC, a comparatively early date in Roman history. Imperial rule was still centuries away, and even the Republic was comparatively young. Indeed, this part of Umbria had not yet formally fallen under Roman rule. Not until 241 do we read in Livy or Velleius Paterculus of a Roman presence at Spoletum – 150 years later, Cicero could still describe it as a *colonia* ('colony').

In all probability, the grove had been in ritual use for centuries by the time the inscriptions were carved – long before Roman times. For much of its history, then, the grove and its sanctity existed outside the Roman cultural context. The dedication to Jupiter, god of the heavens and of thunder and the pre-eminent patriarch of the Roman pantheon, was almost certainly a superimposition, the co-option of a pre-existing shrine.

JUPITER, THE ITALIAN

Jupiter was a more complex, even problematic figure than is usually appreciated; his identification with the Greek Zeus is easily oversimplified. Up to a point, it is true that the Romans imported a ready-made deity: his obvious attributes are all rooted in the Greek mythological tradition. The way we have tended to approach the pantheon in modern times, seeing a 'classical' continuity between the cultures of Greece and Rome, has only underlined this impression. And it is true enough, as far as it goes. At the same time, though, it makes us likely to miss what was distinctively Italic about the Roman gods and the rituals around them.

Some of these attributes were later accretions, clearly influenced by Rome's development as a military state, such as the cult of Jupiter Feretrius (*see pp. 178–179*); others reflected the expansion of the Empire, like Jupiter Ammon, identified with the Egyptian Amun. But others harked back to earlier times. We can only guess at the original rationale behind some of the various prohibitions placed on the Priest of Jupiter. Riding a horse; wearing rings unless plain or perforated; having knots in the headdress or clothing; touching, or even mentioning, a nanny-goat; touching flour mixed with yeast – all these were taboo.

Above: Jupiter was the supreme deity of the Romans. The holm oak was hallowed to him, hence the dedication to him in Roman times of a wood which had almost certainly been sacred to other gods in the centuries before.

Pagan Parallels?

The Romans insisted on the superiority of their civilization. They were especially disdainful of the Celtic cultures of Gaul and Britain. Caesar writes contemptuously of the Druids and their savage rites, the benighted superstition that prevailed among the people. Tacitus testifies to the systematic destruction of sacred groves in Celtic Britain by the troops of Agricola, determined to break the hold of the priests on their communities. Yet the existence of a sacred grove like this one outside Spoleto – and of many others in Italy, Greece and across the Empire – reminds us that the Romans were not themselves far removed from such ancient beliefs. The significance of the 'sacred grove' in a range of cultures, from Scandinavia to the Indian subcontinent, suggests a common origin in a very distant past.

For the Founder

Amidst the ruins of Pompeii was found an inscription to the founder of another city: Rome itself, the centre and origin of the Empire. Its primacy was taken not just as a matter of historical fact but as an inspiration to Romans everywhere.

A Special Exploit

Romulus, son of Mars, founded the city of Rome and reigned over it himself for some forty years. He personally slew Acro, king of the Caeninenses, at the head of his host and consecrated the regal spoils he took from him to Jupiter Feretrius. Received into the company of the gods, he is known as Quirinus.

In the *Chalcidicum*, or record-house, of Pompeii was discovered an inscription that recorded the foundation of the first city of the Empire. It recalled the story of Romulus, who was said by legend to have founded Rome in 735 BC.

MILITARY MYTH-MAKING
The inscription records only one episode of the Romulus myth – and not the most familiar one to modern readers. To the Romans, though, the story of how their founder had slain the king of the Caeninenses in single combat would have been familiar.

The legend harks back to an earlier age of warfare – a time of heroic single combat along Homeric lines. The spirit that had truly made Rome's armies great had, of course, been a collective one: determined, disciplined and tightly drilled. Organization and engineering had been as important as individual valour in the subjugation of most of the known world. But, while recognizing this, the Romans were still inspired by the idea that their founder had fought his enemies hand to hand.

What this inscription calls the *spolia opima* ('rich, or regal, spoils')

were the arms and armour taken from the body of an enemy commander after he had been slain in single combat. Only three Romans ever secured these trophies, and since two were legendary (Romulus himself and Aulus Cornelius Cossus, who triumphed over Lar Tolumnius, king of the Veintes), the feat of Marcus Claudius Marcellus is all the more remarkable. In 222, he took the *spolia opima* from a Celtic chieftain.

But if no one else ever matched the achievement, that was not for want of trying. The ambition was

enshrined at the heart of Roman life by the cult of Jupiter Feretrius. This was supposed to have been the city's first ever shrine, established by Romulus himself as he carried the spoils from the field of battle. As Livy records it, he uttered a famous prayer (see opposite).

SONS OF A SHE-WOLF
King Numitor of Alba Longa, a city-state in the Tiber Valley, was murdered by his brother Amulius, who seized his throne. An oracle told him that his descendants' rule would be threatened by the children of Rhea Silvia, his niece by his brother. Accordingly, he consigned her to the Temple of Vesta as a Vestal Virgin.

But one night Mars descended and slept with the maiden, as a result of which two sons were born: Romulus and Remus. Since they had been born in violation of their mother's sacred status, they were cast into the Tiber as unclean. But a

Right: The Romans seem to have liked the idea that there was a hint of savagery at the roots of their civilization. The story of Romulus and Remus was familiar to every Roman child.

she-wolf found them and raised them as her own. They grew up to avenge their father and established a city of their own. While they were building it, they quarrelled and Romulus killed his brother. He was left as sole ruler – but was branded a murderer and outcast. He gathered around him other outlaws: wanted criminals and runaway slaves. To begin with, there were no women, but Romulus invited the neighbouring Sabines to share a feast – and while the men were distracted, Romulus and his band stole their wives and daughters and took them back to Rome.

ON PUBLIC DISPLAY

Like many items from Pompeii, this inscription has been removed from its site and is on show in the National Archeological Museum in Naples.

> *To you, Jupiter Feretrius, I, Romulus, a victor, bring these spoils. A king myself, I have taken them from a king, and in this sacred precinct, whose boundaries I have imagined and will now mark out, I set up a shrine for these spolia opima, to which will be added other trophies taken from the slain kings and generals of our enemies.*

Above: The original exploit was carried out in Rome, where the original temple to Jupiter Feretrius was also built – but Rome's foundation was seen as a template for that of other Roman cities.

The Roadbuilder

A stela dedicated to Appius Claudius Caecus recalls one of the most illustrious Romans of them all. A victorious general, a committed public servant, he lives on into modern times in the name of that most famous of Roman roads, the Appian Way.

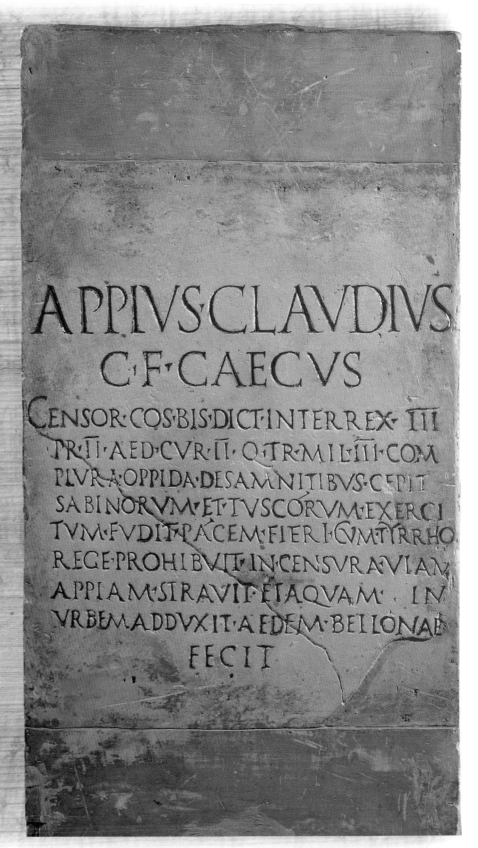

> *Appius Claudius Caecus, son of Caius, censor, twice consul, dictator, three times interrex, twice praetor, twice curule aedile, quaestor, three times military tribune. He took several Samnite fortresses and routed the army of the Sabines and the Etruscans; he brought about peace with King Pyrrhus; in the course of his censorship, he built the Appian Way and organized the aqueduct that brings water to Rome. He built the Temple of Bellona.*

ON PUBLIC DISPLAY

Appius Claudius' greatest monument is still to be seen in the south of Rome, where a section of the Via Appia Antica ('Ancient Appian Way') has been preserved.

Right: This stela sums up an extraordinarily distinguished career: Appius Claudius did as much as anyone to make Rome a major power. Leading Romans were genuinely – if, ultimately, egotistically – 'public-spirited': in service, they knew, lay honour and repute.

ppius Claudius was born around 340 BC, a comparatively early stage in the history of the Republic. Rome was no more than a local power, its emergence – even its existence – threatened by a number of neighbouring tribes. Ironically, Appius Claudius was descended from one of these: his semi-legendary ancestor, Appius Claudius Sabinus, had been born a Sabine, one of Rome's most ancient foes, but had come over to the Roman cause. The Sabines were to be among the enemies Appius Claudius fought in the Samnite Wars, which engulfed central Italy around the turn of the third century BC.

FAMOUS VICTORIES

The Samnites lived in the Apennines, in the southeast of Latium. They fought three tough and wearying wars with Rome. The first was fought between 343 and 341 – just before Appius Claudius was born – and resulted in a Roman victory. But the Samnites were not finished: a second war broke out in 326 and would last for more than two decades. Finally, in 304, this too ended in a Roman victory, thanks in no small part to Appius Claudius' generalship.

As the inscription suggests, the Samnites were allied with Rome's traditional Sabine and Etruscan enemies: this was a struggle for dominance in central Italy. Victory in the Third Samnite War, which raged from 298 to 290, left Rome the dominant power in the peninsula. (In fulfilment of a vow made during the conflict, Appius Claudius later built the Temple of Bellona, in honour of the goddess of war and the sister of Mars.)

Pyrrhus, king of Epirus, invaded Italy across the Adriatic in 280. He won the original 'Pyrrhic victory', defeating wave after wave of Roman legionaries, but sustaining such heavy losses that he was finally forced into a retreat.

WINNING THE PEACE

Appius Claudius' peacetime achievements were, if anything, more remarkable. Elected Censor in 312, he embarked on ambitious public works. He built the 'Aqua Appia', the first great aqueduct to bring fresh water from the hills. He also started work on the 'Via Appia', the first and most famous of the Roman roads, which ultimately linked Rome with Brindisi in southeast Italy. Though the economic benefits it brought were enormous, its original inspiration was military: Appius Claudius wanted an artery for the rapid movement of soldiers and supplies.

In 280, he was suddenly struck blind – the result of a curse, it was rumoured. This was the origin of his agnomen 'Caecus' – 'blind'. He died, deeply mourned, in 273 BC.

Above: The 'queen of roads', in the poet Statius' words, the Appian Way extended across Italy, from the capital to the southeastern 'heel'.

Offices of State

Appius' inscription describes a bewildering array of offices:

• **Censor** The man in charge of the population census. Also overseer of public morality.

• **Consul** Rome's most senior magistrates: there were two at a time, effectively co-rulers of the Republic.

• **Dictator** As in modern times, a one-man ruler with supreme power: in special circumstances (usually war), when the state was considered to be in great danger, he was elected by the consuls to take charge.

• **Interrex** In the earliest times, the regent who took charge between the death of one king and the crowning of his successor. In Republican Rome, the title was used for a member of a committee that met to elect new consuls when, for reasons of war or political crisis, the outgoing consuls had been unable to elect their own.

• **Praetor** A senior judge or general, who could be called on at any time to undertake special military or civic duties.

• **Curule Aedile** 'Aediles' were responsible for looking after public buildings and organizing festivities and public spectacles. Those drawn from the patrician class were known as 'Curule Aediles', from the 'Curule' chair in which senior officials had always sat.

• **Quaestor** A magistrate with special responsibility for public finance.

• **Military Tribune** A military officer of patrician class appointed by the Senate.

A Dictator's Dedication

A mortal threat, a political crisis, a rebellion and at last a hard-won victory over the rampaging Carthaginian forces of Hannibal: a laconic inscription scrawled on a slab of stone in Rome offers no hint of the dramas it commemorates.

> " *To Hercules the Victor Consul Marcus Minucius the Dictator dedicates this stone* "

ON PUBLIC DISPLAY

The dedication was carved into a stone in Campo Verano, Rome, where it can be seen today.

Above: A rough-cut slab, and crudely inscribed, Minucius' hastily fashioned stela resonates with the anxious uncertainty of the time in which it was made.

Excavations outside Rome's church of San Lorenzo in 1862 unearthed a tablet, crudely inscribed, an offering from a 'Dictator', Marcus Minucius, to Hercules the Victor. Terse as it was, the inscription spoke volumes, recalling the darkest days of the Second Punic War, when the very survival of the city had been at stake.

ROME UNDER THREAT
In 217 BC, Roman morale was at its lowest. Things had not been going their way at all. Hannibal, the dashing young Carthaginian commander, had outwitted and outflanked them. Marching his army – elephants and all – up through Spain and France and over the Alps, he had swept aside a

Roman army at the Battle of the Trebbia. Just to make matters worse, this master tactician had managed to entice a second Roman army into a trap on the shores of Lake Trasimeno for a tally of 30,000 legionaries killed or drowned and another 10,000 captured.

With the future of Roman civilization hanging in the balance,

A Long Game

Fabius had snatched stalemate from the jaws of hopeless defeat. It was less than glorious, but it was better than disaster. In time, the value of his 'Fabian Tactics' would be shown, and *Cunctator* pass from being a pejorative to an honorific nickname. In the meantime, though, things were due to get much worse for Rome before they started to get better. Fabius was relieved of his duties the following year. His successors, still itching for a decisive battle, took the fight to Hannibal at Cannae the following year. The result was the loss of over 50,000 legionaries and what is generally agreed to have been Rome's military nadir. It took more than a decade for the Romans to claw back the ground they had lost, but claw it back they did and the Second Punic War ended in victory.

much depended on Fabius Maximus. The commander of the forces defending Rome had been given the title 'Dictator' in the ghastly aftermath of the defeat at Trasimeno. Soon, however, he had been given another name, *Cunctator* – which was certainly not conferred in affection or gratitude. The word meant 'delayer', and at a time when the Romans were desperate for a victory, his strategy found few admirers among the public back in Rome. Rather than risk a pitched battle that he feared (with good reason) he would not win, Fabius dogged Hannibal's steps but backed away from contact.

MINUCIUS' FINEST HOUR
Fabius' tactics had their detractors in the field, too – notably his own second-in-command, Consul Marcus Minucius Rufus. This disunity at the top was hardly helpful to Rome's cause. But Minucius was soon to stumble into the limelight.

Left in command as Fabius faced his critics in the Roman Senate, Minucius caught a group of

Carthaginian stragglers outside their lines and put them to the sword, outside Geronium, in Apulia, southeastern Italy. Rome was in the mood for a triumph, and especially one that showed up Fabius: the propagandists quickly went to work. In one particularly mischievous move, the call went up for Minucius to be appointed Dictator, which made him equal in authority to the *Cunctator*. It would appear to have been at this point that the commemorative stela was erected in Rome on Minucius' behalf.

The 'real' battle of Geronium took place a few days later. This time, Hannibal and his main force were involved. It was another ambush, the Carthaginian commander first setting out his bait and then, when Minucius blundered into his trap, falling upon him with a crack force of infantry and horsemen. Comprehensively outmanoeuvred, Minucius' army seemed doomed to extermination when – in the nick of time – Fabius returned with reinforcements. The Carthaginians were beaten off and the day was saved.

To his credit, Minucius seems to have been chastened by his defeat – and duly grateful to Fabius for his deliverance and that of his men. In the aftermath of the battle, he resigned his dictatorship and served his commander loyally from that time forward.

Left: Fabius Maximus was to need his fabled patience in the political as well as the military sphere: only later would Romans recognize the value of the Cunctator's delaying tactics and accord him the honour he deserved.

Land and Freedom

A bronze plaque discovered in what is now Cadiz brings to light a forgotten moment in the imperial history of Rome. Even as the legions brought their country under the Roman yoke, some in Spain were suddenly to be freed.

Defeat at Cannae in 216 BC brought Rome very close to losing the Second Punic War against the Carthaginians. Very close to its destruction, in other words. Amazingly, just over a decade later, in 202, victory over Hannibal was ultimately secured.

And not only had Rome survived but in the meantime it had acquired an extensive empire. The defeat of the Carthaginians opened the door to Iberia, which quickly became the Roman province of Hispania. New territories were opening up to the east as well,

ON PUBLIC DISPLAY

Aemilius' decree was unearthed near Cadiz in the mid-nineteenth century. It is now displayed in Paris, at the Louvre.

> ❝ *Lucius Aemilius, son of Lucius Imperator, has decreed that the subjects of the Hasta in the Tower of Lascuta shall be set free. Their land and the fort that they had at the time they should have, and they should keep it as long as the People and Senate of Rome agree. Done in camp on 19 January.* ❞

Above: Freedom for the slaves! An inspiring thought, though one that the Romans would apply only selectively. Here, on behalf of the subject serfs of the Spanish Hasta tribe.

where King Philip V of Macedon had imprudently thrown in his lot with Rome's North African enemy. He was defeated in 196, leaving the way clear for an advance on Asia Minor, whose Seleucid king Antiochus III had also been in the Carthaginian camp.

COMETH THE HOUR,
COMETH AEMILIUS
An expedition was sent against him in 190 BC. At this point, though, with all Rome's most experienced military commanders tied up in the east, a rebellion broke out at the other end of the Empire. 'All Spain was up in arms,' Plutarch reports in the account he wrote towards the end of the first century AD:

'There they sent Aemilius… nominally a praetor but accorded the honour of a consul. Twice he defeated the barbarians in battle; 30,000 of them were killed. These triumphs can be attributed to the resourcefulness of the general in selecting the most advantageous ground and, making his attack at a crucial ford, he enabled his men to win an easy victory. After receiving the surrender of some 250 cities, their people swearing their obedience by oath, he left the

province pacified and made his return to Rome. But he himself was not a penny better off for his campaign. He was generally casual about making money, though generous and liberal with what funds he had. But he had so little that when he died there was barely enough to meet his wife's dowry.'

As is his way, Plutarch uses his subject's free and open nature as a reproach to the Romans of his own day – too self-interested, too grasping, in his view. But a bronze

tablet dating from 189 BC and found in what is now Cadiz, Spain, sheds interesting light on a man who does indeed seem to have been humane in his instincts. It promulgates the decree by which Aemilius set free the people who had been held in servitude by the Hasta, one of the region's more powerful tribes.

Below: Hispania (Spain) was one of the great prizes won by Rome as a result of the Second Punic War. Gades (Cadiz) was to become one of its most important and prosperous centres.

Serfs Not Slaves

We should not exaggerate the commitment of Aemilius or of Rome to the cause of liberty – for Romans, yes; for other peoples, no. In setting free the serfs of the Hasta, Aemilius was acting less out of altruistic concern for these bondsmen than out of a desire to reduce the wealth and power of their former 'owners'.

The Hasta's 'subjects' were not slaves as we would normally understand the term; rather, they seem to have been a tribe taken into servitude. The same had happened five centuries before: the Spartans invaded and conquered Messenia, and then put the Helots to work on their own land – enabling the Spartan men to devote their lives to military training and to war.

In Defence of Decency

Had Rome escaped the wrath of Hannibal to fall victim to drunken excess? Was the Empire to be overwhelmed by a wild party? The year 186 BC saw the Senate issuing a stern decree against the Bacchantes, whose orgiastic excesses had genuinely shaken the establishment.

Our ideas of Roman religion often fail to take account of the complexity of Roman society – and, as important, the longevity of the civilization we call Rome. To talk of Jupiter, god of the heavens; Mars, god of war; Venus, goddess of Love…is fair enough as far as it goes, but barely begins to sum up these deities or the various ways in which they were worshipped over time. Though the basic pantheon did endure, cults came and went – sometimes with bewildering rapidity. One of the strangest was surely that of the Bacchantes.

DRUNK AND DISORDERLY

Today, Bacchus is generally regarded as an amiable deity, no more than the god of wine. Like the revelry he stood for, however, he could get out of hand. And there was more to him than drunken jollity. He was the god not just of wine but also of fertility: as such, he was traditionally ambiguous in terms of gender. The thyrsus he carried – a sceptre improvised from a fennel-stalk topped with a pine cone – was only too obviously phallic in its

form. At the same time, however, his followers were mostly women. In Greece, where his cult originated, they had been known as maenads, 'raving ones', their unbridled riotousness seen as an overstepping of all social propriety – of sanity, even.

Such was also the case in Italy, where the cult arrived in the early decades of the second century BC, brought to Etruria by a low-born Greek charlatan, according to the Roman historian Livy. The cult's adherents, in their Bacchanalia, broke all the rules of Roman femininity. Intoxicated on wine, lust, laughter and sheer abandon, they danced madly, committing casual acts of promiscuity and violence with equal heedlessness, rejecting all the proprieties of family, society and state.

Hence the determined action taken by the city's patrician class as represented by the Senate with its decree of 186 BC.

A Threat to Society?

Though Livy offers lurid accounts of an array of crimes, from large-scale fraud to rape and murder, there is no corroboration that such things took place. The problem appears to have been more one of what the French feminist writer Hélène Cixous called the 'Laugh of the Medusa': the sight of women casting off restraint, letting themselves go, giving themselves up to rowdy hiliarity, drunken freedom and sexual licence was profoundly unsettling for a patriarchal society. On top of this, the cult quickly came to admit slaves and lower-class men, mingling not just men and women but the social castes without distinction.

Above:
Merry-making became mayhem in the ritual carousals of the Bacchantes. The cult spread swiftly across Italy in the second century BC.

" The consuls Quintus Marcius, son of Lucius, and Spurius Postumius, son of
Lucius, held discussions with the Senate on 7 October in Bellona's Temple.
Marcus Claudius, son of Marcus, Lucius Valerius, son of Publius, and Quintus Minucius,
son of Gaius, helped to draft this decree…

No one is to have a place dedicated to the worship of
Bacchus…No Roman citizen or anyone possessing his
freedom in Latium, or any of Rome's allies, is to follow
the cult of the Bacchae without first appearing before
the urban praetor and receiving his
permission and that of the Senate,
there being no less than 100
senators present when the case
is discussed.

No man shall be a priest of any such
organization, nor may any man or
woman run such an organization;
no one may keep a fund for such
purposes or appoint any other man
or woman to run such an
organization. No one may take an
oath to join them nor make their
vows alongside them…No one may
perform their rituals, either in
private or in public, within or
outside the city, without first
appearing before the urban praetor
and gaining his permission, to be
agreed by the Senate when no less
than 100 senators are present.

No one may join with more than
five people in total, men and
women, for the purpose of these
rites; nor shall there be more than
two men or three women, without the express
permission of the urban praetor and
Senate, as stipulated above. "

ON PUBLIC DISPLAY

The original bronze tablet in which the
Senatus Consultum de Bacchanalibus was
inscribed is to be seen at the
Kunsthistorisches Museum, Vienna.

Above: The Senatus Consultum de Bacchanalibus came
after months of mounting moral panic among Rome's
patricians, but there was undoubtedly a real basis for
their hysteria. The Bacchantes committed many acts of
vandalism and violence.

Over the Isthmus

Inscriptions have been written to honour great lives and deaths, important battles and building projects. But achievements may be of many different sorts. Even the portage of a fleet of ships across the Isthmus of Corinth? The man who did it certainly thought so.

To the base of an earlier monument, believed to have been erected during the fourth century BC, an inscription was added in 102 BC. It is believed to have been carried out on the orders of Hirrus, the second-in-command to Marcus Antonius, a Proconsul of the time.

Marcus Antonius had been placed in command of an expedition against pirates operating from Pamphylia, on the southern coast of Turkey: Side is the main port along that coast. In order to have sufficient ships on hand to launch a serious attack upon the pirates, Rome's Western Fleet had to be

brought into the eastern Mediterranean.

With the stormy time of year approaching, it was decided that, rather than risk loss or major damage taking them south around the Peloponnese, the ships should be transported overland across the isthmus before proceeding to

> " *Learn here of a feat which no one has attempted before so that we may take with us in fame the deeds of a courageous man. Under the auspices of the Proconsul Marcus Antonius, a fleet was hauled across the isthmus and dispatched over the sea. He himself set out to travel to Side; his propraetor Hirrus had the fleet take harbour at Athens on account of the season. This was all achieved in the space of a few days with a minimum of fuss, with the utmost care and attention to safety. He who is upright praises what is good; the man of envy finds fault. Let them do that, but let them suffer for their spite.* "

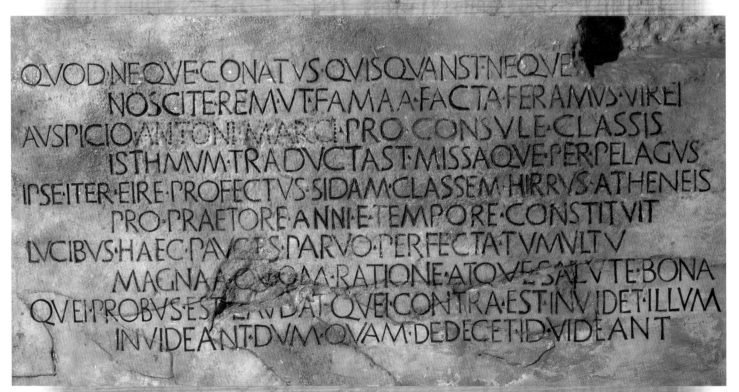

Above: Not content with commemorating his feat, Hirrus had his achievement set down in hexameter verse, as the centred style of the inscribed lines makes clear.

ON PUBLIC DISPLAY

Hirrus' self-advertisement may be viewed today in the Archeological Museum in Corinth.

Below: Thanks to this Mark Antony's misdeeds, the name of the other, earlier Marcus Antonius was largely obliterated in Hirrus' inscription.

Below: Thanks to this Mark Antony's misdeeds, the name of the other, earlier Marcus Antonius was largely obliterated in Hirrus' inscription.

Piraeus, the port of Athens. It was a big and complicated undertaking, and so delighted was Hirrus by the skill and expeditiousness with which he completed it that he had this inscription created in his own honour.

ERASED FROM THE RECORD? When the inscription is examined closely, it becomes clear that an attempt has been made – only partially successful – to obliterate the name of the Proconsul, Marcus Antonius. The most obvious explanation for this is that it was done some seventy years after the placing of the memorial, by supporters of Octavian (later the Emperor Augustus). At that time, in the 30s BC, Octavian was embroiled in his bitter civil war against another Marcus Antonius – the man more widely known as 'Mark Antony'. Was it a gratuitous act of spite against a hated name, or were Octavian's men genuinely under the misapprehension that the Marcus Antonius mentioned was their great enemy? Improbable as this may sound, it is worth bearing in mind that many scholars were similarly confused for a while after this inscription was first discovered in the 1920s.

A Canal for Corinth

The Isthmus of Corinth is tantalizingly slender, at just under 6.5km (4 miles) across, but that little sliver of land put an extra 400km (250 miles) on the voyage round the Peloponnese.

Periander, Tyrant of Corinth, first mooted the idea of a canal in the seventh century BC. In the end, he was defeated by the scale of the engineering task. Even so, he built the 'Diolkos' ('Cross-Portage'), which allowed the transportation of ships, or more often decanted goods. This was a paved way with grooves specially cut for the wheels of carts – almost an early railway.

Demetrius I made a second attempt at cutting a canal in the fourth century BC, but he too was forced to abandon the idea. Julius Caesar was assassinated before he could begin work; it was apparently a pet project of his. In the late 60s AD, Nero's engineers did begin work, using Jewish labour, captured in the First Jewish-Roman War. But this attempt too was unsuccessful. In the end, the dream was not to be realized until well into modern times: the Corinth Canal was finally constructed in the 1880s.

Above: The challenge of carving a canal through the isthmus defeated even the Romans. Not until the nineteenth century was it finally achieved.

The Shield of Virtue

Words of fawning flattery may still be most revealing. Awarded to Augustus, the first of the emperors, by a grateful Senate, the Clupeus Virtutis ('Shield of Virtue') lists the great civic virtues as the Romans saw them.

SENATVS POPVLVSQVE·ROMANVS IMP·CAESARI·DIVI·F·AVGVSTO COS·VIII·DEDIT·CLVPEVM VIRTVTIS·CLEMENTIAE IVSTITIAE·PIETATIS·ERGA DEOS·PATRIAMQVE

" *The Senate and the Roman people dedicated to the Emperor Augustus, son of Caesar the god, in his Eighth Consulate, the Shield of Virtue, Clemency, Justice and Piety towards both the gods and the fatherland.* "

Above: The Clupeus Virtutis lists the Augustan virtues. No doubt they are exaggerated, but there is some evidence that (if only for presentational, political reasons) he tried to live up to them.

ON PUBLIC DISPLAY

This copy of the Clupeus Virtutis is in the Archeological Museum at Arles, in France.

In 44 BC, Julius Caesar had vanquished his enemies both in Gaul and in Rome itself. Having faced the Senate down, he was the object of untrammelled adulation among the populace. And then, just as it seemed his stock could not conceivably soar any higher, he ostentatiously turned down the offer of a royal crown. Causing consternation among the wider patrician class, the cult of Caesar was such that his assassination became inevitable. His adopted son Octavian now determined to avenge his death.

SEIZING POWER BY STEALTH
By 27 BC, after several years of civil war, Octavian had prevailed. Grateful to have peace at last, the people hailed him as a conquering hero. Showing all his adoptive father's political instincts, however, he chose not to make a bid for personal power but instead to renounce the powers already vested in him by the state:

'After bringing the Civil War to a successful conclusion...I handed back authority over the state to the Senate and the people of Rome. In gratitude, the Senate awarded me the title 'Augustus' ['splendid', 'august'], the doors of my temple were decked with laurel leaves and a civic crown placed above the door to my house, while a golden shield was put up in the Senate House, its inscription bearing witness to my virtue, compassion, justice and piety – the merits for which the shield had been awarded. From that time on, I was pre-eminent in influence, though in actual power I was not above those fellow-Romans who held magistracy alongside me.'

This later account by Octavian – now 'Augustus' – is true enough, as far as it goes. He did surrender his authority to the Senate; and his new title of *Princeps* ('Principal' or 'First Man') did make him no more than *primus inter pares* ('first among equals'). But there was no mistaking his pre-eminence. For the rest of his reign, he pulled off the paradoxical feat of displaying both his modesty and unobtrusiveness while also being without doubt the first emperor of Rome.

GOVERNING VIRTUES
The original Clupeus Virtutis has long since been lost, this disc of solid gold a temptation no barbarian despoiler could possibly resist. The marble votive plaque shown here is a copy, but it has preserved the original inscription, which sheds fascinating light on what might be called the 'public virtues' of Roman life. Whether Augustus embodied all (or any) of these qualities is, of course, debatable: they should perhaps be seen as more of a wistful 'wants list'.

Right: Appointed Princeps *in 27 BC, and given the honorific 'Augustus', Octavian effectively invented the office of emperor. It was inevitable, perhaps: for generations now the Republic had appeared politically doomed, with a series of strongmen taking all but imperial power.*

The Roman Virtue

Pietas ('piety') was the ultimate Roman virtue. It comes last the plaque, to give it prominence as the ultimate – as it were, the culminating – quality. The protagonist of Virgil's great epic, the *Aeneid*, is typically referred to as 'Pius Aeneas', and he was the archetypal Roman hero.

Today, the word 'piety' tends to have narrowly religious connotations, but in Roman times its application was much wider. As this inscription demonstrates, it included both respect and reverence towards the gods and a spirit of service to Rome itself. Indeed, it went still further: the Roman was also expected to show the same sense of duty and regard towards his parents – though this is, in any case, implicit in the word *patria*, 'fatherland'. Parents, ancestors, gods, city, state, past traditions, present-day politics – all were aspects of 'Rome' and so to all the Roman owed piety.

Missing in Action

Found near Xanten in the Lower Rhineland, this tablet commemorates the unfortunate victim of one of Rome's rare military disasters. In AD 9, an ill-starred expedition against rebellious tribesmen ended in the loss of an entire army, three legions strong.

Here lies Marcus Caelius – or, at least, here he would have lain if only his mortal remains had been recovered. He was one of thousands to have been lost in the so-called Varian War of AD 9. Rome's Vietnam was supposed to be a punitive expedition against the tribes of the Weser Valley who had launched one too many raids across the frontier into the territory of Roman Germania.

MARCHING TO MASSACRE
The governor on the ground, Publius Quinctilius Varus, mustered an impressive army to teach the barbarians a lesson. Three legions in all were involved: along with Marcus Caelius' Eighteenth Legion, there were also the Seventeenth and Nineteenth Legions. Additional cohorts of auxiliaries and cavalry brought the number of men to around 30,000, all well disciplined and well trained – more than a match for anything the Germani could throw at them.

Or so one would have thought. As events were to turn out, however, Varus' army was destined for disaster. Their years of drilling were of no use to them as they made their way into the densely wooded depths of the Teutoburg Forest. They had no alternative but to break ranks as they picked their way among crowded tree-trunks and thorny thickets, squelching through the boggy mire underfoot. To make matters worse, the rain was lashing down, and the men were thoroughly demoralized when, all of a sudden, they were showered with spears.

Only a few hundred survivors managed to make their way back home to base: the lightly armed Germani had appeared from nowhere, they reported, dancing in and out of the trees to attack them from close quarters. The massacre continued for three full days: Varus himself had fallen upon his sword rather than live with the enormity of the catastrophe that he had set in motion by his own orders. He had good reason to despair: this was a disaster without precedent in Roman history. 'Quinctilius Varus, give me back my legions!' the Emperor Augustus is said to have cried when he heard the news.

Lost Without Trace

The Varian War may not have been the most extraordinary military reverse suffered by the Roman army. At some point around AD 120, the Ninth Legion disappeared abruptly – and unaccountably – from the record. Though serving in the Rhineland at the time, it was not involved in the Varian War; it went on to fight with distinction in several subsequent campaigns. The story that it headed up beyond Hadrian's Wall to fight the Picts of Scotland and was wiped out in some forgotten battle in the mist of a Highland glen has understandably caught the imagination of the more romantic British historians. But it could just as easily have been destroyed in the untrammelled violence of Judaea's Bar Kokhba Revolt (AD 132–135) or the bloody upheavals along the Danube three decades later. Or, of course, it may have simply been disbanded at the stroke of a bureaucrat's stylus: we really have no evidence either way.

Left: The Teutoburg Forest today. Even now, the forests of Germany have an eerie feel. Roman troops would have felt particularly uneasy in this northern wilderness. Torrential rain, barbarian arrows and complete and utter disorientation and panic meant a miserable final few hours for Rome's lost legionaries.

ON PUBLIC DISPLAY

Marcus Caelius' memorial is now among the exhibits in the Rheinisches Landesmuseum in Bonn.

“ *Marcus Caelius'*
freedmen,
Marcus Caelius Privatus,
Marcus Caelius
Thiaminus. To Marcus
Caelius, son of Titus, of
the Lemonia voting
tribe, from Bononia
[probably Bologna], the
First Centurion of the
Eighteenth Legion.
At the age of fifty-three,
he fell in the Varian War.
The bones of his
freedmen are authorized
to be buried here. This
memorial was raised
by his brother Caelius,
son of Titus, of the
Lemonia tribe. ”

Right: Marcus Caelius' family seem to have taken special pains to give him a worthy memorial, given that his body had been lost, they knew not where. The Romans had a horror of their bones being left unburied.

Free – Up to a Point

The *libertus*, or 'freedman', of ancient Rome would surely have celebrated his release from slavery, but he was hardly able to call himself his own master. The owner who released his slaves would remain their *patronus* for the rest of his life, and they his *clientes*, bound to honour him and support any of his public works or political stands. If he was no longer officially their owner, he still had proprietorship over them to such an extent that generally, like Privatus and Thiaminus here, they took his names. So much were they regarded as still 'belonging' to their former master that their bones were an acceptable symbolic substitute for his, which had ended up scattered on some German forest floor. At least they were allowed to live out their lives: in some ancient cultures, of course, slaves were sacrificed to boost their lords' standing in the afterlife.

The Case for the Colonies

Roman democracy could be rumbustious; even rude. The Senate clearly did not stand on ceremony. An inscription from AD 10 records a keynote speech by the Emperor Claudius – word for word, interruption by interruption.

Claudius had been something of a laughing stock growing up at the imperial court: he is thought to have had a mild case of cerebral palsy, or perhaps Tourette's. But his achievements as emperor were not to be derided. Though he inherited the agnomen 'Germanicus' from the father he refers to here, he was to earn his own a few years later, becoming 'Britannnicus' after his conquest of Great Britain. As the speech shows, moreover, he had strong views and expressed them seriously. He was fair-minded: Rome's colonies, he felt strongly, should ultimately become part of the Roman world, with all the rights and privileges that implied. This, of course, was a view he articulated again the following year in relation to the people of Trentino (*see pp. 196–197*).

INTERRUPTION THE NORM?
Opinions differ on his oratory: Suetonius says that he cut a

Above: The inscription of 48 represents a full transcript of proceedings in the Senate. Lines standing out to the left show where the emperor was interrupted.

ON PUBLIC DISPLAY

Claudius' speech – at least a large part of it: the upper part of the inscription is missing – may be seen in the Gallo-Roman Museum in Lyon.

> **"** *Surely it was the intention of my great-uncle, Augustus the God, and of Tiberius Caesar, that the best of the colonies and provincial municipalities – that is, all those with well-born and substantial men – should have a voice in this assembly.*

– What? Does an Italian senator not take precedence over one from the provinces?

surprisingly impressive figure in his public appearances, though there are reports too of a significant speech impediment. Certainly, if we are to judge by this particular address to the Senate, he had some difficulty in keeping to the point. Even so, it is surprising to find, first, that he was so freely interrupted; second, that the fact appears to have occasioned him no surprise; third, and most surprising still, these interruptions made it into the official record, as though no impropriety had been committed, no embarrassment caused.

IN THE SENATE A FIRST AMONG EQUALS

The fact that such vigorous give and take took place goes some way towards renewing one's faith in the Roman political system, which looks a little less authoritarian here than it generally does. Though in theory the emperor was supposed to be no more than *primus inter pares* ('first among equals'), it seldom seems to have been that way in practice. Before the Senate, though, it seems, he really was just another Roman, expected to put his case and hold his corner like anyone else.

Above: The Roman Senate. The office of Princeps *was always supposed to be a publicly accorded honour rather than an entitlement of quasi-royal rank: the idea that the emperor was 'first among equals' did not disappear entirely.*

I will make that clear to you when I submit to the Senate those of my actions which I carried out in my capacity as censor, but I do not see why even provincials should be rejected if they can make an honourable contribution to the doings of the Senate. Take this splendid and important colony of Vienne, for instance: did that not send us senators recently? From there we have Lucius Vestinus, a luminary of the equestrian order and personal friend of mine, my trusted companion and manager of my personal affairs. I beg that his sons should be allowed to become priests, starting at the lowest level, to work their way up the scale with the passing years. As for that thief from Vienne, Valerius Asiaticus, I do not mention his hateful name. I loathe that hero of the gymnasium who had won his family a consulship even before their colony had won the right of citizenship. The same goes for his brother, marked out as unworthy by this relation, so inconceivable as a member of this assembly…

– What is this, Tiberius Caesar Germanicus? Time to tell the Senators where you are actually going with this – you have already reached the farthest borders of Narbonnese Gaul!

–All these young men whom I see before me now – you surely do not regret seeing them among your ranks…And if this is so, what more could you want? Do I have to spell it out? Even the territory beyond the province of Narbonnese Gaul has provided senators, has it not? Surely we have no reason to regret going all the way up to Lugdunum [Lyon] for members?…The time has come when I have to plead openly for Outer Gaul. You will say that Gaul waged war against Julius the God for a decade. But remember too that since then it has shown a hundred years of steadfast loyalty, and the greatest fidelity in many difficulties. My father Drusus was in a position to conquer Germany precisely because to his rear peace prevailed among the Gauls…

"

Worth a War? The Tavola Clesiana

In 1869, peasants digging in a field near Cles in northern Italy's Trentino region unearthed a inscribed bronze tablet, beautifully preserved. Dating back to AD 49, to Roman times, this was a precious antiquity indeed. But still more vital was its significance for Italians of the modern age.

What quickly became known as the Tavola Clesiana ('Clesian Tablet') had been created under the authority of Marcus Junius Silanus and Quintus Sulpicius Camerinus, Consuls, though they in their turn were

ON PUBLIC DISPLAY

The Tavola Clesiana has pride of place among the ancient exhibits in the Civic Museum in Trento.

recording an edict of Tiberius Claudius Caesar Augustus Germanicus – the Emperor Claudius, for short.

Briefly, it ratified the position of the native peoples in what is now the Trentino region. They had been living to all intents and purposes as Romans; Claudius' decree confirmed that status. A minor matter of local government, it might be assumed, but there was really no such thing in an Italy in the grip of

that great upsurge of national consciousness known as the Risorgimento ('Resurgence'). The tablet would always have been interesting enough, but the Tavola Clesiana aroused a euphoric uproar that left its archaeological significance far behind. This part of northern Italy had historically been claimed as an integral part of Austria, whose imperial shadow hung over Italy as a whole. Some in the region even spoke a dialect of

Right: The Emperor Claudius was seen as a laughing stock in Rome, but his image in the Empire was altogether more favourable. Actually a capable man, he took a special interest in provincial affairs.

German. This had long rankled with Italians, and to a generation inspired by the operas of Verdi, the verses of Mazzini and the independence struggles of Victor Emmanuel, Cavour and Garibaldi, it was nothing short of intolerable.

The Tavola Clesiana offered apparent proof that, from ancient times, the people of the region had been Romans, as Italian as any Neapolitans or Milanese. Its discovery gave new impetus to the national reawakening. This did much to impel the 'irredentist' fervour – the passionate patriotic desire to take back land that was believed to have been wrongly taken from them, and which ultimately carried Italy into World War I.

A RECENT ACQUISITION

Trentino's ambiguous status vis-à-vis Rome is no surprise: the region had been conquered by the Romans as recently as the first century BC; only under Claudius was it truly incorporated into the Roman state. A great patron of civil engineering projects, Claudius constructed the roads that finally integrated this remote and mountainous region into Italy.

> ❝ *Bearing in mind that, even in the reign of my uncle, Tiberius Caesar, Pinarius Apollinaris was sent to mediate in those longstanding conflicts (of which my memory only recalls the one between the Commensi and the Bergalei) but subsequently neglected to make his report since my uncle was away from Rome, and that, even after, in the reign of Caius [Caligula], no one asked him for his findings, and having then been informed by Camurius Statutus that most of these lands and forests fall under my authority, I dispatched my friend Julius Planta to investigate the matter in consultation with the procurators, the peoples mentioned above and those of neighbouring territories. He was asked to report to me and entrusted with the authority to act in my name to resolve things.*
>
> *As regards the legal situation of the Nauni, Tuliassi and Sinduni tribes, some are in alliance with the Tridentini while others are not. Though the origins of this latter group are uncertain, they have mixed so long with the Tridentini, enjoying the rights of citizenship, that they could not now be separated out without serious detriment to that splendid municipality. I therefore decree that they should be allowed to remain in possession of these rights, which they have so long believed they had. I do this freely, since I hear that so many have served as soldiers in my own guard, whilst others have served in the legions or played a part in civic life as jurors at trials in Rome. I bestow these rights so that any transactions they may have performed as Roman citizens, either with the Tridentini or with others, should be legal, and so that they might keep any Roman names they may have adopted.* ❞

Left: The Tavola Clesiana meant even more to the people of nineteenth-century Trentino than it must have done to their forebears in Roman times, providing what seemed conclusive proof of their Italian nationality.

197

A Son of Empire

Dedicated with evident pride, a funerary inscription from Ravenna reminds us of the sort of faithful sons and unsung heroes who built the Empire. Marcus Apicius Tirone had put in years of military service before moving on to make a contribution in the civic sphere.

> *To Marcus Apicius Tirone, son of Tirone of the Camila clan. Primipilus of the Original 22nd Legion. Pious and faithful Prefect of the 13th 'Twin' Legion. Centurion of Apollo's own 15th Legion. Called to the office of Registrar in the Military Prison with responsibility for wage-lists, he was a city-father for the Municipality of Ravenna and a priest.*

ON PUBLIC DISPLAY

Marcus Apicius' funerary stela is one of the exhibits in Ravenna's San Vitale National Museum.

Many years of familial devotion and tireless public service are distilled into the modest little inscription that memorializes Marcus Apicius Tirone of Ravenna. Like many ancient inscriptions, it leaves us in the dark about a great deal – even dating it is difficult, though he appears to have lived and died around the middle of the first century AD.

The Thirteenth Legion became known as *Gemina*, 'the Twin', only in 31 BC, when its depleted forces had to be bumped up with men from other legions during Octavian's civil war against Mark Antony. That means Marcus Apicius missed the legion's finest (or, at least, its most notorious) hour, as the force which 'crossed the Rubicon' with Julius Caesar in 49 BC. Summoned back to Rome to face charges of insubordination, the conqueror of Gaul decided to bring an army with him as he crossed the river that marked the border with Italy: technically, therefore, he was invading his own country – an irrevocable step.

FRONT-LINE SERVICES
But Marcus Apicius must have seen plenty of excitement of his own: *Primipilus*, his title in the Twenty-second Legion, literally means 'first javelin'. It was given to the centurion of the legion's first century – the vanguard unit that led the others into battle. Though the *Legio XV Apollinaris* had been founded by the Emperor Augustus, the *Legio XXII Primigenia* was not created until AD 39, when the Emperor Caligula raised it for his campaigns of conquest among the German tribes. The Fifteenth Legion was stationed in Pannonia (Hungary) at this time – a tough posting in itself, but the legion was also sent to put down uprisings further east in Armenia, Parthia and Judaea.

Left: Summing up not just one man's career, but an entire ethic of public service, the stela his family put up for Marcus Apicius Tirone is simultaneously proud yet modest, assertive yet unassuming.

Above: Today, Ravenna is more famous for its Byzantine-era mosaics dating from the reign of Theodoric (454–526).

But if the vocation of the Roman citizen was to serve, and that service was epitomized by the soldier's sacrifice, it is striking how seamlessly this inscription shows Marcus Apicius eventually moving into military – and ultimately civil – administration.

COLD COMMEMORATION?
Also striking to the modern view, however, is the impersonality of an inscription clearly placed in love. Of course, we have no way of knowing quite what this signifies. Was this memorial dedicated to Marcus Apicius by the municipality? Did his close relations commemorate him in a different way? Did their affection and their grief at his loss simply 'go without saying'?

It must be remembered that a range of written sources offers abundant evidence that the distinction between 'public' and 'private' life did not hold for the Romans in the way it does for us. The citizen had one overriding object in life: to achieve *existimatio*. This term may be translated easily enough as 'reputation' or 'civic honour', but to translate it is to miss the point to some extent. Most interesting to us now is the way the word brings together our ideas of 'existence' and 'esteem'. It is drawn from the same root as the verb *existere* – literally, to 'stand out from' – its importance underlining the indivisibility of the person and the public persona. Without his reputation, the Roman did not exist.

On the Menu at Asellina's

Outside a *caupona*, or 'food-bar', in Pompeii, the proprietress offers her brief bill of fare. Handwritten, but with care and with a certain effort at decorative appeal, it has a friendly, familiar charm even after 2000 years.

> *Shoppers, in the kitchen we have chicken, fish, pork, peacock.*

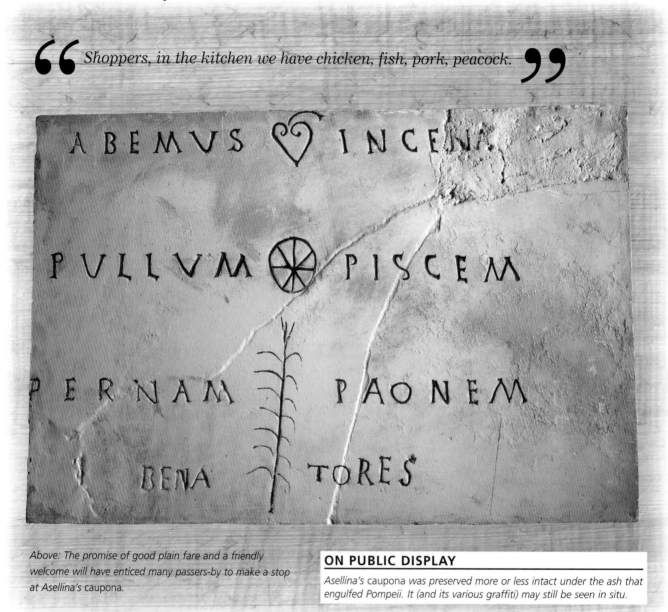

Above: The promise of good plain fare and a friendly welcome will have enticed many passers-by to make a stop at Asellina's caupona.

ON PUBLIC DISPLAY

Asellina's caupona *was preserved more or less intact under the ash that engulfed Pompeii. It (and its various graffiti) may still be seen in situ.*

With a counter open to the street, Asellina's *caupona* would have offered drinks and snacks to passing customers. There was also space for more leisurely diners and drinkers to sit inside. Excavated in 1911, it is one of scores – very likely, hundreds – of what we might call 'fast-food' bars: a very important part of the Roman scene. Only the richest Romans had space in their homes for cooking; most lived in overcrowded tenements, or *insulae*. Even if there

had been room for a stove, it would have been insane to have one: these tenements were wooden – and often jerry-built – and were notorious for their fires. At home, then, most Romans would have done no more than browse on goat's cheese and olives, tomatoes and herbs: for hot food, they turned to the *tabernae*.

This was not of course 'eating out' in the modern sense, so no effort was made by proprietors at cultivating glamour or mystique. On the contrary, the idea was to create

a sense of home from home. Hence the handwritten graffitied bill of fare with its engagingly amateurish attempts at decoration: a stylized heart, a spoked wheel, a squiggly plant or herb. Whether there would have been a more detailed menu, or whether customers had to be content to take their chicken, fish, pork or peacock 'as they came', we can only guess.

Working in a bar like this was a low-status occupation: the staff of Asellina's were not just women but

Opposite the menu is a bit of election graffiti. Again amateurishly but clearly carefully done, it throws the weight of the *caupona*'s women staff behind one Caius Lollius:

 The girls at Asellina's – especially Zmyrina – ask you to vote for C. Lollius Fuscus as duovir for roads and for sacred and public buildings.

In what appears to have been a conventional arrangement, the letters DVAS (*duovirum aedibus sacris publicis*) and OVF (*oro ut faciatis* – 'I ask that you make') have been interposed between the letters of Lollius' name.

Above: Though ordinary people – still less alien women – would not have had a vote in Roman times, they still felt closely involved in the political process.

aliens. At the same time, it seems likely that, as the years went by, they would have come to command a degree of affection and respect with their regular customers – as though they were members of their own families. 'Asellina's girls' clearly felt they had a genuine stake in their community – hence the graffitied electoral message they also displayed on the outside of the bar.

Also on the Menu?

The claim has several times been made that Asellina's was a *caupona-lupanar*, or a 'bar-brothel'. And so, for all we know, it might have been. How much more this rests on than stereotyping is far from clear, though: the evidence is circumstantial at very best. It is true that prostitution was part and parcel of Pompeiian life: more than twenty bordellos have been found in the excavation of the city. If Pompeii is a guide, Roman civilization was sex-obsessed: statues of Priapus, the god of lust, with his outsize phallus, have turned up everywhere. And since staff in the catering industry were poorly paid and, generally speaking, aliens – and therefore ineligible to marry citizens – it has been argued that they would have had to pay their way as prostitutes. This, of course, ignores the possibility that they had married or quasi-marital partnerships with male foreigners. Ultimately, we have no real way of knowing.

A Man of Substance

Marcus Holconius Rufus was pretty much 'Mr Pompeii': an entrepreneur, a patron and a politician. He had his name and resumé carved into the steps of the Great Theatre, just as he stamped his mark upon the city as a whole.

> **"** *To Marcus Holconius, son of Marcus Rufus, five times Duumvir (of which two Quinquennial), voted <u>Military Tribune by the people</u>, Flamen of Augustus, Patron of the Colony. By the decree of the Decurions.* **"**

ON PUBLIC DISPLAY

Marcus Holconius Rufus' details are still to be seen in the steps of the Great Theatre in Pompeii.

Above: The theatre evidently enjoyed enormous popularity in Roman times. Prominent patricians made generous benefactors. They came themselves – not just to see but to be seen.

Though much about him remains mysterious, we know from several sources that Marcus Holconius Rufus was one of the most important personages in late first-century Pompeii. He owned a brickworks and ran a thriving wine-business, supplying the capital; he evidently amassed a considerable fortune. Wealth was little use to the successful Roman without fame, however – or at least that *fama* which meant 'respect' and 'reputation'. Like any important magnate of the Empire, Marcus Holconius Rufus made it his business to put his riches at the service of his city: in return, he was to garner many honours.

HONOURS LIST
The Duumviri – literally the 'two men' – were the leading magistrates in any Roman colony. Elected officials, they had a role equivalent to that of the consuls in Rome itself. They presided over court cases and had responsibility for collecting taxes. But they were effectively taxed in their turn: the prestige of being one of the Duumviri was dearly bought, since it was expected that the successful candidate would be lavish in his largesse. Festivals and shows were just the beginning. A Duumvir might well find himself funding major building projects – as Marcus Holconius Rufus appears to have funded this theatre.

His pre-eminence in his community is indicated by his election as Duumvir not once but five times – and, on two occasions, not for the usual term of one year but for five years. His election to the office of Military Tribune was unremarkable and would almost certainly have happened early in his public career – probably his first step on the political ladder – but the office of Flamen was of a different order entirely. The Flamen was an official priest, appointed to oversee one of the various gods of the Roman state. As 'Flamen of Augustus', however, Holconius Rufus represented the imperial cult – his was the first known appointment of this sort in Italy.

His final title, Patron of the Colony, is another important one: he was entrusted with the task of representing the city of Pompeii in Rome. This made him a sort of Pompeiian ambassador to the imperial capital, a vitally important function given the constant tensions between the provinces and the metropolitan centre.

On Show

Superficially, the Roman theatre was just an amphitheatre or stadium cut in half – the same sweeping curves, the same raked seating, and the same free-standing walls. Where a Greek theatre was generally carved out of the contours of a hillside, its Roman equivalent tended to be built on a level site. Like the Greek theatre, though, the *theatrum* had to be built to demanding acoustic standards. Roman drama would have seemed static to an audience today: tragedy in particular seems to have been more about the

Above: The Roman theatre was closely modelled on Greek examples: its curvature made for fine acoustics; its raking seats allowed everybody a good view.

declamation of long speeches than physical action, so the way sound carried was crucially important. The *cavea*, where the audience sat, was divided by staircases (*scalae*) into triangular sections (*cunei*): Pompeii's Great Theatre had three of these.

As in many a modern theatre, being seen was as important as seeing: the auditorium was segregated according to social hierarchy. The first few rows were reserved for senior dignitaries, behind them sat military officers and citizens; and at the back were packed non-citizens and women. This inscription appears to have marked Marcus Holconius Rufus' *bisellium*, or 'double seat' – the equivalent of a box in a theatre of today.

Pompeiian Politics

Graffiti scrawled on a shopfront in Pompeii offers revealing insights into an ancient society in which city politics appears to have encroached into just about every area of daily life and to have excited the interest and enthusiasm of all.

Marcus Vecilius Verecundus is described in one inscription as a *vestiarius*, or 'tailor', and it does seem possible that he or his workers made clothes. There is evidence too that wool was woven here for use in making blankets and woollen garments. But paintings on the walls of his workshop show his slaves heating up wool, which would imply that he was primarily a *coactilarius*, or 'manufacturer of felt'.

True Believers?

Quite what part religion played in Roman life has been a longstanding subject of debate. Sophisticates seem to have worn their 'beliefs' comparatively lightly, if truth be told. Some scholars have suggested that educated Romans regarded their pantheon in pretty much the same way we regard it twenty centuries on – as a colourful collection of characters, the subjects of some splendid stories. To judge by Verecundus' frescoes, the gods may have been more than this, but perhaps not a great deal more: Mercury and Venus here seem to be little more than good-luck charms.

Above: Venus was famously the goddess of love, but it was in the nature of Roman religion that deities multi-tasked: she seems to have had an important proprietary role over trade and industry in Pompeii.

BLEST BY THE GODS

On the frontage of the shop is a fresco that was probably intended as a talisman, featuring Mercury, the messenger of the gods. The painter has shown him coming out of an ornate temple: his identity is clear from his *petasus* (sun-hat) and – more particularly – the *caduceus* (serpent-rod) carried in his left hand. In his right, he holds a bulging *marsupium*, or 'pouch', emblematic of the money a prosperous business might bring in.

Underneath, only just discernible, another picture shows a woman behind a shop-counter. She is holding a pair of shoes or slippers as she talks – or, perhaps, disputes – with a seated young man, who is apparently a customer. In front of the counter, barely visible, stands a wooden rack of the sort used for drying textiles and other items in the open air. Another painting across the passage shows Venus Pompeiana on a quadriga, a four-horse chariot shaped like a vessel's prow and pulled by a team of elephants. Scholars have speculated that this refers to the import of Egyptian linen from Alexandria. If so, it would make this particular painting not just a talisman but an advertisement of sorts, suggesting the far-flung provenance of Verecundus' more prestigious wares.

PROFANE POLITICS

Fascinating from the modern point of view is the juxtaposition of such sacred images with voting-slogans. Whilst those who wrote these graffiti apparently took care to avoid actually disfiguring or obscuring the pictures of Mercury and Venus, they do not seem to have worried that their political slogans would be in any sense unseemly. Indeed, the slogans have been squeezed in between the paintings at very close quarters.

One intriguing anxiety is, however, suggested by the fact that an attempt has been made to obliterate Cuculla's name (though, fortunately from our point of view, with only a thin coat of limewash). Was this because she was seen as a woman of ill-repute, or was female support considered a liability for a candidate? The political process

ON PUBLIC DISPLAY

Verecundus' shop can be visited today, looking much as it must have done almost 2000 years ago: that is the peculiar miracle of Pompeii.

explicitly excluded women, but – here, as at Asellina's (*see pp. 200–201*) – we see an indication that Pompeii's women took an eager interest in politics.

Little is known of the candidates themselves: Gaius Julius Polybius seems to have been a descendant of one of the men who marched with Octavian in the Civil War of the first century BC. It appears to have been in gratitude for his service that the future Emperor Augustus admitted his family into the patrician class. Polybius' candidacy can be dated only approximately, to the period of the Flavian Dynasty – that is, between AD 69 and 96. Marcus Holconius Priscus was a scion of that same powerful Pompeii clan which produced Marcus Holconius Rufus (*see pp. 202–203*). He is known to have stood for the duumvirate alongside a certain Caius Gavius Rufus in the elections of AD 79.

> **❝** *Cuculla asks that Caius Julius Polybius be duumvir.*
>
> *I ask that you vote for Holconius Priscus as duumvir. He is worthy of that position in the state.* **❞**

Right: Though the religious painting here was only roughly done, it was treated with respect by subsequent graffiti-writers who made sure of steering clear when they came to write their slogans.

Citizen Julian

A letter from Marcus Aurelius to one of his provincial governors set so important a precedent that it was inscribed as a decree. The Tabula Banasitana established new criteria for the awarding of citizenship, redefining what it meant to be a 'Roman'.

Right: So important a precedent did the ruling on Julianus' request for citizenship seem to set for comparable cases across the Empire that Marcus Aurelius' letter was inscribed on this bronze plaque.

" *We have noted the request of Julianus, of the Zegrenses, as referred to in your letter; and, whilst it is not our custom to give citizenship to members of these tribes except where imperial indulgence appears warranted by especial merit, given your assurance that they are leaders among their people and that they have shown outstanding loyalty in submitting themselves to our interests; considering further that, even among the Zegrenses, there are scarcely any groups whose services could be set above theirs…we have no hesitation in granting Roman citizenship, without prejudice to the laws of his own tribe, to Julianus himself, to his wife Ziddina and to their sons Maximus, Maximinus and Diogenianus.* "

ON PUBLIC DISPLAY

The Tabula Banasitana is among many other intriguing artefacts from Roman times to be seen in the Archeological Museum in Rabat, Morocco.

Towards the end of the second century AD, the Emperor Marcus Aurelius received a letter from his governor in Mauretania (now Morocco). It requested Roman citizenship for a certain tribal chief. Julianus, as he called himself, was a leader of the Zegrenses, who lived around Banasa. The emperor's reply was deemed so important that it was inscribed in full on a bronze plaque, which was discovered by archeologists in 1957.

A TALE OF TWO CITIZENSHIPS

Under Hadrian (117–138), the emphasis had already shifted from imperial expansion to the fortification of the Empire's frontier. Now, under Marcus Aurelius, it would appear, efforts were being made to ensure the loyalty of remoter and 'wilder' territories like Mauretania. The stick of military conquest was being replaced by the carrot of citizenship, the promise of being part of the world's most splendid civilization.

But to modern eyes the most striking thing about the inscription is the emperor's scrupulous observation that Julianus should have his citizenship 'without prejudice to the laws of his own tribe'. This amounted to a sort of 'dual citizenship': Julianus was being invited to be a Roman without at the same time ceasing to be a man of the Zegrenses. The dilemma about how far citizenship might be handed out to members of the subject nations had been a live one for as long as Rome had had its empire. In the first century BC, we find Cicero accepting that a citizen from a subject province might have loyalties both to Rome and to his homeland – but insisting that Rome had to come first in his affections. By the end of the first century AD, however, Pliny the Younger is markedly more indulgent to the divided loyalties of 'foreign' citizens.

CIVILIZING BY STEALTH

This sort of cultural sensitivity is not something we should necessarily expect to find among the Romans, whose patriotic pride was immense and whose

Above: Roman ruins in Mauretania. 'Civilization is seductive', as Tacitus was to note. The coming of the Romans – their architecture, their amenities, their lifestyle – irrevocably altered the values and aspirations of the Mauretanians.

chauvinism was often unabashed. But they were also supremely practical, and the great builders of roads and aqueducts were equally happy to try their hand at social engineering. The hope here appears to have been that if Julianus' loyalties were to be secured by citizenship, his countrymen would want to emulate him and, in time, the whole of Mauretania would be 'civilized' along Roman lines.

ASPECTS OF IMPERIALISM

Tacitus was a wayward genius: Rome's greatest historian could often be withering in his account of his own society and its ways. His *Agricola*, published around AD 98, was written partly in praise of his father-in-law, the Agricola who conquered Britain. It was also, however, a fulmination against all he saw amiss in his own society – not least its military aggression, an audacious choice of target, given the centrality of the imperial ideal to

Rome. But Tacitus saw with searing scorn how empty such conquests could be: 'They create a wasteland and call it peace,' he wrote. Critics of modern, guns-blazing imperial interventionism still quote that passage, but while Rome did indeed take its territories by force, the real 'conquest' actually took place more slowly and insidiously. As Tacitus himself points out when he describes Agricola's actions in Britain:

'He gave the chiefs' sons a liberal education…so much so that the same people who had so recently hated our language now loved its literature. Our modes of dress were esteemed, and the toga was worn. Little by little, they succumbed to the appeal of vices, covered porticoes and baths, and all the refined elegance of the banquet. To all this, in their ignorance, they gave the name of civilization, though it was really a part of their slavery.'

Strange Deities in Dacia

Sarmizegetusa, the Roman capital of the province now corresponding with Romania and Moldova, was very much a frontier region for the Empire. From here, however, comes an inscription which clearly illustrates that the army was divided by religious frontiers of its own.

> *For the worship of the ancestral gods Malakbel and Bebellahamon and Benefal and Manawat, Publius Aelius Theimes, one of the colony's duumviri built this shrine by himself and at his own expense. He did it for himself and for all his people, on the orders of the gods, in gratitude for their love for him. He added a kitchen too.*

Above: The typography may be Roman through and through, but the deities it deals with are more exotic. Out on the frontier, the Roman cultural writ did not run quite as absolutely as has often been assumed.

ON PUBLIC DISPLAY

This inscription is housed in the Deva Museum of Dacian and Roman Civilization, in Romania.

The rule of the Romans was highly regimented. Wherever they went, they brought uniformity: in art, in architecture, in engineering. Give or take a grey sky or a chilly wind, and a Roman city in Britain might as well have been a Roman city in Morocco. So effectively had they brought the earth to order that it was no idle boast when a poet insisted that the Romans had 'made a city of the far-flung world'.

EQUAL OPPORTUNITIES
The greater the Empire grew, however, the greater the number of nations it encompassed: something was going to have to give. What gave first, of course, was the independent spirit of the conquered peoples. Having first been forcibly subjugated, they were then seduced by the benefits of Roman culture. Those were considerable: stable governance, peace and prosperity, and the opportunity for individuals

Right: The need to replace Italians with aliens in the Roman army has been suggested as one of the causes of Rome's eventual 'decline and fall', but it arose comparatively early in the Empire's history. As long as – like Publius Aelius Theimes – soldiers accepted Roman values, it hardly mattered what their ethnic origins were.

to rise. For if the Romans were aggressive in imposing their political culture, they seem to have been largely free of what we would now call 'racism': Africans and Asians were well-represented among the imperial elites.

The Romans also seem to have been indulgent about the continuation of traditional religious practices, as long as these were incorporated within the overall framework of Roman worship. More than this, there are indications that metropolitan Rome was curious about 'exotic' foreign cults, which were often taken up with enthusiasm. Hence, for example, the emergence of Jupiter Ammon, who took on aspects of the Egyptian deity Amun, and the widespread worship of Mithras, a Persian god of fire. The latter was especially popular in the military – partly because it was a 'macho' cult that appealed to soldiers but also because an army that was reliant on men recruited from every corner of the Empire, learned to be tolerant from an early stage.

PALMYRA ON THE DANUBE
At first glance, the inscription placed by Publius Aelius Theimes at

a temple in the garrison town of Sarmizegetusa, Dacia, might have been put up in any other shrine. Until, that is, we read the names of the gods: no Jupiter or Juno here; no Mars, no Minerva or Aphrodite.

So are these Dacian gods? There is evidence from elsewhere that the Romans co-opted indigenous cults: in Britain, at the springs of Bath (Aquae Sulis), the local Celtic goddess Sulis became identified with Minerva. The evidence here suggests that Publius Aelius Theimes, though very much a

Roman in most of his attitudes, remained true to 'ancestral deities' associated with the Middle East.

Malakbel was a mysterious god, worshipped alongside Aglibol as one of the two gods of the 'Sacred Garden'. This appears to have been one of the four main shrines of Palmyra, Syria: it seems likely that it was some sort of sacred grove, though we cannot be certain of this. Neither can we be sure why Malakbel should appear here on his own – and heading the list of Theimes' ancestral deities. In any normal circumstances, we should expect 'Bebellahamon' to lead the line. Assuming, that is, that he is to be identified with Bel-Hamon, the great god worshipped at the main temple at Palmyra – possibly associated with Baal, the ancient god of the Canaanites. The goddess Manawat was usually taken to be Bel-Hamon's consort and worshipped with him at his Palmyra shrine.

Intriguingly, the inscription informs us that these deities ordered Theimes to build his temple. (Did he have a vision?) Engagingly, he adds that the kitchen was his own initiative.

The Wrong Goddess?

As if Publius Aelius Theimes' inscription were not mysterious enough already, the name of one of the deities he claims to be honouring is unfamiliar even to scholars of the period. Who was 'Benefal'? One historian, Ted Kaizer, has suggested that this is a reference to 'Fenebal', an ancient goddess of the Phoenicians. It is a suggestion that raises as many questions as it answers, however. How did this deity come to be worshipped at a shrine in eastern Europe more than a millennium after her heyday? And why was her name changed? Just an inscriber's 'typo', or did the letters have to be rearranged for some superstitious reason? Or, of course, does Theimes' inscription refer to another deity entirely?

Here Lies Lutatia

From a city in Roman Spain comes a crudely worked, but strangely affecting little inscription, on the gravestone of Lutatia, a teenage girl. As so often, the ancient epitaph raises more questions than it answers, but it still brings Lutatia's memory to life.

This is a monument to a musician, but it sends out dissonant signals: the conception is expensive, the execution clumsy and cheap. This was a lavish monument commissioned at a budget price. The crabbed, crooked lettering is oddly spaced and the lines slant slightly to the right. The sculpted figure is inept: the framing arch seems too tight a fit, exaggerating the size of a head that seems to loom out of all proportion to its body. The fingers strumming the strings have all the life and flexibility of plasticine sausages. And yet, the overall effect of the memorial is irresistibly human, genuinely moving. Absorbed by the music she is making, and with the merest Mona Lisa-like suggestion of a smile playing across her lips, Lutatia Lupata plays to us across the centuries.

> *In the name of the gods and the ancestral spirits. Lutatia Lupata, aged sixteen. Lutatia Severa set this up in memory of her foster-daughter. Here she lies. May the earth rest lightly upon you.*

ON PUBLIC DISPLAY

Lutatia can be seen, still strumming away after so many centuries, at the National Museum of Roman Art in Merida, Spain.

Right: Lutatia Severa's memorial for her departed alumna might have been more accomplished in its execution, but it still speaks to us of the love and grief she felt.

PROFESSIONAL RELATIONSHIP? This extraordinary stela comes from Merida, in southwestern Spain: it was found during the excavation of a Roman necropolis, to the east of the city. When it was discovered in 1956, it was lying face down, having presumably fallen some time soon after it was erected in the middle to late second century AD. That almost certainly explains how it came to be so well preserved.

The relationship between Lutatia Severa, who set up the stela, and the late Lutatia Lupata is unclear. The dead girl appears to have been a freed slave and her foster daughter, as well as her pupil (*alumna*), presumably in music. Was she also her apprentice? Scholar Eve D'Ambra argues as much.

Whilst patrician Roman women (like young ladies of later times) did devote themselves to learning musical instruments, women who played professionally were hired as entertainment for banquets. Theirs was generally an ambiguous role; they were not just performers but what we might also call 'escorts', doing whatever it took to make the party go with a swing.

Lutatia Lupata's music, then, is no aristocratic accomplishment – how could it be, with such an amateurishly fashioned stela? And

besides, however interested in the art, how many patrician women would have chosen to have themselves remembered by their hobby? Music was Lutatia's skill, a source of professional pride: we see her instrument here as her 'trademark'.

As for Lutatia Severa, hers is the tribute of a woman who, while she may have trained her *alumna*, almost certainly exploited her. And yet who, at the same time, evidently loved her.

Above: Today it is just a small town in Spain's most provincial province, Extremadura; in the Roman age, Merida was one of the world's great cities. A splendid theatre is just one of the architectural monuments remaining from those times in a centre which has earned the status of a UNESCO World Heritage Site.

Classical Guitar

The instrument on which Lutatia plays has been variously described as a lute, a *cithara*, or a *pandurium*, but it is hard to identify it with any certainty. Strictly speaking, the 'lute' of the Renaissance was introduced to Spain by the Moors in medieval times and found its way into Western musical culture by that route.

The *cithara* was introduced to Rome from Greece; the Greeks in turn had adopted it from their Persian enemies. Its eastern origins are evident in the similarity of its name to that of the Indian *sitar*. As played in the Roman world, though, the *cithara* was more like a lyre. The neck of the instrument on which Lutatia is playing, however, is more like a *pandurium*, an early mandolin. Even there, though, the resemblance is incomplete: the *pandurium* typically had just three strings. All we can really say is that Lutatia appears to be playing some early version of the modern Spanish guitar.

The Catch with Caracalla

It was the poet Virgil who reminded Romans to fear the Greeks when they bring gifts. Mauretanians learned to exercise the same caution with Roman emperors. The tax relief granted by Caracalla to the people of Banasa in 216 came with a painful sting in its fiscal tail.

> *As a reward for your enthusiasm and loyalty, I hereby cancel any debts you may owe the treasury, whether in grain or cash; the same applies to any cases currently pending, unless judgment has been given and no appeal made. Beyond this, I am extending my indulgence to any suits in which it can be demonstrated that an appeal has already been lodged, even if it has yet to be granted. I do this because I know my generosity will be amply rewarded when you have properly considered the grace I have shown you; that you will show your gratitude in your turn – not only with the service of the brave men of your loyal communities, who have proven themselves invaluable both as civil servants and as soldiers but with the products of your forests, full as they are of celestial beasts. I also expect that, from now on, you will be more punctual with your regular taxes than you have been, conscious that I gave you – unexpected and unasked – this unprecedented and generous grace.*

Above: To all appearances, Caracalla's offer to the people of Banasa was indeed one of 'generous grace', but as Roman subjects they were quick to read between the lines.

ON PUBLIC DISPLAY

The Caracalla Inscription can be found in the Archaeological Museum of Rabat, Morocco.

The Emperor Marcus Aurelius Antoninus was better known as 'Caracalla', after a kind of hooded Gallic cloak he had worn in his youth. Now remembered for his unpredictable moods and his murderous rages, it can come as a surprise that he conducted any official business at all.

The inscription found at Banasa – then in Roman Mauretania, today in Morocco – gives some indication of Caracalla's priorities as emperor. He had offered some fairly transparent hints before: in AD 212, few were fooled when his *Constitutio Antoniniana* extended citizenship to all free men of the Roman Empire, and also granted to free women the same rights as their Roman sisters. He did so not for heartwarming reasons of inclusiveness and brotherhood, but for altogether more hard-bitten motives.

ANIMAL TAX

The 'celestial beasts' referred to in Caracalla's edict are believed to have been elephants, in which Mauretania's forests were said to abound. Writing six centuries before, the Greek historian and traveller Herodotus had remarked on the region's richness in wildlife. 'The country is nurse to great snakes, elephants, antelope,

buffalo…and to lions and panthers.' All of these would have appealed to the Romans as fodder for the gladiatorial arena. It is typical of Caracalla in particular that, amidst his most pressing preoccupations of fiscal policy, he should have been able to spare a thought for games and shows.

BUILDING A TAX-BASE

Quite simply, Caracalla needed to extend the citizen body. It may be facetious to point out that this was a self-inflicted problem, although it is true that he had slaughtered over 20,000 in his recent purges.

Till 211, the overriding priority of Caracalla's reign had been to get rid of his younger brother Geta, with whom he had been forced to share the throne. Theirs had been an implacable hatred, nursed since they were boys, the sons of the distinguished soldier-emperor Septimius Severus. The two were appointed as his co-successors, in the hope that they would find a way of working together, but their mutual antipathy prevailed.

So what really lay behind the *Constitutio Antoniniana*? Both political and economic necessity. Citizenship brought with it responsibilities as well as rights. Caracalla was strapped for cash,

Above: Caracalla's need for tax revenues was even greater than his predecessors', so profligate was he in his funding of spectacles and games.

and the first duty of the citizen was to pay taxes to the emperor. The second was to do military service, and the overstretched army was in need of recruits.

DESPERATE MEASURES

He had already been reduced to debasing the Empire's coinage, reducing its silver content by 25 per cent, in order to be able to pay the legions' wages. He had also embarked on one of the greatest building projects of antiquity, Rome's famous Baths of Caracalla.

Frantic now in his attempts to find whatever funds he could for the imperial coffers, he embarked on a reign of terror, imprisoning and executing well-born Romans on flagrantly trumped-up charges so as to be able to confiscate their estates and possessions.

His edict to the people of Banasa seems comparatively rational in the circumstances: he effectively writes off funds he knows he is not going to get, but warns his newly minted citizens that he will be back for much, much more before they know it.

A Gladiator's Grave

Akhisar, in modern Turkey, was once the Greek colony of Thyatira, in Roman times a bustling city and a centre for the dyeing trade. Here was found a simple stela, placed by a widow for her gladiator husband. Killed in the arena, or the eventual victim of a quiet old age?

> *Ammias, for Araxios, also known as Antaios, of Daldis. To her husband in memory.*

ON PUBLIC DISPLAY

Araxios' stela may now be seen – along with a great many other ancient treasures – in Paris at the Louvre Museum.

Left: A gladiator goes into action, risking life and limb for the entertainment of others. His heavy armour was no guarantee of safety. Even so, many men succeeded in making a career of the arena – some respectable husbands like Araxios.

The image is all violence, the text all quiet devotion: Ammias could be any wife, tenderly mourning a beloved husband. Roman gladiators, notoriously, were the dregs of society: condemned criminals, desperadoes and ruthless killers.

How do we get the two elements in this inscription to add up?

ORDINARY, DECENT KILLERS?
To read the mainstream historical accounts, Roman gladiators were a class apart – outstanding stars and at the same time outcasts; adored

and despised in just about equal measure. The Emperor Commodus spent much of his life posing as a gladiator, hanging out in their uncompromisingly masculine company and taking part in (carefully staged) contests with the top fighters. Commodus was notoriously demented, of course, but many Roman men must at least to some extent have shared his secret admiration for the desperate, swaggering machismo of fighters born to live on the edge, to triumph or to die. Aristocratic women, notoriously, threw themselves at gladiators – so, at least, the satirists liked to claim. This is hardly the sense we have of Ammias' relationship with Araxios – a beloved husband and, it seems, a very ordinary one.

We have, perhaps, to make a distinction between the imperial metropolis and the provincial cities – even so important a centre as Thyatira. We also have to recognize the effects of the passage of time and a gradually growing manpower crisis. At a time when the Roman legions were enduring a semi-permanent shortage of recruits, the Empire did not have unlimited lives (even criminal lives) to waste. The Romans may have staged and enjoyed spectacles but, suggests the historian Mary Beard, their importance has been exaggerated in accordance with a modern obsession. In reality, she argues, such shows were few and far between in the provinces: the people of Chester, in Britain, would have been 'lucky to see a handful of B-team gladiators twice a year'.

Evidence from Augusta Rarica, near Basel in modern Switzerland, suggests that a pragmatic solution was found to the problem, using 'semi-professional' gladiators in the way that a lower-league football team might do today. Gladiators were given a month or more of intensive training; after that, they got on with their ordinary working lives, whilst remaining 'on call' for any major festivities. Such men were not the desperate outcasts of the metropolitan arena but ordinary – even respectable – members of their communities.

ARMS AND THE MAN
In early Republican times, it is thought, prisoners of war would have been made to fight for their lives in the gladiatorial arena, using some version of their traditional weaponry and armour. This tradition was reflected in the later conventions of the arena, when different categories of fighter were named after different subject peoples. The 'Galli' (or 'Gauls') and the 'Samnites', for instance, were heavily armed, and fought with the *scutum* (a rectangular shield) and a sword or lance. From the beginning of the imperial age, the Samnites were allies of the Romans, so for reasons of political correctness these gladiators were renamed *Secutores*, or 'Chasers'. By this time, the gladiatorial class names did not necessarily indicate ethnic origin: just a certain set of arms and armour and style of combat.

Araxios is generally said to have been a 'Thracian' gladiator: his stela shows him wielding a wicked-looking *sica*, a short, curved dagger-sword, the trademark weapon for a gladiator of his class. In other respects, though, he departs from the norm. The 'Thraeces', or 'Thracians', were lightly armed but mobile: besides the *sica*, they carried a small round shield (*parma*)

and they wore leg-greaves. Araxios is heavily armed and peers over the top of a big, rectangular shield. A sign of 'mix-and-match' in the Lydian arena? Or – which is perhaps more likely – the 'generic' gladiator of a jobbing sculptor?

Above: Commodus' obsession with machismo and violence was extreme even by Roman standards. Not only did he dress as Hercules/Heracles, he believed he was the hero. But his patronage promoted gladiatorial contests throughout the Empire – a welcome boost for men like Araxios.

A Greco-Roman Wrestler

Araxios' nickname originates in the old Greek myth of Antaios, the giant wrestler who was reported to have lived in the Libyan desert of North Africa. Supposedly the son of Poseidon, god of the sea, and the earth-mother, Gaia, he had his father's stormy temperament and his mother's earthbound strength. As long as he stayed in contact with the ground, indeed, he was absolutely insuperable. Waiting by the roadside, he challenged everyone who passed to wrestle with him. Invariably he triumphed, and then killed his victims, saving their skulls in the hope that he could accumulate enough to build a temple to his father. He finally met his match in Heracles who, allying cunning with his own immense strength, hefted his adversary high above the ground and held them there. Antaios crumpled, powerless to resist as the Greek hero crushed the breath out of his helpless body.

The Politics of Persecution

From Arycanda, in southwestern Turkey, comes a heartfelt plea for protection from the evils of that shameless, godless crowd, the Christians. It is ironic that it was inscribed around 311, just about dead-heating with an imperial decree that the new religion should be granted toleration.

> " *To the saviours of all humanity, the divine Augustuses, the Caesars Galerius Valerius Maximianus, Flavius Valerius Constantine and Valerius Licinianus Licinius, the solemn prayer and plea of the loyal peoples of Lycia and Pamphylia. The gods of your fathers having shown, O glorious rulers, that they look after those who see to the defence of religion, we believe that, for the sake of your eternal fortune, supreme lords and masters, you should summon up your immortal and imperial power. And, calling on that power, you should insist that the Christians – so long rebellious, even into our own time – should be destroyed, and forced to renounce their crazy notions of removing the honours to which the true gods are entitled. Though of the greatest benefit to your loyal subjects, this can be achieved only if you step in and use your immortal and divine authority to put a stop to these wicked atheists, enemies of true religion, and insist that, for the remainder of your incorruptible reigns, they practise the rites due to the ancestral gods.* "

ON PUBLIC DISPLAY

The Arycanda Inscription today forms part of the exhibition at the Archeological Museum in Istanbul.

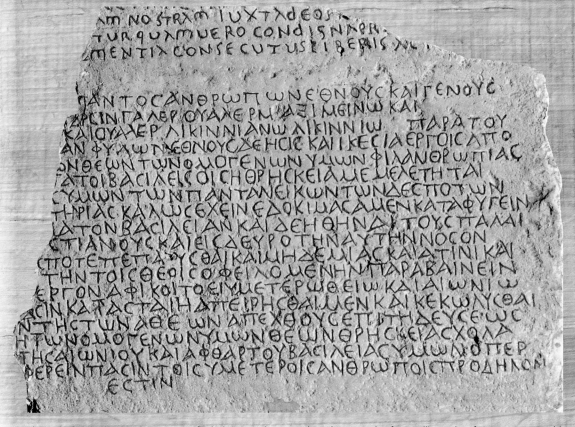

Above: Today it seems incongruous to find Christians denounced on the grounds of ungodliness, but for many respectable Romans Christianity was another barbaric cult, as unsettling in its way as that of Bacchus centuries before.

That Christians in the Roman Empire were 'thrown to the lions' is one of those things that 'everyone knows' and, as far as it goes, the claim is true enough. The Emperor Nero, notoriously, used the Christians as scapegoats for the Great Fire of Rome (AD 64); further attacks were instituted during the reigns of Domitian, Trajan, Septimius Severus and Decius. In 303, Diocletian proclaimed his 'Edict Against Christians': churches were to be demolished and Christians enslaved. That was just the start: even allowing for the Christian chroniclers' exaggerations, thousands must have died in the 'Great Persecution' that followed.

A COMPLEX PICTURE

But those examples are drawn from a period of well over two centuries: the real picture was considerably more complex. Crackdowns corresponded with moments of economic crisis or other difficulties: for lengthy periods, there was little or no official interference. Where there was persecution, moreover, it came, as often as not, not from the state itself but from a general public convinced that the authorities were not clamping down anything like harshly enough. Christians were jeered at, harassed – perhaps physically attacked – by pagan neighbours, who clearly saw their views as being anything but inoffensive. Sometimes there were more serious and sustained outbreaks of mob violence, with or without the connivance of the authorities.

That respectable opinion was genuinely outraged – and that lawgivers were felt not to be acting with sufficient resolution against the Christians – is clear from an inscription placed in Arycanda, Turkey, around 311. This was the copy of a letter sent by the concerned citizens of Pamphylia and Lycia, and the main text – after a Latin preamble – was in Greek.

WHEELS WITHIN WHEELS

At official level, there was confusion: whilst the Christians could provide a useful focus for public resentment, they were becoming a factor in the politics of the Empire. Once a single realm, this was now clearly divided between Eastern and Western sections; meanwhile, there was manoeuvring between the different 'tetrarchs' who were supposedly sharing power. It was dawning on the main rivals for power that the Christians had become a 'lobby' whose support it might prove advantageous to enlist.

In the West, Constantine's father Constantius Chlorus had already shown himself an unenthusiastic tormentor of the Christians; his main rival Maxentius (Maximian's son) also felt the need to curry their favour, despite personal misgivings. In the East, the persecution continued to rage unchecked, but even there questions were beginning to be asked. Galerius, once ruthless in his pursuit of the Christians and the main power in the East, was coming to the conclusion that they would be better assimilated into the official culture. In April 311, he issued his 'Edict of Toleration'. From that time forth, Christians could live, practise and hold their gatherings unmolested by the state, though they should 'in consciousness of the indulgence they have been granted, offer prayers to their God for our protection and for the security of the state'. The news took a while to get through (a single day in May saw the execution of Silvanus, Bishop of Gaza, and 39 followers), but the Arycanda Inscription was already behind the times when it was written.

Below: The time-honoured image of the Christian condition under Roman rule in a nineteenth-century artist's impression: few, in reality, were ever 'thrown to the lions'

Palmyran Pretensions

An impressive tomb, and an impressive trilingual inscription from a part of the world just coming into the Roman sphere. But Hairan's monument would have been more imposing still had it not been for the fact that his Latin let him down.

There had been a Roman province of Syria since 64 BC, but eastern-lying Palmyra had not formed a part of it. Not until the 30s of the first century AD had it been incorporated into the Empire. Recently conquered and still comparatively un-Romanized, it maintained most of its old traditions (including its calendar) when Hairan passed away in the year 363 – AD 52.

Those traditions also included the construction of lavish underground tombs, or *hypogaea* – often decorated with busts or statues of the deceased. If Hairan's had one of these, it has not survived: instead, its occupant has been immortalized by the fact that his linguistic shortcomings seem to capture a crucial moment in Palmyran history.

A TRILINGUAL TEXT
The scale of his *hypogaeum* would have made it clear enough that Hairan was a man of wealth and rank, but this, apparently, was not

> *In the month of Nisan [April] of the year 363, this tomb of Hairan, son of Bonne, son of Rabbel, son of Bonne, son of Athenatan, son of Taimai, a Tadmorean from the tribe of the sons of Mita, which he built for Bonne his father and for Baalthega, daughter of Bolsori from the tribe of the sons of Gadibol, his mother, and for his sons, in their honour.*

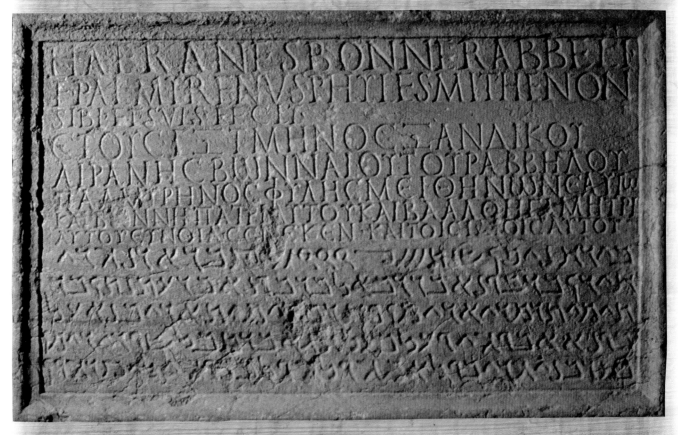

Above: This fascinating inscription is representative of a Palmyra in transition. Latin, at a cultural premium, comes first in Hairan's trilingual sequence, though as yet it is still imperfectly grasped.

ON PUBLIC DISPLAY

Hairan's Inscription, along with many other stunning finds from the nearby ruins, are to be seen in the Palmyra Museum.

enough. Hairan had himself commemorated by a trilingual inscription, announcing his proprietorship in Latin, Greek and Palmyran. The Palmyran version (given above) is much the fullest, giving details of lineage, which would have made sense only to someone of Hairan's own Palmyran background. That a version in Greek is given is no surprise, because this part of the world had been thoroughly Hellenized under the rule of the Seleucid Dynasty in the centuries after Alexander's death.

The Latin text is shorter still. Even so, as James Noel Adams has noted, it contains a number of surprising lapses. The first line – *Haeranes Bonne Rabbeli* – should, we know from the Palmyran, tanslate to 'Hairan, son of Bonne, son of Rabbel', but while 'Rabbel' is given a correct genitive form (meaning 'of'), 'Bonne' is not. As for line 2, after a promising start ('f.' is the correct abbreviation for *filius*, 'son'), it ends with Hairan completely confused. Apparently unable to find the Latin for 'sons of Mita', he throws in the towel and gives this particular phrase in Greek: *phyles Mithenon*. He ends on safe ground with *sibi et suis fecit*

Above: Palmyra was a meeting-place, commercial and cultural, between Asiatic east and Roman west. Even today, the sense of romance amidst these ruins is overwhelming.

('built it for himself and his own') – an established formula which he had presumably seen somewhere.

What we have here, Adams suggests, is a Palmyran magnate attempting to give himself airs, to create a *persona* for himself as a Roman. So new and unfamiliar is the Latin culture, though, that he finds himself fumbling, literally lost for words.

Betwixt and Between

Palmyra was situated on the main trading route between east and west, between Persia and the Mediterranean: economically and culturally, it looked in both directions. Part of the vast swathe of territory taken by Alexander the Great in the fourth century BC, it had fallen into the hands of his general Seleukos in the fighting that followed the conqueror's death. But the Greek culture of Seleucid Asia was a Greek culture that had 'gone native' – very much a Euro-Asian hybrid. Many of its traditions were clearly Persian in origin, and it held out strongly against Roman rule – almost a century after the rest of Syria. Even then, it retained a wayward streak: in 267, Zenobia, the widow of Odenathus, the city's client king, rose in rebellion. It took the Romans seven years to suppress the independent kingdom of Palmyra she proclaimed.

Bibliography

Books

Adams, James Noel. *Bilingualism and the Latin Language.* Cambridge: CUP, 2003.

Armstrong, Karen. *A History of Jerusalem: One City, Three Faiths.* London: HarperCollins, 1996.

Austin, M.M. *The Hellenistic World from Alexander to the Roman Conquest: A Selection of Ancient Sources in Translation.* Cambridge: CUP, 1981.

Austin, M.M. Austin & Vidal-Naquet. P. *Economic and Social History of Ancient Greece: An Introduction.* London: Batsford, 1986.

Bahn, Paul G. (ed.) *The Story of Archaeology: The 100 Great Discoveries.* London: Phoenix, 1996.

Bédoyère, Guy de la. *Roman Britain: A New History.* London: Thames & Hudson, 2006.

Blanshard, Alastair. 'The Problems with Honouring Samos: An Athenian Document Relief and its Interpretation', in Newby, Zahra and Leader-Newby, Ruth (eds). *Art and Inscriptions in the Ancient World.* Cambridge: CUP, 2007.

Camp, John and Fisher, Elizabeth. *Exploring the World of the Ancient Greeks.* London: Thames & Hudson, 2002.

Collins, Paul. *From Egypt to Babylon: The International Age, 1550–500 BC.* London: British Museum Press, 2008.

Curtis, John, and Tallis, Nigel. *Forgotten Empire: The World of Ancient Persia.* London: British Museum Press, 2005.

Downs, Jonathan. *Discovery at Rosetta: The Ancient Stone that Unlocked the Mysteries of Ancient Egypt.* London: Constable, 2008.

Eagleton, Catherine and Williams, Jonathan. *Money: A History.* London: British Museum Press, 2007.

Fagan, Brian M. (ed.) *Discovery! Unearthing the New Treasures of Archaeology.* London: Thames & Hudson, 2007.

Fischer, Steven Roger. *A History of Writing.* London: Reaktion, 2001.

——. *A History of Reading.* London: Reaktion, 2003.

Gordon, Arthur E. *Illustrated Introduction to Latin Epigraphy.* Berkeley and London: University of California Press, 1983.

Green, Peter. *A Concise History of Ancient Greece, to the Close of the Classical Era.* London: Thames & Hudson, 1973.

Grummond, Nancy Thomson de. *Etruscan Myth, Sacred History and Legend.* Philadelphia: University of Pennsylania Museum, 2006.

Grummond, Nancy Thomson de, and Simons. Erika, *The Religion of the Etruscans.* Austin: University of Texas Press, 2006.

Haynes, Sybille. *Etruscan Civilization.* London: British Museum Press, 2000.

Lefkowitz, Mary R. *Greek Gods, Human Lives: What We Can Learn from Myths.* New Haven and London: Yale, 2003.

Lefkowitz, Mary R. and Fant, Maureen, B. *Women's Life in Greece & Rome.* London: Duckworth, 1982.

Matszak, Philip. *The Enemies of Rome: From Hannibal to Attila the Hun.* London: Thames & Hudson, 2004.

Miller, Stephen G. *Ancient Greek Athletics.* New Haven and London: Yale, 2004.

Rankin, H.D. *The Celts and the Classical World.* London: Routledge, 2nd edn. 1990.

Reeves, Nicholas. *Ancient Egypt, The Great Discoveries: A Year-by-Year Chronicle.* London: Thames & Hudson, 2000.

Robinson, Andrew. *The Story of Writing: Alphabets, Hieroglyphs and Pictograms.* London: Thames & Hudson, 2nd edn 2007.

Schmidt, Michael. *The First Poets: Lives of the Ancient Greek Poets.* London: Weidenfeld & Nicolson, 2004.

Schnapp, Alain. *The Discovery of the Past.* London: British Museum Press, 1996.

Spawforth, Tony. *The Complete Greek Temples.* London: Thames & Hudson, 2006.

Spivey, Nigel and Squire, Michael. *Panorama of the Classical World.* London: Thames & Hudson, 2004.

Tyldesley, Joyce. *Chronicle of the Queens of Egypt, From Early Dynastic Times to the Death of Cleopatra.* London: Thames & Hudson, 2006.

Whitley, James. *The Archaeology of Ancient Greece.* Cambridge: CUP, 2001.

Woolf, Greg (ed.). *Cambridge Illustrated History of the Roman World.* Cambridge: CUP, 2003.

Websites

British Museum: www.britishmuseum.org/

Egyptian Museum, Cairo: www.egyptianmuseum.gov.eg

Forum Antiquum (gateway site for ancient history resources): www.sas.upenn.edu/~ekondrat/ForumAntiquum.html

Internet Ancient History Sourcebook: www.fordham.edu/halsall/ancient/asbook.HTML

Israel Museum, Jerusalem: www.english.imjnet.org.il/HTMLS/Home.aspx

Louvre Museum: www.louvre.fr/llv/commun/home.jsp

National Archaeological Museum of Athens (includes specialist epigraphic museum): www.culture.gr/h/1/eh154.jsp?obj_id=3249

National Museum of Beirut: www.beirutnationalmuseum.com

National Museum of Iran: www.nationalmuseumofiran.ir/

Perseus Digital Library: www.perseus.tufts/edu/

University of Pennsylvania Museum: www.museum.upenn.edu/

Internet Ancient History Sourcebook: www.fordham.edu/halsall/ancient/asbook.HTML

Index

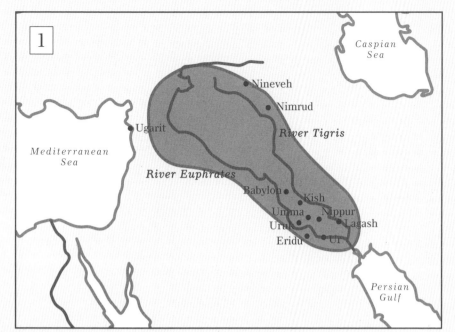

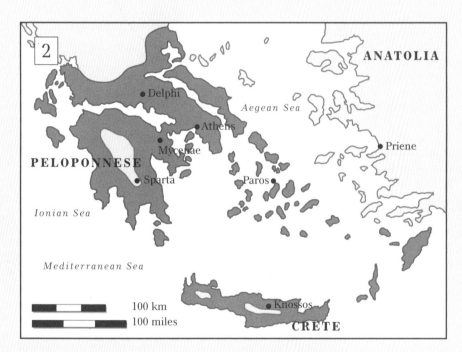

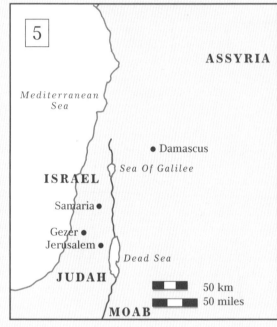

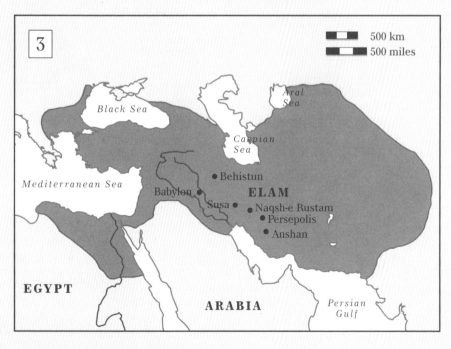

Map 1 (Mesopotamia)

Caspian Sea

Nineveh

Nimrud

Ugarit

River Tigris

Mediterranean Sea

River Euphrates

Babylon • Kish

Umma • Nippur

Uruk • Lagash

Eridu • Ur

Persian Gulf

Map 2 (Mycenean and Minoan)

ANATOLIA

Delphi

Aegean Sea

Athens

Mycenae

Priene

PELOPONNESE

Sparta

Paros

Ionian Sea

Mediterranean Sea

Knossos

100 km
100 miles

CRETE

Map 3 (Persia)

500 km
500 miles

Aral Sea

Black Sea

Caspian Sea

Behistun

Mediterranean Sea

Babylon • ELAM

Susa • Naqsh-e Rustam

• Persepolis

• Anshan

EGYPT

ARABIA

Persian Gulf

Map 4 (Egypt)

• Byblos

Mediterranean Sea

CANAAN

Rosetta

SINAI PENINSULA

Giza

Dahshur

Nile

EGYPT

Abydos • Karnak

Thebes • Luxor

Hierakonpolis

200 km
200 miles

NUBIAN DESERT

Red Sea

Map 5 (The Holy Lands)

ASSYRIA

Mediterranean Sea

• Damascus

ISRAEL

Sea Of Galilee

Samaria •

Gezer •

Jerusalem •

Dead Sea

JUDAH

50 km
50 miles

MOAB

ANCIENT CIVILIZATIONS

1. MESOPOTAMIA
   3500 BC

2. MYCENEAN AND MINOAN CIVILIZATIONS
   1500–1000 BC

3. PERSIA
   500 BC

4. EGYPT
   1200 BC

5. THE HOLY LANDS
   AD 10

6. GREECE, ETRUSCIA, CATHARGINIA
   500 BC

7. ROMAN EMPIRE
   AD 100